D1210650

brary

ULTRALIGHT
winter travel

THE ULTIMATE GUIDE TO LIGHTWEIGHT
WINTER CAMPING, HIKING, AND BACKPACKING

JUSTIN LICHTER | SHAWN FORRY

FALCON

GUILFORD, CONNECTICUT
HELENA, MONTANA

An imprint of Globe Pequot

Falcon and FalconGuides are registered trademarks and Make Adventure Your Story is a trademark of Rowman & Littlefield.

Distributed by NATIONAL BOOK NETWORK

Text copyright © 2017 by Rowman & Littlefield

All rights reserved. No part of this book may be reproduced in any form or by any electronic or mechanical means, including information storage and retrieval systems, without written permission from the publisher, except by a reviewer who may quote passages in a review.

All photos by Justin Lichter and Shawn Forry unless noted otherwise

British Library Cataloguing-in-Publication Information available

Library of Congress Cataloging-in-Publication Data
Names: Lichter, Justin, author. | Forry, Shawn, author.
Title: Ultralight winter travel : the ultimate guide to lightweight winter
   camping, hiking, and backpacking / Justin Lichter and Shawn Forry.
Description: Guilford, Connecticut : FalconGuides, [2017] | Includes index. |
   Identifiers: LCCN 2017033263 (print) | LCCN 2017039415 (ebook) | ISBN
   | ISBN 9781493026104 (paperback) | ISBN 9781493026111
   (ebook)
Subjects: LCSH: Snow camping—Equipment and supplies. | Hiking—Equipment and
   supplies. | Backpacking—Equipment and supplies.
Classification: LCC GV198.9 (ebook) | LCC GV198.9 .L54 2017 (print) | DDC
   796.9—dc23
LC record available at https://lccn.loc.gov/2017033263

The authors and Rowman & Littlefield assume no liability for accidents happening to, or injuries sustained by, readers who engage in the activities described in this book.

♾️™ The paper used in this publication meets the minimum requirements of American National Standard for Information Sciences—Permanence of Paper for Printed Library Materials, ANSI/NISO Z39.48-1992.

Printed in the United States of America

This book is dedicated to the endless pursuit of wild places, the curiosity of the unknown, the draw of self-propelled adventuring, and the humility to see mistakes as milestones in judgment.

CONTENTS

Justin Lichter

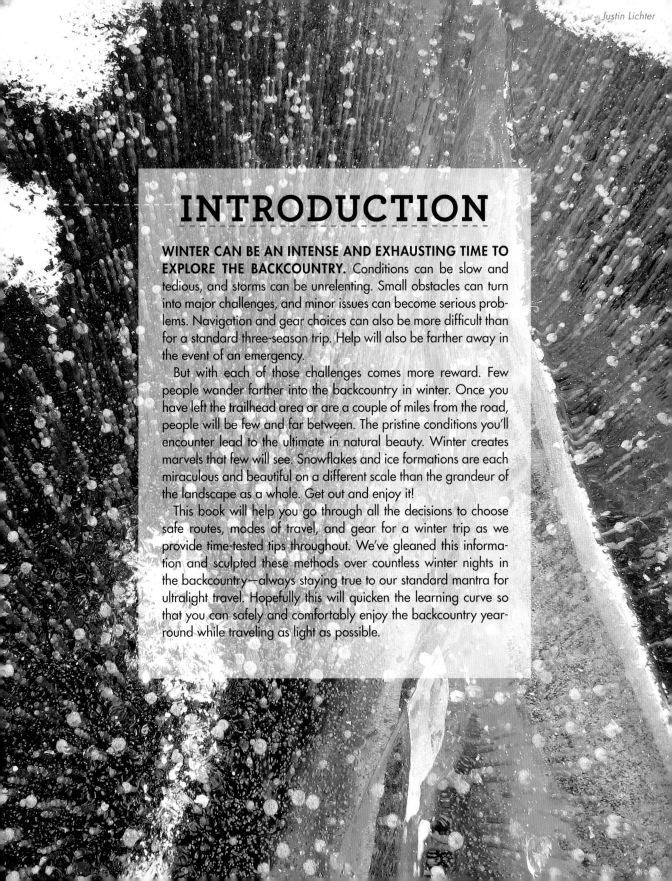

Justin Lichter

INTRODUCTION

WINTER CAN BE AN INTENSE AND EXHAUSTING TIME TO EXPLORE THE BACKCOUNTRY. Conditions can be slow and tedious, and storms can be unrelenting. Small obstacles can turn into major challenges, and minor issues can become serious problems. Navigation and gear choices can also be more difficult than for a standard three-season trip. Help will also be farther away in the event of an emergency.

But with each of those challenges comes more reward. Few people wander farther into the backcountry in winter. Once you have left the trailhead area or are a couple of miles from the road, people will be few and far between. The pristine conditions you'll encounter lead to the ultimate in natural beauty. Winter creates marvels that few will see. Snowflakes and ice formations are each miraculous and beautiful on a different scale than the grandeur of the landscape as a whole. Get out and enjoy it!

This book will help you go through all the decisions to choose safe routes, modes of travel, and gear for a winter trip as we provide time-tested tips throughout. We've gleaned this information and sculpted these methods over countless winter nights in the backcountry—always staying true to our standard mantra for ultralight travel. Hopefully this will quicken the learning curve so that you can safely and comfortably enjoy the backcountry year-round while traveling as light as possible.

CHAPTER 1

BACKGROUND AND TRAVEL CONSIDERATIONS

IT SEEMS TRITE TO SAY THERE ARE MANY DIFFERENCES BETWEEN SUMMER AND WINTER TRAVEL, but it is important to point out some of those critical differences. Some are often overlooked and can lead to unrealistic goals and expectations. It is important to try to be realistic in planning your trip to avoid disappointment or poor decisions in the backcountry.

GOALS OF THE TRIP

It is crucial to address your motivation and goals for the trip before you set out. Is this a day trip, an overnighter, or something longer? Are you ski touring for the day to reach a nice spot for a picnic lunch? Are you looking for some good snow to make some turns? Are you simply traveling from point A to point B? Going for distance or just seeking out a specific location?

These will all factor into your travel techniques, equipment choices, and even your safety decisions.

MENTAL PREPARATION

There are crazy people out there! There are lions, tigers, and bears! There's no TV and no Internet. No showers! No cell phones and no Facebook! Oh, no!

What are you subjecting yourself to when you decide to go on a thru-hike? The negatives are quick to pop into our minds and slow to disappear. The positives are fleeting. Despite some people's rosy, glorious, and admirable view of backpacking and thru-hiking, it is not all peaches and cream, not all rainbows and sunny skies. However, many of the common concerns are not actually issues once you are out there. It is tough to prepare mentally, but some mental preparation is critical.

Justin Lichter

EXPECT A TRANSITION PERIOD

Day 1 will not be easy. Nor will Day 2, Day 3, or Day 4 for that matter. But as with life, a routine will begin to take form. You are free and flexible, and your routine is truly your choice. Sculpt it to make your days fun and enjoyable, and give your body time to recover during the first few weeks. Get used to being unplugged and outside. Enjoy and connect with your surroundings, the friendships, the exercise, and the experience. As the days progress, your body will begin to get used to the routine and the walking, skiing, snowshoeing, or whatever you are doing. Things will become easier. For me, Day 1 is usually one of the most difficult mentally and Day 2 one of the most challenging physically.

Day 1 is hard mentally because it is an abrupt transition from what I was doing the previous day. The day before, I am usually scrambling to get ready for a trip—packing resupply boxes, organizing gear, and trying to tie up any loose ends with work. You are connected to all the modern amenities, food when you want it, a roof, heat, air-conditioning, Internet; and then, all of a sudden, you aren't.

Day 2 is hard physically because I am usually a little too reliant on general conditioning and cross-training and not on specific, targeted training while wearing a weighted pack. I feel good physically Day 1 because I am excited and fresh. Naturally that leads to a bit of fatigue and soreness on Day 2.

EMOTIONS

Expect an emotional roller coaster. This is one of the hardest things to prepare for mentally, but it is important to know that thru-hiking, and any winter travel, is difficult. Going in with a realistic mind-set is important. Winter travel is not always a walk in the park. You often have to trudge through soaking rains and numbingly cold winds. Your shoes and feet can be wet for days on end, and at some point you will likely have to pry on cold, wet clothes

Trying to get a ride to town for resupply while completely exhausted after making it through the High Sierras
Justin Lichter

on a frigid morning. Be ready for challenges. Be ready for fear, boredom, and time for your mind to wander. Be ready and open. Be accepting of whatever comes your way. Learn about yourself.

THE GOAL

As you plan your trip, you will likely have a goal in mind—complete the entire trail, ski a specific slope, summit a peak, see a lake, or whatever it might be. Plan for the trip as a whole so that your itinerary, calendar, mail drops, and savings reflect that; but keep in mind that the trail is an evolving feature. Start by creating micro-goals instead of looking at a long trail as a whole.

When I began the Appalachian Trail (my first thru-hike), it seemed inconceivable to walk 2,175 miles. I knew it would take six months—a mind-blowing amount of time and distance to be walking and thinking about each day. I quickly learned to divide the trip into smaller, more manageable segments that coincided with each individual resupply, or every major resupply. I was achieving these micro-goals every five to ten days and was able to count down the days until the achievement and reward of reaching each town's bounty. Before I knew it, I was halfway into the journey and chipping away at these incremental goals at an even faster clip.

Without intermediate goals, the distance of the Appalachian Trail is almost crushing, even demoralizing. Some days you might push as hard as you can, be utterly exhausted at the end of the day, and get only 5 miles in, barely chipping away at 0.2 percent of the 2,175 total miles. Don't look at it this way. That is a recipe for disaster. I've met countless people who felt the weight of the trail in its entirety, only to see them start down the rabbit hole of skipping miles.

As you are drowning in overwhelming emotional distress, which will inevitably happen at some point, remember that without these low points, the high points wouldn't be as rewarding. Without the valleys, there would be no mountains. You need to persevere through these moments. You can endure one step at a time. And that's what will make the thru-hike what it is: an agglomeration of steps, of days, of challenges that bind together to create a journey. An adventure that is different for everybody. A life-changing experience with memories you never expected. A hike in winter is no different.

SAFETY

Safety is always the number-one priority and needs to take precedent over everything else. You need to be ready to adjust your plans and the goals of the trip accordingly. Don't be so goal oriented that you become stubborn. Let the conditions help make your decisions. In winter this is imperative and much more critical than in summer. Dangers can range from hypothermia to avalanches, and things can spiral downward extremely fast. Winter storms can be more intense, and since many access roads are closed in winter, emergency evacuation or rescue can take longer. You need to be prepared and have the equipment and knowledge to be completely self-sufficient.

WINTER AND SNOW CONDITIONS

Snow and other winter conditions should be incorporated into your plans. They will affect your mileage, pace, and equipment choice, as well as your exertion and calorie needs. It is imperative to check the weather and avalanche forecasts leading up to the trip and before you head out. Know how the snow conditions have been changing and how the impending weather may affect them. Incorporating this information into your plans will greatly increase your safety.

If a storm rolls in and the avalanche conditions skyrocket, you may have to find a safe place to wait out the storm and let the snow conditions settle. If you get a good crust, you may be able to cruise and make really good time. If you are dealing with spring conditions, you may have a fast crust for the first few hours in the morning before things soften up and get edgeable and perfect, and then turn to mush in the afternoon.

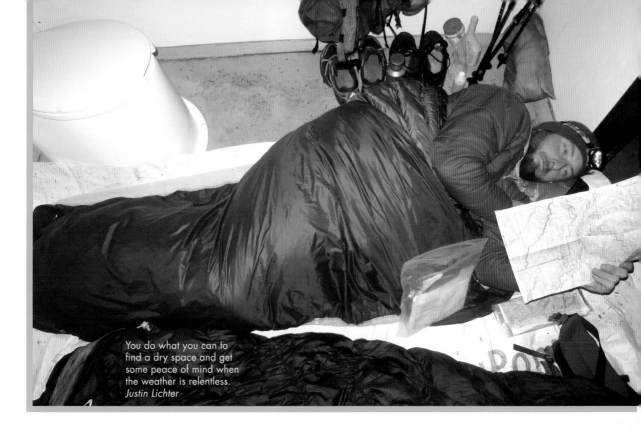

You do what you can to find a dry space and get some peace of mind when the weather is relentless. *Justin Lichter*

Snow levels and snow line can also play a key role in a trip. In mountainous areas the snow levels can fluctuate with each storm and even throughout a storm. If the trail or route you plan to follow is going to drop below the snow line, this will probably affect your gear choices and your daily mileage. For example, in many places in New Zealand, you will have to hike up to snow line before you can throw your skis or snowshoes on. It can be very uncomfortable to hike that approach in your ski boots, but if you wear shoes or hiking boots, you will have to carry them when you hit the snow and put your ski gear on. Decisions, decisions, decisions.

Likewise, if you know a storm is coming in, you will need to be ready for the adverse conditions. Have you buried your waterproofs? Have your storm gear and your layers accessible so that you can easily add layers or rain gear without having to dig through your whole pack, while still packing these items so they don't get wet. It is hard, and often painful, to stop for a long time in winter when it is cold, so efficiency and planning when packing is critical.

If you know a storm is coming, you will want to plan your route accordingly. Conditions in the mountains can often deteriorate well before the weather forecast says the storm is supposed to swing through. Gusty winds, low visibility, and dropping temperatures can start before the clouds move in. If your route is along an exposed ridgeline or you planned to summit peaks, you may want to look for an alternate route that is more sheltered and below tree line. Snow conditions change rapidly, and additional snowfall can reduce your pace to a crawl.

Make sure to check the avalanche forecast for the area you are headed. Avalanche conditions can change rapidly. Looking at the forecast will give you a baseline of the conditions and help you determine what layers, aspects, elevations, and additional factors you need to keep an extra close eye on. This will help you plan your route to be as safe as possible and give you a solid understanding of what's happening within the snowpack—especially important if you are not out in it every day or are heading out into the backcountry from a completely different region.

For example, if the avalanche forecast and "avalanche rose" show a high risk on north-facing slopes above tree line, you can plan to minimize your time in these areas. If you do have to travel through those areas, you can plan to be either on the ridgeline or in an area with a slope below 30 degrees. Keep in mind that avalanche danger can change dramatically by aspect, elevation, slope, and terrain, and it is quickly affected by such factors as solar radiation, temperatures, wind, snowfall, and precipitation, to name a few.

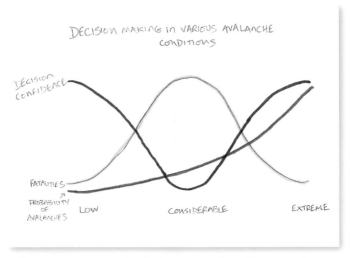

Making decisions when avalanche danger is rated considerable can be difficult. When the danger is rated low, the probability is low for slides, giving us decision-making confidence. When the danger is rated extreme, it's the exact opposite, and there are often many obvious signs that the dangers are high. At the considerable rating, many of the dangers are not evident, making it easy to underestimate the risk.
Justin Lichter

TEMPERATURES

Temperatures play a huge role in your routine during a winter trip. When it is very cold, it can be tedious to take breaks and even just to tie your shoes. Layer changes or other times that require finger dexterity and the need to remove your gloves must be minimized and sped up. You can quickly lose sensation in your fingers. You also must maintain a keen sense of your toes throughout the day and be proactive at the first signs of frostbite. This can be counter-intuitive, since sensation loss can mimic the feeling of walking without problems. Having a proper layering system, and keeping those layers handy for quick additions, is essential.

Beautiful feathers, but they can lead
to very dangerous conditions if they
haven't been knocked down before
the next snowfall.
Shawn Forry

In temperatures of -20°F, exposed skin can get frostbite in 30 minutes. Add in some wind, and that time can plummet to as little as 5 minutes.

Cold temperatures can also destabilize the snowpack. If temperatures persistently remain below freezing, the snow crystals will become increasingly less bonded and more "sugary." This can lead to a weak, dangerous snowpack and persistent weak layers. Also, on cold clear nights a surface hoar (or hoarfrost) can develop on top of the snowpack. This is similar to dew in summer, but instead it is frozen ice formations on top of the snow. This surface hoar, if not "knocked-down" or melted before the next snowfall, is a menacing beauty. These fragile featherlike formations are absolutely stunning, but they can lead to VERY dangerous avalanche conditions.

Cold temperatures present challenges, but warmer winter temperatures can sometimes be even more dangerous. You will sweat more, and there's nothing more conducive to hypothermia than a steady, cold rain or very wet snowfall where the temperature is hovering right around freezing. A "warmer" snow or cold rain can be much more uncomfortable and challenging to deal with than a cold snow, since you won't be able to just brush it off. Dressing appropriately is key in both situations.

Warmer temperatures can increase stability within the snowpack by allowing the snow crystals to round and bond better. However, warmth can also have a destabilizing effect. Wet avalanches are common in spring as temperatures begin to warm and cause point releases. Rapid warming can trigger avalanches. Furthermore, warm storms that come in as rain or heavy, wet snow can add a lot of weight to the snowpack in a short amount of time, triggering weak layers and leading to very unstable conditions and potentially devastating avalanches.

Warming temperatures can also cause free water to flow through the snowpack or along crust layers or the ground-snow interface, lubricating the slope and causing an avalanche. I have seen this firsthand while ski patrolling in Colorado.

It was early April, and we had a pretty good snowpack that was stable and skier compacted. Since it was the first night of the season when the temperature did not fall below freezing, thereby not allowing the snowpack to re-bond, we decided to do some avalanche control. We were skeptical that anything was going to happen, but with the conditions in mind, we went out and threw some explosives. On the third explosion, the entire slope ripped out and slid to the ground. It tore through a bunch of trees at the bottom. In one east-facing bowl, the entire winter's snowpack was gone; we couldn't reopen the bowl for the rest of the season.

Warming temperatures during a snowstorm can be a major red flag for increasing avalanche danger. If snow gets "upside down" because of warming temps, the new snow layers will end up with lighter powder below heavier snow. This can be a very dangerous situation. Use extreme caution, and follow all avalanche safety and travel precautions when traveling during and after these conditions are in place.

Proper layering and managing your body heat accordingly, as discussed in more detail later, play a critical role in dealing with all temperatures while traveling and can also affect your expectations, route selection, and choices on modes of travel.

WIND

Winter winds can stop your forward progress in its tracks and chill you to the bone. It can be flat out dangerous, as well as terribly unpleasant, to travel during wind events, storms with driving snow, or freezing, windy conditions. Heavy winds make it nearly impossible to stop

Wind Chill Chart

TEMPERATURE (F)

WIND (MPH)	0	40	35	30	25	20	15	10	5	0	-5	-10	-15	-20	-25	-30	-35	-40	-45
	5	36	31	25	19	13	7	1	-5	-11	-16	-22	-28	-34	-40	-46	-52	-57	-63
	10	34	27	21	15	9	3	-4	-10	-16	-22	-28	-35	-41	-47	-53	-59	66	-72
	15	32	25	19	13	6	0	-7	-13	-19	-26	-32	-39	-45	-51	-58	-64	-71	-77
	20	30	24	17	11	4	-2	-9	-15	-22	-29	-35	-42	-48	-55	-61	-68	74	-81
	25	29	23	16	9	3	-4	-11	-17	-24	-31	-37	-44	-51	-58	-64	-71	-78	-84
	30	28	22	15	8	1	-5	-12	-19	-26	-33	-39	-46	-53	-60	-67	-73	-80	-87
	35	28	21	14	7	0	-7	-14	-21	-27	-34	-41	-48	-55	-62	-69	-76	-82	-89
	40	27	20	13	6	-1	-8	-15	-22	-29	-36	-43	-50	-57	-64	-71	-78	-84	-91
	45	26	19	12	5	-2	-9	-16	-23	-30	-37	-44	-51	-58	-65	-72	-79	-86	-93
	50	26	19	12	4	-3	-10	-17	-24	-31	-38	-45	-52	-60	-67	-74	-81	-88	-95
	55	25	18	11	4	-3	-11	-18	-25	-32	-39	-46	-54	-61	-68	-75	-82	-89	-97
	60	25	17	10	3	-4	-11	-19	-26	-33	-40	-48	-55	-62	-69	-76	-84	-91	-98

FROSTBITE TIMES: 30 MINUTES   10 MINUTES   5 MINUTES

and take a break, and wind chills can make the raw temperature feel even more bitter. You need to keep close tabs on the sensation of your fingers, toes, cheeks, nose, and any other exposed skin. If you are traveling with a partner, periodically look for blotchy, white spots on his or her face.

Most locations have typical wind patterns during and immediately after storms that can help you forecast a storm and determine a good campsite or spot for a potential break. Many locations in the Northern Hemisphere have strong winds from the southwest that arrive prior to the storm. These winds shift to northerly, easterly, or northeasterly following the passing of the main low-pressure area.

Terrain or trees can act as great windbreaks. If you are getting cold, seek out these areas and alter your route to stay in them. Continue moving to help build and maintain body heat once you are out of the wind, or quickly set up your shelter and get into your sleeping bag (depending on how cold you are).

Finding a spot out of the wind for a break can help keep you warm. Here we found a huge windrow and a nice tree along an otherwise exposed ridge traverse.
Justin Lichter

Setting up your shelter in a very windy location can be extremely tricky and can lead to a poor night's sleep, as well as the chance for your body heat to spiral downward as you fight to set up your shelter. The shelter will probably rattle constantly in the wind, and the extra air movement will remove a lot of the heated air within your shelter, leading to a colder night's sleep. If you can, find some shelter from the strongest winds to set up. This will also help keep you significantly warmer.

As you set up your shelter, set its narrow portion to the windward side, and stake it down firmly. Your shelter should now automatically get spread out by the wind. Spread out and stake down the other corners tightly. If you are using a tent or tarp with a pole, now place the pole into the setup. If you are using a tent, repeat the same process to get the fly in place.

MINIMAL DAYLIGHT HOURS

When planning your trip and your daily expectations, keep in mind that the daylight hours are extremely short in winter. Many locations have 10 hours or less of daylight during mid-winter, and it can be extremely hard to travel at night. Plus, because the sun is setting at a steeper angle, dusk is shorter than in summer. During storm conditions, darkness can set in even earlier. Navigating at night, dealing with colder temperatures, skiing in the dark in variable conditions, and thinking about facing an unexpected situation, such as potential burial in an avalanche in darkness, make nighttime travel very risky. Plan your trips to incorporate reasonable daily mileage so that you don't get left out in the dark. Remember that everything takes longer in the winter—packing up, getting water, cooking, setting up your shelter, getting ready for bed, changing your clothes, and taking off or putting on your gear. As a result, there will be more downtime where you aren't traveling, but a decent amount of time may be occupied by doing all the daily chores that take longer than with an average summer trip.

Consider bringing a paperback book, crossword puzzles, or some other lightweight entertainment for the long nights, unless you are okay with going to sleep at 7:30 or 8 p.m. On the other hand, you may be flat out exhausted by the time you finish eating dinner and be ready for bed.

TERRAIN

Terrain is a huge factor in scheduling your travel plans, making an itinerary, and determining daily mileage goals. Depending on conditions, slogging on flat ground in winter can take as long as ascending the steepest technical slope, while at other times you may be able to cruise on top of a frozen lake unimpeded, picking the straightest distance to get to the other side and cutting off summer trail mileage. Conditions can change frequently as you hit different elevations, aspects, slopes, tree cover, or varying temperatures. The speed you are traveling one hour may not be the same rate of progress you'll maintain for the rest of the day or the remainder of the trip.

Without going into too many specifics, another item to keep in mind is that terrain will drastically affect your route choices. You may not be able to preplan all the specifics about your route. Route selection on a smaller scale once you are on the ground is very important. Don't get tied to any preplanned details, since you will need to factor in snow and weather conditions to decide your safest and best route choices. This may end up adding extra distance or additional vertical gain to your initial route estimates, but safety is the number-one priority. Skirt that avalanche slope if necessary, or climb up onto the ridgeline to bypass steep, unsafe terrain.

Depending on the scale of your maps, some terrain features may barely show up. If you have a map with 100-foot contour lines, a 50-foot cliff might "disappear" in the scale. Or that cliff area may have completely filled in with winter snowpack and is now a safe, gentle slope of snow. Keep your eyes open, and be ready for changes on the fly.

MODE OF TRAVEL

You'll likely take multiple factors into account for choosing your mode of travel for the trip. This will be detailed in a later chapter as we discuss the pros and cons of each option. Whatever means you choose will permeate most of the rest of the planning decisions, including your gear choices, pack weight, and potential rate of travel; the ideal route; and the daily mileage you may be able to do.

For example, if you choose to snowshoe, your maximum rate will be limited to 3 miles per hour. It is hard, if not impossible, to move much faster than that, except for maybe in short bursts. If your mode of choice is snowshoeing, you may want to avoid any contouring or sidehilling. It can be extremely tedious to cross slopes on snowshoes, especially in firmer conditions.

With skis you may move more slowly through some types of terrain, but if downhill conditions are good, you may be able to move upwards of 10 miles per hour—although I would still be cautious about planning how much distance you can cover on skis. Skiing may seem glorious and fast, but it is also often fairly slow. An average pace for skis through variable conditions and terrain is probably still 2 to 2.5 miles per hour.

OTHER FACTORS

When looking at your route beforehand, it is very important to look at the details of the trail, cross-country route, summertime dirt roads, or other roads you may be using for your travel paths. These may help tell you the conditions of the route or trails you are going to be using, which will help you determine potential distances you can cover each day, or period of each day.

Many dirt roads or closed winter roads become playgrounds for snowmobiles in wintertime. Is the area a popular snowmobile recreation area, or are they permitted there? How far might your route overlap the snowmobile trails? Is there an area more frequented by skiers or other recreational users? Following their tracks can drastically increase your rate of travel and reduce your exertion over that distance. Sometimes it can even double your speed. Depending on your goals for the trip, it may be worthwhile to sidetrack out of your way and add mileage if you believe that a nearby forest service road or area will have tracks to follow.

To decide if you should add distance, weigh the distance out of the way versus the time it will take to get there, the likelihood that there may be tracks or broken trail to follow, plus your overall frustration and fatigue level from endlessly breaking trail. Sometimes you may just want to do this for a mental break. When you are breaking trail incessantly and navigating all the time, you aren't able to zone out and let your mind wander. Your mind is racing constantly with route selections and thoughts about choosing the safest and most efficient way. You may choose to add miles for the opportunity to make a known amount of progress and mentally "check out" for a little bit.

GROUPS AND GROUP DYNAMICS

When planning your trip, be sure to evaluate the skill level of each individual in the group. If people are not able to travel at the same speed or are of varying skill levels, this should be taken into consideration to help shape and define the goals of the trip. You'll need to plan to the slowest person's ability. Attempting to cover long distances when someone is out of shape and crawling can lead to frustration for the rest of the group.

In winter you can use the variety of skill levels to help level the playing field. If you have people who are cruising and people who are slower, you can have the faster people break trail. Or you might alternate breaking trail at specific time intervals according to the difficulty and exertion required to break trail. For example, in deep snow you might be completely fatigued from breaking trail for 15 minutes, whereas in shallower new snow conditions, you may be able to break trail for 3 hours.

Also take into account people's comfort levels. It is not necessarily a bad thing to get someone slightly out of his or her comfort range, but make sure everyone in the group is aware that this may be the case—it can slow travel drastically when someone is pushed to the limit.

It is best to know one another's strengths and weaknesses beforehand. People's perception and decision making are commonly influenced by the group dynamics and the group's perception of an individual. Even the most inexperienced person in the group should vocalize his or her thoughts and concerns. Don't rely solely on the most experienced members of the group. Experienced members can sometimes get a group in trouble because they try to show off, "prove" their comfort level, or simply rely on their experience. The classic line is "I've skied this slope or a slope like it a million times, so this one will be fine."

Typically, the more people in a group, the slower you will travel and the fewer miles you will be able to cover. Be mindful of the tendency for no one to speak up, assuming someone else is making the decisions or keeping an eye on the group. Keep in mind that the umpteenth person on a potential avalanche slope is not necessarily any safer than the first person. We are all in charge of one another's safety. If you want a free ride, hire a guide.

You may have to cater the group's mode of travel toward snowshoeing if some members are not proficient skiers. A group on a mishmash of different equipment will lead to different route selection, inefficiencies in breaking trail and setting a track, different speeds of travel, and an overall reassessment of the trip and evaluation of the goals. In winter it can be frustrating and tedious, even slightly dangerous in cold conditions, for faster members to wait around for slower members. There are options, such as adding additional mileage or taking an extra lap and making some turns, but these should all be planned for so that the group's expectations can be successfully managed.

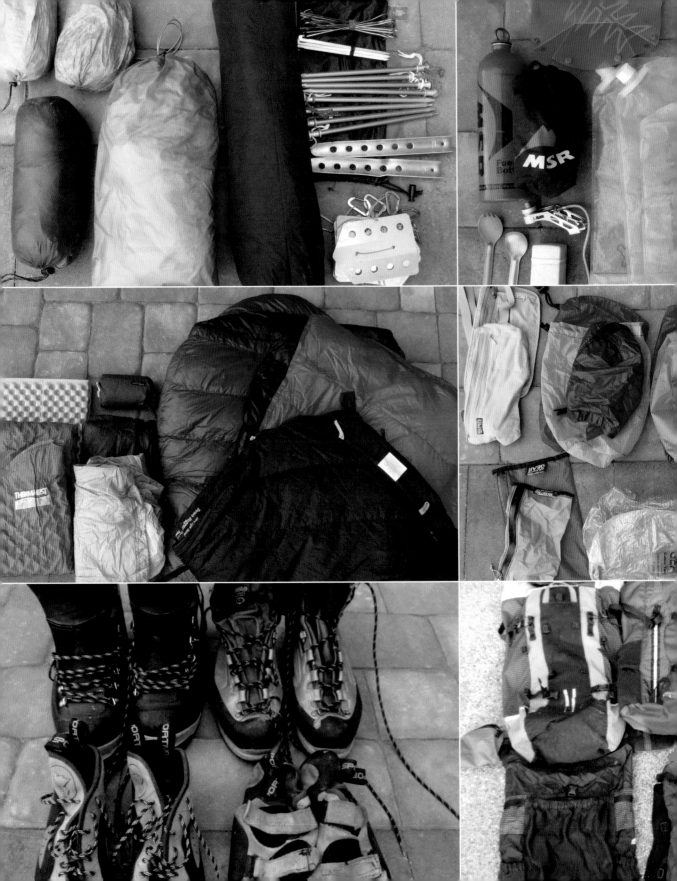

CHAPTER 2

CLOTHING AND EQUIPMENT ARE ESSENTIAL PARTS OF A WINTER TRIP. Along with your skills and experience, they create the foundation you will rely on. Making the correct choices with these items for the conditions you will encounter is critical.

CLOTHING AND EQUIPMENT

Let's talk about clothing and equipment for a second. It's exciting, it's fun; it may even be the chapter you instantly flipped to peruse in this book! We all do it, sorting through myriad product catalogs, critiquing every online review, and mimicking what others use. The reality is that these things will be only one pillar of the foundation of your overall success in crafting an appropriate winter kit. There are more variables, more conditions to consider, and the consequences are greater.

As with most things, the "how" and "why" will play a larger role in your happiness and success than the "what." Mistakes in winter travel are greatly extenuated and expedited. Your brain is going to be the essential item that is worth every ounce. Picking the best gear for the circumstances is important, but it also is imperative that you understand the limitations of every piece of equipment you rely on. This will have a direct correlation to your comfort and ultimate safety.

Winter conditions are unpredictable. Gear alone will not prevent incidents. The most important things you can carry into the backcountry are your experience and judgment.
Justin Lichter

I'm a huge fan of testing clothing and equipment around town and in the backyard before feeling confident this *thing* will do what all the marketing jargon claimed it would. One of my fondest memories from my time in the Great North Woods in wintertime is of having slumber parties on the porch with other Outward Bound staff, testing out our new "secret weapon" sleep system for the winter. When it's -40°F, you learn pretty quickly that your handcrafted Mylar vapor barrier jacket isn't going to cut the mustard for heat retention, not to mention that the crinkly cacophony has annoyed your friends all night. That's when sneaking back into the house at 2 a.m. with your tail between your legs has its merits. By experimenting like this on various systems, you can quickly and safely dial in a system that will keep you comfortable and heighten your enjoyment of winter outings. There's no greater feeling than knowing your system is going to work perfectly when Mother Nature throws you her worst.

Does that mean you can't make mistakes when it's below freezing, the wind is howling, and you just realized you forgot to bring a lighter? Absolutely not! What else are you going to brag to your friends about after eating crunchy ramen with icicles on your eyelashes?

The key is to transition through this trial-and-error period in a controlled environment. If you're working off a solid summertime foundation with your systems and gear choices, you will only need to translate what is working for you into the new conditions you are (hopefully) going to enjoy. If the polar bear plunge/trial by fire is your preferred method of entry into winter pursuits, just know that the learning curve will be slightly longer; your patience level should be too.

The aim of this chapter is to provide a broad overview and synopsis of winter systems as they pertain to clothing, equipment, and the use thereof. We are relying on our experiences of thousands of nights and

Bluebird ski outings still require proper forethought and precaution to ensure the day will be all smiles.
Shawn Forry

Sometimes you don't know until you try. Experimenting with using a dogsled as a sleep system and shelter: These types of experiments are low consequence and easy to do within close proximity of a warm house.
Shawn Forry

many thousands of miles traveled in winter, and we'll share these time-tested preferences with you. We hope to clearly lay out the differences between products, the conditions they are best suited for, and the limitations you should come to expect in their application. Some of these opinions may seem biased, but they are clearly rooted in our personal experiences. As with most things, your mileage may vary.

SHELTERS

The first thing that likely comes to mind with winter camping is the S-word: *snow*, and lots of it. This can be a huge psychological barrier to grapple with. The very sound of it conjures up images of swirling spindrift, soggy sleeping bags, and bone-chilling sleepless nights. The reality that you are sleeping on miniature ice cubes is reason enough to pause and consider your approach to a comfortable night dwelling. For most regions of the world, winter

The Mountain Laurel Designs Cuben Duomid proving its worth high in the Himalayas along the Great Himalaya Trail. Ultralight shelters can be successfully utilized with careful consideration to design, campsite location, and know-how.
Shawn Forry

daylight hours will likely limit half your day, if not longer, to darkness. A winter shelter should be a reprieve from the conditions of the day's travel—a place to dry out, get warm, and regain your sanity.

Winter comfort can be just as cozy as any other season. Just think, no bugs and no hot sweaty nights! This section will dive into the myths and methodology of winter shelters to ensure your selection is appropriate to not only meet the conditions but also your objectives and spectrum of comfort.

Nothing creates more debate than which type of shelter is appropriate for winter use. With so many types to choose from, the obvious choice is: It depends. Everyone has a personal spectrum of comfort, so additional consideration should be taken before you drop large sums of cash on your next outdoor abode. Anticipated weather conditions are at the forefront of forethought. Rather than simply asking yourself what shelter will be right for you, ask what conditions you'll likely need to endure. The nighttime anxiety of not knowing when your shelter is going to collapse, burying you alive, or be blown away is a recipe for a sleepless night and a grumpy morning.

FABRICS

Within the realm of ultralight travel, nothing trumps the unilateral advantages of Dyneema® Composite fabrics (formerly Cuben fiber, also known as DCF). While marginal for pack use because of the probability of abrasion, DCF truly shines as a choice fabric for shelter use. Chosen for sails on high-end racing yachts because of its high-tenacity strength, nothing else has the comparative tensile or tear-strength-to-weight of a DCF tarp. However, with prices for a DCF shelter easily in the $300 to 700 range, DCF obviously doesn't fit within everyone's outdoor budget. When analyzing the cost per dollar of DCF versus other applicable fabrics, the argument to save a few ounces of pack weight becomes negligible unless one considers the fabric's collective high strength, minimal stretch, and water absorption. In applications where ultimate strength and weight saving are a priority, DCF should not be overlooked. As always with featherweight gear, knowledge of application, limitation, and care is a must to ensure an appropriate margin of error is preserved should conditions turn south.

Silnylon and coated nylons are still the most represented fabrics in the shelter market. While cost-effective and lightweight, these fabrics are prone to eventually "wetting out"— being saturated from the elements. This water weight will freeze within the tent fabric and eventually become part of your overall pack weight. Similarly, silicone and polyurethane coatings on various nylon blends are prone to delaminating over time due to UV damage. Less common on higher-end brands and shelters, this adverse characteristic is further highlighted by the high stretch tendencies of nylon as it reaches its saturation point. This tendency means that you'll likely have to adjust and tighten your guylines more frequently, potentially even multiple times per night.

TENT VS. TARP VS. HYBRID

The great debate of winter shelters really boils down to three words: tent, tarp, or hybrid. There is a direct correlation between weight and a shelter's suitability during extreme conditions. Additional factors like campsite selection, experience, and technique can highlight or alleviate each shelter's shortcomings. This section will help highlight the pros and cons of each shelter choice.

Choosing the right shelter is a balance of personal preference and conditions. There will always be a compromise in weight, protection, and square footage.
Michael Vaz

Tent

By far the most stable and heaviest winter shelter is a tent. Commonly lumped under the term "four-season" or "mountaineering tent," these types of shelters typically have a double-wall construction and many overlapping poles. This category can be further defined by tunnel versus hoop design. Think of a four-season tent as an ordinary three-season tent on steroids. Panoramic views of a tent with the fly removed and copious amounts of bug netting make for nice advertising, but these features have no place on a full-blown winter tent. Higher on the priority list are more square footage to organize the additional gear required in winter, a comfortable place to cook when the weather turns foul, and the reassurance that your living quarters will stay erect throughout the night whatever the conditions.

The dual advantages of a true double-wall construction are moisture management and increased warmth and insulation. By "double wall," we mean an outer waterproof tent fly over a inner windproof fabric devoid of any bug netting. The inner tent fabric really is the workhorse, minimizing the likelihood of the elements coming in via spindrift and drafts. Additionally, on extended outings the added barrier between the accumulating condensation on the outer tent fly and your trusty sleeping bag will ensure that your bag maintains optimal warmth. Obviously, the fabric of a double wall tent will be twice as heavy as a three-season single-wall tent.

Single-wall tents rely on a single layer of waterproof fabric to shield you from the elements. True to ultralight ethos, single-wall tents are generally quicker to set up and much lighter than an equivalent double-wall tent, but they are much more demanding when it comes to controlling condensation. Single-wall tents are best suited for high alpine environments where conditions are generally cold and dry. Some single-wall tents are tailored to these conditions and use more water-resistant, breathable fabrics like eVent to address

The multiple overlapping poles of dome tents create exceptional strength when you're faced with accumulating and drifting snow conditions. While not a replacement for digging out your tent throughout the night, dome tents provide exceptional peace of mind to safely weather the night. They are the warmest option and minimize exposure to condensation, thanks to their inner and outer tent fabric, at the expense of being one of the heaviest options.
Rudy Muliana

The best-designed double-wall tents allow you to rig the inner tent under the protection of the rain fly, keeping everything dry while packing and unpacking, leaving only the rain fly to stow before departure.
Hilleberg the Tentmaker

TIP

Companies like Fibraplex offer custom carbon fiber replacement poles for nearly any preexisting shelter. For most applications, the substitution of carbon fiber poles usually yields a weight savings of at least half over traditional lightweight aluminum poles without sacrificing strength.

the burden of moisture management inside the shelter. While effective to some degree, the narrow range of use and generally high cost of these fabrics make them a specialized tool.

You will see far more poles incorporated into a four-season shelter. While a common summertime three-season tent can get by with a single arching pole design, the amount of force applied at all angles to this single pole design is quite minimal compared to multi-pole construction. A shorter span and greater overlap between pole sections will generally yield a more stable design. Having large spans of unsupported tent fabric diminishes a shelter's ability to absorb and resist the punishing effects of snow and wind. A common trick to bulk up the strength of a three-season tent is to double up the poles if design allows. Obviously, double the poles, double the weight. It should be noted that incorporating the factory guyout points will greatly contribute to the tent performing as advertised and will help the shelter maintain its respective shape. Every time a guyline loosens, a pole droops, or the fabric begins to sag is a chip at the overall foundation of shelter's design and strength.

Tunnel tents like this Hilleberg Nallo GT are amazingly well suited for windy environments. The secret to their strength lies in a taut pitch thanks to multiple guyouts. Tunnel tents are generally quicker to pitch during stormy conditions, and the integrated vestibules are often roomy.
Petra Hilleberg

The last design consideration in a tent is hoop versus tunnel. A hoop tent, with its overlapping free-standing pole design, creates a rigid tent structure at the expense of the weight of all those poles. Quick to erect in calm conditions, things become exceptionally tricky when the winds pick up. You could end up chasing your tent across the snow if you're not careful! Their design is much less aerodynamic by nature than a tunnel tent's.

Tunnel-shaped tents truly shine in their weight versus square footage and inherent ability to not only shed high winds but also alleviate some of the headache of setting the tent up in unfavorable conditions. The long slender design creates ample vestibule space on either end of the shelter, which can further distinguish cooking from storage areas under the tent fly.

One desirable design element of either hoop or dome tents is the ability to anchor and erect the tent fly first. The process for setting up most three-season shelters is to set up the inner tent first utilizing the tent poles, donning the waterproof fly as an afterthought. This design minimizes the exposure time of the inner tent from saturating and succumbing to the elements while you're setting up in blizzard-like conditions. The last thing you want to do is start your evening by shoveling out the inside of your tent! Similarly, morning pack-up becomes more comfortable, allowing 90 percent of all morning chores to be achieved while under the protection of the tent fly. Leaving the final pack-up detail to break down the fly, stuff it in the pack, and GO! maximizes your ability to maintain comfort and dryness over multiple days.

Tarp

The far opposite end of the shelter spectrum for wintertime use is a tarp. Nothing beats the unmatched ventilation and minimalist weight of a scant tarp design. On winter outings where the weather is forecast to be mild and/or the consequence of heavy snow falling from the sky is minimal, the use of a tarp can not only be appropriate but downright rewarding. The unlimited square footage available for cooking, organizing, and even middle-of-the-night bathroom trips can have its advantages. Keep in mind, however, that the weight and warmth of your sleep system will need to be bolstered to offset the lack of climate control while under a tarp.

Ultralight tarps can successfully be implemented in the wintertime. Plan on increasing the size of your tarp by around 50 percent for additional coverage. Using all available guylines will add stability in the wind and strengthen the tarp for any additional load from snow. Note the use of ski poles to help support the side panels from crosswinds.
Calvin Croll

In general, it is advantageous to increase the coverage and size of a winter tarp compared to a summertime equivalent. The flexibility in setup designs also helps cater the equipment to the conditions. The airy ventilation of a lean-to can quickly be modified to a buttoned-down A-frame if weather conditions go south.

With the plethora of über-light DCF tarps currently on the market, and depending on the goal and dynamics of your trip, carrying a dedicated kitchen tarp for winter use is nothing to scoff at. These types of shelters will put a bigger dent in your wallet than in your pack weight, only setting you back 4 to 8 ounces. They pack smaller than a can of Coke and can even offer quick protection during breaks and emergencies.

Pyramid

Pyramids offer a compromise of versatility, convenience, and comfort between a tent and a tarp. The inherent wind- and snow-shedding design allows for full protection from the elements while keeping overall weight to a minimum. If incorporating tie-outs at each side

Likely the most commonly used ultralight winter shelter, pyramid tarps offer incredible strength and versatility. Pyramids offer the ability to dig into the snowpack to create even more headroom, while also maintaining easy access to snow for melting and nightly bathroom visits. (Be mindful not to mix the two!) Note the added custom spindrift skirts around the perimeter to minimize drafts and retain warmth by weighting with snow.
Shawn Forry

wall, the strength-to-weight ratio of a pyramid is hard to beat. Circular footprints maximize the uniform tension across the fabric for increased strength at the expense of livable space optimized in a square or rectangular pyramid design.

Pyramids have the added advantage in their ability to dig into the snow. It's easy to stand up in a pyramid because of its floorless design. Some pyramid shelters have a fixed or removable floor option, but the versatility of the floorless design should not be overlooked. Extremely easy to set up and dismantle, it's easy to see why pyramids are commonly utilized for many winter pursuits.

A key design component to keep in mind is the use of a single central pole to hold the tarp fabric erect. There is an immense amount of pressure on this pole when weighted with snow. Care should be taken to properly prep the footprint of the snow by compacting the surrounding area and removing any accumulated snow at regular intervals. A lapse in either effort could result in a slowly sinking pole and/or a complete failure caused by a break in the pole or fabric from being overloaded. Trekking poles can be lashed together with a Voile Strap to substitute for a dedicated pyramid pole; they can even be doubled up if you're hiking with a partner to strengthen the support structure. If using a single pole set, you can build a riser out of snow, your shovel blade, or your cooking pot to perch the poles atop.

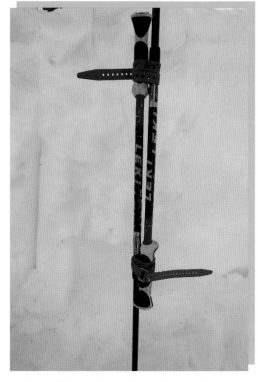

Lash two trekking poles together with two Voile Straps to increase the center pole height of pyramid tarps. Additional height is handy if digging a floor into the mid or raising the mid high for extra ventilation.
Shawn Forry

All smiles after surviving a long night, during which we nearly got buried alive.(See sidebar on page 26.) Long expeditions are a mantra of staying positive through the hardships and enjoying the moments of reprieve.
Shawn Forry

Shelter Collapse

Nearing the summit of Mount Thielsen, as we pushed higher the snow continued to accumulate. By noon we were postholing in our snowshoes up to our knees. Conditions continued to deteriorate throughout the day, limiting our visibility to only a few hundred feet at best. In these conditions along the Pacific Crest Trail, navigating through the trees in limited visibility becomes a test in patience and intuition. Every blob of snow sticking on a tree gives the illusion of a reassuring trail marker.

The objective for the day was to push as far as possible, in hopes of passing 9,183-foot Mount Thielsen early the next morning. The long-term forecast predicted continued accumulation at these elevations. We would find intermittent reprieve in lower elevations once past Crater Lake, about 40 miles to the south. Mentally the motivation was there, persistently trumped by the physical reality of tenuous winter travel.

By nightfall we carved out a protected area to call home within the canopy of several large firs. Routine kicked in to the rhythm of our nightly ritual. A tarp platform was stomped and prepped. Deadman was sourced (in this case broken tree branches) to stake out the corners of our Mountain Laurel Designs Duomid, and within 5 minutes we found ourselves distanced from the wintery maelstrom, divided by only a thin sheet of DCF fabric.

Once all the evening chores are completed, the din of swirling winds and the metallic scraping of meal prep become an eerie calm as one sinks deeper into the warmth of a sleeping bag within the serenity of the shelter. Heavy eyed with exhaustion, this cocktail of environmental factors can turn one from keen aptitude to dire complacency.

As any shelter is slowly buried, the isolative factors of the thickening snow increases the respective warmth and isolates the exterior distractions. Both are prime conditions for deep, uninterrupted slumber. By midnight, the pitter-patter of snowflakes on the DCF long forgotten, we were both startled awake by a crisp and violent SNAP! The ensuing panic of trying to make sense of matters was blurred by the sedative of deep REM cycles. Basic motion was burdened and heavy. The familiarity of my headlamp tucked routinely in my shoe by my head was oddly misplaced. Everything felt damp and disoriented. Snapped back to the present, the pieces of the puzzle were beginning to indicate that either the pole had busted through the tarp fabric because of the weight of accumulated snow or our single Leki carbon fiber trekking pole holding the shelter erect had exploded into several pieces, likely the result of the nearly 2 additional feet of heavy, wet snow that had fallen since we'd fallen asleep.

Miraculously the pole had not pushed through the DCF fabric, as we'd first assumed, further testament to the sheer strength of the fabric. Our efforts were futile to prevent our precious down sleeping bags from absorbing any more moisture from the immense condensation that had accumulated under the tarp—a direct result of continued exhalation without proper ventilation. Digging oneself out from the inside out while wrestling with a wet blanket is an exhausting, claustrophobic affair at best.

Fool us once, shame on us. For the remainder of the expedition, nightly straws would be drawn on storm days to determine who would be assigned shovel duty. We narrowly escaped a more consequential outcome. Tails between our legs, we rounded Mount Thielsen the next morning and descended to the nearest reprieve from the conditions, Diamond Lake Resort, for three days to dry sleeping bags, replenish lost calories, and continue to treat our recent frostbite.

WALL TENTS

Most commonly associated as the shelter of choice for early pioneers, trappers, miners, and hunters, nothing beats the overall comfort of a full-blown wall tent. As defined, these shelters are typically accompanied by an internal heat source, most commonly a compact, collapsible wood-burning stove. Lending themselves better to expeditionary base camp models, modern day wall tents have been modified to meet the needs of the ultralight winter trekker. Traditional wall tents weighed about 100 pounds for the tent and stove, but modern wall tents designs like the TiGoat setup are less than 3 pounds. Wall tents can easily become downright balmy, even during the harshest conditions. It's not uncommon to be down to a T-shirt when external temperatures are in the extreme negatives. I've been in some expedition-style wall tents that have achieved a 150°F difference between external and internal temps!

Is this photo from 1816, 1916, or 2016? Wall tents have been a proven concept for hundreds of years. By incorporating a heat source inside an enclosed shelter, exceptional warmth and comfort can be achieved. By taking these concepts and utilizing ultralight fabrics, wall tent systems can weigh less than 3 pounds versus the 100-plus-pound canvas version seen here.
Calvin Croll

A modified DCF Mountain Laurel Designs Supermid is able to accept an ultralight wood-burning stove to create the perfect combination of warmth, versatility, and weight for ultralight winter camping. A sewn-in flame-retardant boot jack for the chimney adds around 3 ounces to the already light and roomy 81-square-foot shelter.
Shawn Forry

Shell fabric can range from ultra-traditional Egyptian cotton to modern-day nylons and DCF. The application and weight are obviously key talking points. While the use of cotton is seemingly counterintuitive, the fabric excels at ultimate breathability when external temperatures are well below zero. At these extreme temps, the priority of full-blown waterproofness becomes less advantageous and can actually become more burdensome. At these temps, the moisture content of snow and ice is so low that the "wetting" ability of the precipitation becomes negligible. Extremely heavy in application, a waxed-canvas wall tent can easily weigh 10 to 40 pounds! We mention the use of highly breathable canvas here and throughout the book for historical context so as to not overlook the applications that cotton and canvas can bring.

More to the point, by incorporating the use of an ultralight pyramid shelter and an ultralight titanium or aluminum cylinder stove, true winter comfort can be had for as little as 2.5 pounds. Yes, that's lighter than most stand-alone three-season tents! The ability to fully dry out articles of clothing and equipment, in addition to having a comfortable dwelling, is highly appealing. It should be understood that with such a high heat source within a non-breathable shelter fabric, condensation can quickly overwhelm the shelter unless proper ventilation takes place at frequent intervals. Commonly, roof vents help dissipate some of this internal moisture but do not fully remedy it. The ability to open a door or tent flap to help promote cross-ventilation is desirable.

The cylinder stove is the true workhorse. Amazingly compact in design, lightweight cylinder stoves like Ti Goat's Vortex Cylinder Stove can serve jointly as a heat source for the shelter and as a cooking stove. Most pyramid-type shelters can be retrofitted to accept the required heat-resistant Kevlar stove boot. It should be noted that the comfort of an ultralight wall tent can be offset by the inconvenience of setup times. The increased time needed to source and secure appropriate, dry fuel to burn for the evening, in addition to the tedious nature of assembling some stove designs, means that extra time should be allotted for camp setup until proficiency is achieved. Obviously, this choice in shelter design is best suited to areas with ample access to fuel such as sticks, twigs, and small branches.

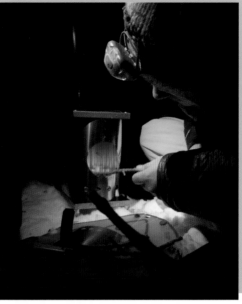

At just under 20 ounces, the Ti Goat WiFi stove offers amazing comfort on chilly nights, allowing you to not only efficiently dry gear but also melt snow and cook meals. A small armful of kindling will suffice for several hours of burn time. Prevent the stove from sinking into the snow by propping two rotten sticks under the corners of the stove base. Be mindful of rogue embers coming off the chimney and landing on your shelter fabric!
Shawn Forry

Extreme care must be taken when within close proximity to heat sources such as cylinder stoves. It is all too easy to accidentally brush up against the stove with your coat sleeve or, worse, your sleeping bag! Oversizing the choice in pyramid design helps allow ample square footage under the tarp for better maneuverability. Soot and burn holes are an inherent reality when incorporating any wood-burning product into a tent. Spark arrestors atop the stove chimney add marginal protection, but repair tape such as Gear Aid's Tenacious Tape should become a staple in your repair kit. Likewise, carry a dedicated stuff sack to help quarantine the spread of soot across the rest of your kit.

BIVIES

Probably more so than any other shelter system, bivies seem to be the most often misused and misunderstood form of shelter. In principle, wrapping one's sleeping bag into the confines of a fully waterproof bag appears as the "be-all and end-all" of bag protection. Much like fully waterproof (and/or waterproof "breathable") rain gear, the limitations of breathability are quickly revealed. Conditions must be just right to not wake up and discover pockets of dampness and moisture saturation across your sleeping bag.

Much like during the day's travel, albeit in smaller quantities, the body is constantly expelling moisture in the form of perspiration. There is a delicate balance of being warm in your sleeping bag but not so warm that you begin to sweat. Our perception of warmth commonly

Mountain Laurel Designs / Stove Use for PCT

The High Sierra felt like the most committing section along the Pacific Crest Trail during winter. Here we would cross the highest and most remote terrain along the entire trail. Due to winter road closures, the required 200-mile roadless stretch during the summer months would be extended to well over 440 miles, reliant on a single resupply midway via the town of Mammoth Lakes. Knowing this reality, we went into the Sierra section with a mind-set of being far to the conservative end of the ultralight spectrum.

Knowing that access for emergency services would be extremely delayed due to proximity and conditions, we planned our strategy according to the "what ifs." Answering these hypothetical questions not only informed our route choice and bail-out options but also, more importantly, the proactive measures we could put in place if things took a turn for the worse, namely cautionary risk assessment and proper gear and equipment.

The single highest factor we were accounting for was the impending multi-foot, multiday storm events that can reduce travel to a crippling pace and increase avalanche danger to unacceptable levels. The only practical and logical remedy for these situations is to wait until conditions become more favorable. This directly affects not only your food and fuel rations but also the means by which you can stay safe and warm during these times.

One of the proactive solutions we drafted was to always carry an emergency ration of food, not to be taken lightly when we were objectively factoring food carries of up to ten days at a time. When food can weigh up to 3 pounds per person per day, the logic of carrying even more food was a hard pill to swallow.

It takes a huge reserve of fuel to prepare all these meals, melt snow, and have a precautionary reserve for emergency fire starting when natural fuels are saturated and frozen. A key benefit to our choice of stove was its multifuel capability. A simple alcohol stove that can revert to wood-burning mode allowed us to utilize fuel sources we would have access to rather than laden our packs further with liters of denatured alcohol.

The final ingredient to our ability to hunker down for days on end was a proper shelter system. Utilizing my experience with traditional wall tents and stove systems working winter courses with the Voyager Outward Bound School, we were able to adapt these principles through an ultralight lens. Rather than using traditional (re: heavy!) 10.9-ounce cotton duck canvas, we reached out to Mountain Laurel Designs to modify one of their DCF Supermids by adding a fire-resistant Kevlar boot to access a wall tent stove and spindrift skirts around the perimeter. Instead of having to lug a 40-pound traditional wall tent around, our shelter tipped the scales at just under 1.5 pounds.

The workhorse of the entire shelter system was the Ti Goat WiFi stove we would carry. At just over 1.5 pounds, this little wood-burning giant would not only heat up the interior of the shelter to a balmy 80+°F but also allow for clothing, boot liners, and sleep systems to be fully dried. Additionally, the flat-top design permitted cooking and snow melting capabilities by utilizing the top surface as a cooktop. In terms of comfort and sanity while sitting out a blustery storm cycle, it's hard to beat the 3-pound system's weight penalty on an ultralight wall tent system.

exceeds our body's perception of warmth. By the time your feet "warm up" within your sleeping bag on a chilly night, they are likely already beginning to sweat in minute quantities, let alone condensation caused by the temperature change between the inside and outside air. Over the course of an evening, these small quantities will accumulate into a measurable amount, usually noted as the dampness you feel in the footbox of your bag.

Fully waterproof bivies can shine when used in collaboration with vapor-barrier clothing or liners (see sleeping bag section). This combination, in effect, will create a protective and fully waterproof barrier between external moisture sources and the effects of internal perspiration. You have essentially eliminated the ability of moisture to encroach on the sleeping bag's insulation.

For winter use, the intent of a bivy is to further minimize the dampening effects of spindrift and increase the overall margin of error when sleeping in close proximity to snow. To better achieve these desired effects, a compromise must be struck. Rather than relying on the misnomer of waterproof/breathable fabric, it is far better to utilize highly water-resistant fabric for at least the top fabric. This design factor will shunt the effects of spindrift blowing around and minimize brushing up against any damp interior shelter walls from condensation by greatly increasing the breathability of the fabric itself.

Using a waterproof floor in a bivy can be favorable in certain applications. Since directly sleeping on any waterproof fabric will result in poor moisture transfer, if the bivy is large enough, it is favorable to incorporate the sleeping pad directly inside the bivy. This approach will not only help keep your sleeping bag drier (a consideration for morning pack-up) but also will increase the heat retention of the sleeping pad itself. Most ultralight bivies are not sized for this application, so care should be taken during purchase to maximize the bivy's utility. Some bivies are available in XL sizes; if in doubt, ask the manufacture how the bivy was sized and for what applications. Having a bivy that is slightly too large will increase the usability of the design at the expense of only 1 to 2 ounces' weight penalty (if using ultralight fabrics).

Additional design features to consider are the incorporation of bug-netting and waterproof zippers. While the former can seem unnecessary for winter use, for fully enclosed

A properly chosen style and application of a bivy can increase the versatility and warmth of your sleep system. Shown here is a 6.3-ounce Montbell Breeze Tec fully waterproof bivy and a custom 5-ounce Katabatic Bristlecone bivy with DCF floor and breathable Pertex Quantum top. Bivies should be sized for their intended use, factoring in anticipated sleeping bag and pad combinations.
Shawn Forry

bivies, at a minimum, a small window of netting over the face area will allow proper ventilation of exhalation while sleeping and add flexibility for use in the buggier summer months. Waterproof zippers are often incorporated as an up-sale and are largely not required, for many of the same reasons discussed above regarding fully waterproof bivies.

A bivy of choice is one with a waterproof DCF floor with highly breathable Pertex Momentum fabric on top, sized to incorporate the use of both a NeoAir sleeping pad and a thin overbag to extend the seasonal use of the sleep system.

GROUNDSHEETS

Depending on your choice of shelter, your sleep system may require the addition of a groundsheet. While floorless shelters will obviously lack a proper barrier between you and the elements, fully enclosed four-season tents can also benefit from additional protection in certain conditions. Similar to summer outings, a groundsheet serves the simple purpose of adding a moisture barrier between you and the ground while also adding a layer of protection for inflatable sleeping pads. Sleeping on ice and snow can be equally as abrasive as sleeping on duff and debris.

The additional consideration with winter groundsheets is how quickly they can turn into an ice rink. Regardless of how thermally efficient your sleeping pad is, body heat will inevitably begin to seep into the surface layer of snow or ice, quickly turning things into a glazed-over debacle. Oversizing your groundsheet by several inches on each side will help ensure that you have adequate protection as things begin to slide around and bunch up, as well as give you some room to set your stuff on.

Tyvek is a great lightweight groundsheet material that is as durable as it is waterproof. Once Tyvek loses its glossy finish, it is much less slippery on snow. Cut the footprint of your wintertime groundsheet larger than you would for summertime use to make sure you have adequate protection for camp chores.
Justin Lichter

Material choice can be limited as you try to find something that minimizes both the lack of traction and water permeability. Heavy-gauge painter's plastic is 100 percent waterproof, but it's slicker than snot and slightly heavier than other materials. Tyvek has a bit more traction but is only water resistant. As Tyvek breaks in and begins to take on its "fuzzy" characteristics, snow and ice will want to stick to the individual fibers and/or try to freeze the groundsheet to the ground. On well-worn Tyvek groundsheets, the once-hydrophobic tendency of the fabric will begin to retain moisture, causing excessive bulk and weight to be carried throughout the day.

Cuben Fiber groundsheets are by far the lightest option, but their poor abrasion resistance qualities cause them to wear prematurely. It should be noted that I've found them to be longer lasting in winter environments than with use on more-abrasive ground surfaces in the summer. Despite the attractive weight specs, über-light polycro groundsheets are universally a poor choice for winter. The abrasive nature of the ice and snow crystals will tear them to shreds, and they are much too slippery.

Our personal preference is to utilize Tyvek, under the assumption that it will be retired more frequently to maintain the fabric's positive attributes. Shortly after it begins to get worn and fuzzy, it's time to cut a fresh piece.

Some die-hards will eschew a groundsheet altogether. In theory, if utilizing a closed-cell foam ground pad, there is no need for a vapor barrier, since the foam material itself is waterproof. While this is true, there are other trickle-down considerations. In general, winter sleeping bags are bulkier and can hang over the edge of the sleeping pad, especially as things get more slick. Additionally, if you're using a floorless shelter, there will be limited options on what to do with the remainder of your gear to minimize it getting further saturated if placed directly on the snow. There is a time and place for such applications, but the window of error is greatly narrowed. Competency in your personal systems should be prioritized. Overall, in our eyes the lack of personal comfort trumps the approximately 6-ounce weight penalty.

GUYLINES

For us ultralighters, the most common thing to be trimmed from a shelter in the interest of cutting pack weight is the exorbitant amount of guylines that can accompany a new shelter. For winter travel, strongly resist the temptation to trim every last gram from your shelter. The reality is that sufficient guylines will greatly add to the strength and usability of most any shelter. When fierce winds and harsh conditions directly correlate to the amount of suffering and consequences you may incur, the wise winter traveler not only utilizes every single guyline but also makes sure there is ample length and diameter to said lines. Cordage as thin as dental floss is a nightmare to tie and untie with gloves on, and cordage that is too

Guyline tensioners like the ones from Mountain Laurel Designs are lightweight time savers, but they can be prone to icing up.
Shawn Forry

short limits your ability to anchor to deadman and other buried snow-staking devices. Take the time to learn simple tensioning knots, such as a trucker's hitch or clove hitch, or pre-rig your guylines with simple guyline tensioners. A favorite are the tensioners commonly found on most Mountain Laurel Designs tarps, and there are dozens of other well-thought-out designs. Keep in mind that the smaller and more complex the tensioner, the higher the probability of its icing up.

For specifics, a 2 to 3 millimeter spectra core, brightly colored guyline is hard to beat. At a minimum, leave at least 4 to 6 feet of cordage per corner and 6 to 8 feet for guylines to ensure you have enough length. Consider setting the narrowest portion of your shelter and/or the side with the most guylines into the wind to maximize their effectiveness. One trick is to add a small loop of elastic bungee cord to add a bit of shock absorption on extremely windy conditions.

STAKES

One often-overlooked addendum to setting up a textbook winter shelter is how to effectively anchor the shelter to the ground. The convenience of dirt is usually buried under snow, and if you are ambitious enough to shovel to ground, the earth is so frozen that getting even a titanium needle stake into the ground can prove challenging. There are several methods for getting your shelter properly anchored. Each has its own unique drawbacks and considerations.

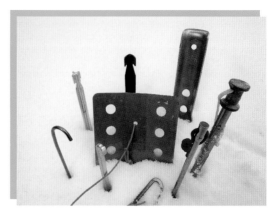

Leave the ultralight titanium skewers at home! Not all tent stakes are created equal or suitable for wintertime use. Anticipate deep snow and/or frozen ground when setting up your shelter. Staking to natural deadman and features like rocks, trees, and branches is the most secure and lightest option.
Shawn Forry

One universal truth is that you will need to add cordage to the tie-outs of your shelter. The added flexibility and convenience of being able to tie off your shelter to far-off or deeply buried anchor points will greatly offset any weight penalties. Additionally, it will be time to remove that dental floss guyline material for summer. The ultimate test for how thick your guylines should be is how much dexterity your hands have while wearing gloves. Trying to untie temperamental knots in dental floss with frigid hands will become the bane of your existence.

DEADMAN

This technique utilizes the snow as an asset. By burying any object and allowing the snow to firm up, you effectively create a nearly impossible to remove anchor point. The T-slot is the most robust form of deadman, but even slotting an object into the snow at a 45-degree angle can be adequate for some conditions. The T-slot technique entails digging a T-shaped trough

The Eerie Calm of Being Buried Alive

While on the PCT during winter, we followed one golden rule to a T. As a result, we commonly became complacent. There were two tidbits of information we were constantly monitoring: the forecast and the elevation profile of our maps. These two pieces of data would generally point to the travel conditions for the day. Deterrents such as where the snow line was subsequently indicated how soggy we would be from sleet or rain, or how much we would be postholing from accumulation. By the time we got to camp, we generally knew what kind of night we were in for.

There is a gentle, eerie calmness to the melodic pattern snowflakes make on a shelter's taut fabric. The calmness alludes to the fact that you are no longer directly in those conditions; the eeriness stems from the reality that those conditions are trying desperately to get into your safe haven. The silent night killer I speak of is when you no longer hear the pitter-patter of snow on the tarp. This can only mean one of two things: (1) The storm has blown over and a starry night may soon present itself, or (2) you are slowly being buried alive. The night we found ourselves just north of Mount Thielsen proved to be the latter.

The actions we failed to interlink with the golden rule on this particular night was that the forecast was completely wrong for the high terrain we were traveling, and we failed to leave the warm confines of the sleeping cocoon and head into the harsh conditions for shovel duty. There is always the convenient assumption that the other person will take the high road and initiate the process. The other contributing factor to this level of laziness is that as the snow continues to pile atop the tarp, the shelter takes on fabulous insulator characteristics. Not only are you sleeping warmer, but the deafening silence reduces the odds of being roused from your slumber.

Simultaneously hearing a sound reminiscent to a gunshot and feeling the sudden slump of weight blanketing our bodies sent us into a state of confusion. My first thought was that the trekking pole holding up our DCF Mountain Laurel Design Duomid had shot through the apex of the tarp like an arrow exiting a bow. Wallowing in a sea of frosty, deflated tarp fabric, we quickly realized how damp our sleeping bags had become and were continuing to get. The accumulating moisture due to the lack of air movement was quickly mopped up by our lofty 800-fill down. Scrambling to locate our headlamps, enough probing around revealed that the tarp was intact but that the carbon-fiber trekking pole formerly holding up the shelter had exploded into several pieces.

Having nearly been buried by more than 2-feet of accumulated snow had proven a valuable lesson to not only the importance of shovel duty as a whole but also the frequency in which it must occur during a storm night. Roles would be clarified for all subsequent nights by a vicious game of Rock, Paper, Scissors.

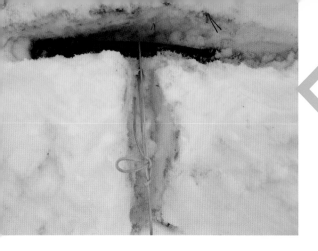

Using a branch as a T-slot deadman is the lightest and fastest means to secure a shelter. Branches should be at least 1 inch in diameter and 1 foot in length. Using a trucker's hitch to secure the guyline negates the need to dig the branch up in the morning for removal. Just untie, pull, and pack!
Shawn Forry

at a 45-degree angle on both planes to the corner of your shelter. Undercutting the lip of where the deadman will nestle will further increase its strength and prevent the object from pulling out. Any object can serve as an anchoring point, but a material of choice is a simple 1- to 2-inch branch that is approximately 12 to 16 inches long. The beauty of this system is that in the morning you can simply untie your shelter's guylines and leave the branches in the snow. This is most effective when you use a slipknot like a trucker's hitch. There's no need to dig the branches out or carry them during the day.

Other commonly used objects are skis, trekking poles, or even stuff sacks filled with snow. Mountain Hardwear and Big Agnes sell snow/sand anchors, which fall into this category. The caveat with these objects, unless utilizing the simple deadman, is that they will necessitate excavation in the morning, which can be an arduous task depending on how the snow firms up overnight. It's a great way to warm up, but a complete waste of time and effort to the efficiency minded.

Utilizing a ski as a horizontal deadman in shallow sugary snow. In deeper, more consolidated snow, the ski could be oriented in a vertical fashion to make retrieval easier. Using deadman is the most bomber way to secure a shelter, albeit tedious to prep and dig out in the morning.
Justin Lichter

T-slot anchors have amazing holding power in consolidated snow. Skis, ice axes, and pickets can be used in conjunction with a section of cordelette for anything from staking out shelters to establishing a belay anchor for crevasse rescue.
Shawn Forry

Side view highlighting an undercut lip to reduce the chances of the deadman failing due to vertical forces.
Shawn Forry

Also of note, the more sugary the snow, the larger and longer the deadman material will need to be. Digging deeper and/or waiting longer is another factor to ensure that your anchor point is solidified.

Snow Flukes

Companies like MSR and SMC make premade snow flukes that weigh around 7 ounces and 1 ounce per stake, respectively. These wedge-shaped pieces of aluminum or titanium generally have exceptional holding power for their size. By design, they are meant to sink deeper in the snow as force is applied to them, if anchored at the correct angle (approximately 60 degrees). Too acute an angle and they become like mini stingray torpedoes propelling through the snow. Too obtuse an angle and they will rip right out under the most ginger of tugs. Unless you are planning on base camping above tree line, where the access to natural anchors and deadman materials is limited, the weight and bulk of snow flukes is generally prohibitive. They can be especially tiring to dig out every morning. If you've ever camped in the freeze/thaw of "Sierra Cement" overnight, you know you'd better have a proper metal shovel to boot in the morning.

Snow flukes like the SMC T-Anchors work by driving deeper the more pressure is applied to them. Made of aircraft-grade aluminum, these snow flukes weigh 1 ounce but are quite bulky. Snow must be consolidated for them to hold, and they are prone to icing in by morning.
Shawn Forry

Ice Screw

If you're camping on a frozen lake or a glacier, the ultimate holding power is an ice screw. Your shelter will simply be pulled to shreds before an ice screw pulls. Note that ice screws have a narrow window of application, since they are only effective in extremely hard packed snow, névé, and ice. Similar to climbing considerations, radiant heat will cause ice

Nothing is more secure than an ice screw when camping on frozen lakes or glaciers. Fairly narrow in their scope of use, the lightest models weigh about 3 ounces each. Similarly bulky to snow flukes, they have multiuse capabilities if you're traveling in technical terrain.
Shawn Forry

screws to begin to melt out if exposed to the sun for several hours. Protect them by adding a covering of light snow. As with snow flukes, ice screws can be bulky and cumbersome for general travel, but they do have the added advantage of being multipurpose if your day's travel requires ice protection. The lightest and cheapest ice screws available are generally the Russian-made titanium Irbis ice screws, weighing it at 100 grams for a 15-centimeter screw. They do come with a few caveats though. Their applications are pretty limited for true technical ice climbing. Their sub-par design makes them prone to dulling quickly, and they have marginal holding power on water ice. If only intended for shelter staking, they fit the bill nicely.

Aluminum Gutter Nails

Some folks have had success with inexpensive aluminum gutter nails from the hardware store. These lightweight nails usually come in a ten-pack for about $7 and are around 7 inches long. Where they really shine is when you're camping in cold environments where the ground will have very little snow cover. The nails can be hammered into the frozen ground for exceptionally good holding power. A rock can usually suffice as a hammer, and these gutter nails can take more of a pounding than your traditional tent stakes.

TIP

Why camp on ice? It's hard and cold and potentially unstable and dangerous. Well, it's by far one of the least impactful camping methods on the environment. Come springtime your camp will literally melt away. If you know the bulk of your camping will be exclusively on ice, you could bring a single ice screw to "drill" placement holes in the ice to accept natural anchors like sticks.

NATURAL SHELTERS

In winter you can also look for a natural shelter or make one using the snow in combination with what you have. Snow is a very good insulator. This can help keep the temperature just below freezing inside your shelter so that it won't plunge into the single digits or even below zero.

You can make snow caves, igloos, trenches, or quinzhees. All are great options for winter camping; however, they can be time-consuming to make. If you're building one by yourself, allot about 2 to 3 hours.

A trench is the fastest system to build. An igloo is the most time-consuming and not the best method for lightweight hiking and backpacking; it can require a snow saw, and packing the snow takes a lot of work. A quinzhee is basically a snow cave, except you pile snow into a dome because there isn't enough snow to dig out a cave. If you're making a quinzhee, make sure the snow settles enough to bond together. This can take a few hours, so you'll need to check it over time. Without proper snow consolidation, the roof may collapse. Also make sure to mark the thin points of the roof so that you don't accidently walk over them.

Snow shelters like this quinzhee can be exceptionally warm compared to the ambient temperature. For additional warmth, keep the main sleeping platform inside slightly higher than the entrance, blocking the wind and allowing for a cold air sink. Note the use of sticks to indicate the depth of the snow walls while excavating. Plan on 1 to 2 hours for construction.
Calvin Croll

Snow caves require a lot of snow and a spot that's out of avalanche danger. Look for a snowbank or drift to build a snow cave in. Start by digging a tunnel for the cave. The tunnel should be wider than your shoulders and should slope up toward the cave. That way, cold air will settle outside the cave opening. Hollow out a cavity in the snow for the cave. Make it tall enough for you to sit upright in and big enough for you and your companions to lie down in.

Pack the roof of the cave, and smooth the surface so that snow doesn't drip on you or your gear.

If you have space in the cave, you can make benches out of snow, keeping you off the ground and above some of the cold air. Poke a trekking pole, ski pole, tree branch, or avalanche probe through the ceiling of the cave for ventilation. Cover the floor or the benches with waterproof material. Put your backpack in the doorway to block cold air and keep the cave warmer.

Snow trenches are the easiest and fastest winter shelters to make, but they're not as comfortable or as warm as a snow cave. Also, they're not recommended if you're

TIP

Before carving into your snow pile to build a quinzhee, break off several branches about 12 inches in length and insert them into the outer layer of snow. As you begin to carve out the interior, these branches will act as indicators so that the roof does not become too thin and collapse.

expecting a lot of snow, because they don't have strong roofs. Dig a trench at least 3 feet deep, 6 feet long, and 3 to 4 feet wide for each person, with an entrance at one end. Lay your poles, skis, or smooth tree branches across the width of the trench. Spread your tarp, rain fly, or emergency blanket over the trench. Anchor the sides by covering the edges with snow, tree branches, or rocks.

If you're considering a natural shelter of any sort, anticipate getting wet in the process of constructing it. It can be physically demanding to shovel for hours, especially with full-on snow caves. Snow will be dropping on you throughout the excavating process, and expect a pair of gloves to be completely saturated by the end of the process. The downside of increased warmth and protection at night is the necessary evil of construction.

TIP

As your body heat begins to warm up the interior of a snow shelter, the walls will become iced over. To prevent water from dripping on you throughout the night, make sure the roof line is in a smooth arch so that water will run to the edges instead of dripping. Tea candles do a phenomenal job of warming the inside of a natural snow shelter, provide ambient light, and double as an emergency fire starter.

COOKING AND STOVES

Nothing brings luxury into winter backpacking more than the nightly ritual of sipping a hot beverage. Hot drinks not only provide a vital morale boost, they provide warmth and an inviting means to stay hydrated in the backcountry. Additionally, where some ultralighters may go sans stove for their meal preparation during the summer months, being able to enjoy a hot dinner not only adds to the palatability of each meal, but the ability to rapidly warm water becomes an effective risk management tool to ensure quick and easy access to heat.

Similar to effective sleep systems, everything in a cook system has to work in concert. The key components to consider are the stove and cooking pot. Lesser but equally important components to review are windscreens and pot supports. As we dive into this section, it will be important to define what style of cooking is preferable and how efficient the preparation time should be.

COOKING POTS

With a plethora of designs, materials, and features to choose from, similar to backpack selection, the starting point will be capacity of the pot. In general, plan on roughly doubling the size pot you would typically use in the summertime. This will largely be dictated by the ergonomics of melting snow for water. Knowing if your preferred cook style is solo or group will further define your volume needs. For weight saving purposes, sharing a cook set between travel partners is the most economical approach. The compromise will be reduced into longer wait times and/or a unified dietary preference. Plan on at least 1.3 to 2 liters per person when selecting an appropriate size winter pot.

The shape, size, materials, and style of cooking should all be considered when selecting a winter pot. From left to right: Evernew 900-milliliter titanium; Vargo 900-milliliter titanium with titanium pot grippers; Vargo 1.3-liter; Antigravity Gear 1.5-liter aluminum pot.
Shawn Forry

Titanium has become the gold standard in pot material due to its high strength-to-weight ratio. Titanium pots can have incredibly thin walls, yet are nearly indestructible. First-time buyers will likely cringe at the high retail cost of any titanium pot, but the lifetime durability make them a standard in any ultralight kit.

Aluminum pots are cost-effective and even lighter than titanium. Because of the softer characteristics of aluminum, dings and dents will be far more prevalent, even after just a few outings. For price comparison, the common grease pots found at large box stores typically run around $5. For longer-term durability, opt for a hard-sided anodized aluminum, of which the common grease pot is not.

Stainless steel is yet another option, but it has little application for ultralight endeavors. The heaviest of the options, a comparable stainless steel pot can easily weigh double that of a similar titanium or aluminum pot—cheap and effective, but by far not the lightest option out there.

Worth noting is the heat transfer rates of each of these materials. Science tells us that dark-colored pots along with select material choices are more effective at overall heat transfer. This, in effect, will both decrease your boil times and fuel consumption. Thin-wall aluminum demonstrates the highest, most even cook rates in the lab, but you'll need to invest more energy in proper wind protection and stove choice to achieve real-world cooking efficiency. Titanium has the worst heat transfer and is notorious for creating hot spots and uneven cooking—proof that you can't have your cake and eat it or, at the very least, eat from it.

The shape of the pot is also worth considering. Wider, stouter pots tend to cook faster because of their increased surface area across the flame and are generally easier to cook in, stir, and clean. The shape can feel bulkier when packed compared to taller, narrower pots. Some narrow-mouth pots are even sized to perfectly fit a fuel canister inside, further maximizing space efficiency inside the backpack. The space efficiency that can be realized by carefully packing contents into an empty cooking pot is considerable. The hard-sided vessel additionally creates a safe container for transporting delicate items like alcohol stoves and windscreens.

Another minor consideration up for debate is the style of pot handle. Most pots have a foldable handle, with or without a silicone coating, to further reduce the possibility of burning your fingers while handling the pot. Bail-style pot handles allow you to cook over fires at the expense of less stability while adding ingredients and stirring. A simple DIY option is easy to craft with a drill and some simple thin-gauge bailing wire or metal cable. Some pots eschew handles all together to further minimize weight. The common solution is to utilize dedicated pot grips. Even the lightest option, like the Vargo Pot Lifter, can weigh close to an ounce yet serve only one purpose.

Ergonomics will dictate compromises, and creativity can breed multifunctionality. Bandanas, multi-tools, and/or liner gloves can serve the same purpose for the skilled chef. Be prepared for an increase in kitchen mishaps when compromising simple kitchen features. The choice will be yours whether to cry over spilled ramen.

For the most dedicated backcountry chefs, options for pot lids that double as skillets can further expand the culinary options. Nesting cook sets and dedicated mugs and eating vessels largely fall outside the common ultralighter vocabulary. A far better option would be to swap that heavy pot lid for a few layers of doubled-over aluminum foil. A simple titanium spork or spoon will nicely round out the ultralight cooking kit.

Swapping the stock lid for a DIY aluminum foil lid can save up to 1 ounce without much compromise.
Shawn Forry

STOVES

A stove's sole job is to create a source of heat to effectively heat an object. Sometimes stoves are complicated gadgets that sound akin to rocket ships; sometimes they are elegantly simple, completely devoid of moving parts and chaos. Careful selection and a keen awareness of the pros and cons of each stove design will help you craft a best-case scenario to suit your cooking needs.

The physics of any stove are simple: igniting an object in gas, liquid, or solid state to release energy as heat. The effectiveness of the potential energy in this equation can sway drastically depending on the ambient temperature outside. Obviously, the colder it is outside, the more energy is going to be required to raise the temperature of water even one degree. How this energy is released can dictate your preferred cooking style, namely to boil or simmer? We'll boil the range of options down to discern when and how different models should be utilized.

Liquid Fuel

By far the most commonly used traditional stove type is the liquid-fuel stove. The MSR WhisperLite has long been the reigning champ of the liquid-fuel family, not so much by weight and performance as by outright recognition. These types of stoves burn ultra-refined gasoline known as white gas. They burn hot, sip fuel, and perform well at subfreezing temperatures. Most models are even capable of burning common, internationally available "multifuels" like kerosene, gasoline, and diesel fuel by swapping out a simple jet within the stove. This can be hugely advantageous when heading into extremely remote corners of the world. These stoves can take a beating and are built for expeditions. Some models have a higher emphasis on fast boil times, while others are geared toward flame control in the way of simmering. Since they are all designed around a remote fuel bottle, the designs tend to be low and stable—crucial when juggling larger winter-size pots.

Where liquid-fuel stoves crumble is their upfront cost and tendency toward frequent maintenance (which typically requires carrying a dedicated spare parts kit and tools) due to their sooty by-product. They are the heaviest option with the most moving pieces; in other words, things that can go wrong. Despite the time involved and fuel wasted to prime the stove, a weight versus fuel efficiency gain is usually realized after fourteen or more days of fuel is carried. Quite the load, but worth noting.

Most liquid-fuel stoves require a satellite bottle and fuel pump. Various size fuel bottles are available and help cater the fuel requirements to the length of the trip. Common size bottles are 11, 20, and 30 ounces, ranging in weight from 3 to 8 ounces. All current models on the market are made of aluminum, but there are a few elusive MSR Titan titanium versions floating around that shave a few grams from a comparable aluminum model.

The MSR SimmerLite is currently the lightest liquid-fuel stove on the market and a worthy candidate for winter solo or group use. At 6.4 ounces for the

While the MSR WhisperLite has been around seemingly forever due to its multifuel capabilities, rugged construction, and ability to be field maintained, there is little reason to select this stove over the lighter, more user-friendly MSR SimmerLite, currently the lightest liquid fuel stove on the market. *Shawn Forry*

stove alone and the ability to fully simmer, this stove has a large range of versatility and function.

Canister Stoves

The most common scenario for first-time winter trekkers using an upright canister stove is getting set up for a night's dinner and lighting the stove, only to see the roar of the flame die down to a sputter. Canister stoves are amazingly light, simple, and compact, not to mention their fuel source stores the highest potential energy via BTUs. It's no wonder that the appeal of these advantages would translate over to winter use. Where canister stoves fall flat on their flame is that once temperatures drop below freezing, chemistry trumps effectiveness.

Snow Peak Gigapower titanium canister stove converted to remote liquid feed using a Brunton remote converter and the wire from a coat hanger. Liquid-feed canister stoves are capable of operating at much lower temps than standard upright stoves. Note the use of an avalanche shovel to provide a stable platform to cook on in the snow.
Shawn Forry

All fuel canisters are composed of a mix of butane and propane. Without dusting too much off the seventh-grade science textbook, both fuel types boil (turn to a gaseous state) at different temperatures. Butane's boiling point is around 31°F, with chemically altered "isobutane" boiling at around 11°F. You'll have plenty of wiggle room with propane, as it will continue to boil all the way down to -43°F! Below that, and you should seriously reconsider your life choices.

It is important to know this because upright canister stoves rely exclusively on the pressure of compressed liquid gas to boil (i.e., evaporate) and turn into a gaseous state, ready for ignition by the stove's flame. The other compounding science kicker is that due to the process of vaporization, it takes considerable energy to change from the physical state of liquid to gas. This is noted in a fuel canister by cold, sometimes icy sidewalls. The irony is that the longer your stove is running, the colder the canister is getting, further challenging the already handicapped realm of vaporization. Most canisters will be composed of a ratio of approximately 80 percent isobutane to approximately 20 percent propane. The effectiveness of the canister stove is reliant on this ratio for optimum burn. At some point the easily excitable isobutane will completely burn off, leaving the heavier propane behind. This is the point at which the flame will begin to flicker, resulting in yet another night of crunchy ramen. ***Note:*** Burning 100 percent propane would seem like the obvious solution, but the thick-walled steel canister required to safely transport the high pressure and high flammability of propane would quickly negate the performance-to-weight category.

If we sidestep this limiting factor of vaporization and mirror the advantages of a traditional liquid-feed stove, herein lies a solution. Enter the world of remote canister stoves. The key design difference is that the stove operates separately from the canister via a fuel line. Not all remote canister stoves are created equal. Some merely address the tippy nature of standard upright stoves by lowering their center of gravity. If you've ever tried to stir your 2-liter pot filled to the brim using a canister stove connected to a 16-ounce canister, you'll know why (i.e., the "tower of power").

Close-up of stove modification using a common household coat hanger. The wire will draw heat from the stove down to the fuel line, preheating the liquid fuel to a gaseous state for normal operation.
Shawn Forry

The Kovea Spider is the lightest remote canister stove on the market. The preheat tube allows the canister to be inverted (not shown) to transition into liquid feed, further extending the temperature range at which the stove can operate.
Shawn Forry

Look at any liquid-feed stove and you will notice a preheat tube where the fuel line is directly routed through the flame before exiting the jet for combustion. This quick blast of heat through preheating expedites vaporization and, in turn, transforms the fuel from a liquid to a gaseous state. Any remote canister stove with this built-in design feature will be able to capitalize on the option to transform the stove to liquid feed. By simply inverting the canister, gravity replaces the dependency on pressurized fuel. As with a liquid-feed white gas stove, some priming will be required before inverting the canister to allow ample time to preheat the tube and to minimize flare-ups.

The right models of remote canister stoves are a great option for winter use. They burn extremely clean and quiet compared to traditional liquid-feed white gas stoves, with very few moving parts or pieces to maintain. The availability of different canister sizes makes it possible to dial in your fuel use to carry the minimal amount of fuel (and weight) required. It should be noted that canisters can be more challenging to locate and purchase when you're on the go outside of dedicated sporting goods stores. Additionally, some brands like Gaz and Coleman have proprietary canister valves, where compatibility between brands is limited.

MSR sells a dedicated canister support to conveniently invert any size canister for ease of operation. Conversion kits to adapt a common upright canister stove to liquid feed used to be commonly available. Brunton used to make a conversion kit for upright to remote canister use. A simple DIY project to modify this remote stand to incorporate a preheat tube is relatively straightforward. This used to be the de facto solution for die-hard winter canister users. Today, with more options from manufactures catering to this niche market, there are lighter, and arguably safer, options on the market. The following table lists some of the lightest available.

Make	Model	Weight	Price
Kovea	Spider (KB-1109)	5.9 oz	$64.95
Optimus	Vega	6.3 oz	$94.95
MSR	Windpro II	6.6 oz	$99.95
Snow Peak	GeoShield (stove only)	7.4 oz	$99.95
Primus	Express Spider	7.1 oz	$69.95

One of the main drawbacks of canister stoves is the inability to refill the canisters themselves. This can leave you with dozens of half-filled canisters or the need to carry multiple half-empty canisters on a single trip. The canister's weight alone negatively offsets the weight efficiency of the stove design. Additionally, the negative environmental impact of non-refillable canisters is a consideration for the environmentally conscious trekker—and a million-dollar endeavor for the intrepid entrepreneur who invests time and energy into resolving this obvious drawback to canister stoves.

While DIY solutions for refilling canisters from home are available, it is not advisable given the dangers surrounding overfilling, inevitable leaks, and the potential for damage to the valves themselves. Currently, it is possible to recycle empty canisters if appropriately punctured.

Alcohol Stoves

Alcohol stove—aka, the little engine that could. Nothing is more elegant, utilitarian, and simple than an alcohol stove. Whether home built or manufactured, alcohol stoves are the lightest option, with absolutely zero moving pieces. These stoves are the clear winner in nearly every category, including weight, maintenance, noise, and cost. Where alcohol stoves have lost credibility is in winter use, which is more accurately related to the inherent characteristics of the fuel at hand.

Denatured alcohol or methanol products like HEET have a lower potential BTU count than most any other stove fuel. For comparison, alcohol stoves effectively output half the heat as a white gas or canister stove. This translates to having to carry twice as much fuel for the equivalent cook time. However, because of the extremely low weight of the stove, the additional fuel weight is not offset until longer carries of a week-plus are required. For summertime use, alcohol stoves are hard to beat when weight and simple cooking are prioritized.

For winter use, the inherent limitations of alcohol stoves are further highlighted. A long-time myth is that alcohol stoves will not work at extreme elevation or low temperatures,

TIP

Prior to using your canister stove, warm the canister in your jacket while setting up camp, or in your sleeping bag overnight if planning on cooking in the morning. By pre-warming the canister, you will delay the negative effects of cold on the canister, ensuring that you maximize each canister's use. Resting the canisters on a small section of foam pad or creating a small cozy will further delay the cooling effect if the canister is warm to begin with.

neither of which is accurate. As with all stoves at low temps, proper priming is required. Either utilizing a priming pan or pouring a small amount of fuel on the exterior of the stove will effectively prime the stove. Preheating the fuel in a jacket pocket or sleeping bag prior to use will further expedite the priming process. Alternatively, you can light a piece of paper or toilet paper and hold it to the fuel to act as a wick and help it heat up.

When minimal weight and reliability are of the utmost importance, alcohol stoves should not be overlooked. They will take double the time to melt snow and boil water, but in winter, when there are more hours of darkness than daylight, what's the rush?

Since alcohol stoves output such little heat, the higher priority becomes containing and focusing the heat source. Windscreens are an absolute must for alcohol stove use. By far the most efficient model on the market is the Trail Design's Caldera Cone. This cone serves as both a pot stand and windscreen, further highlighting the multiuse ethos of ultralight hiking. The funnel design of the cone creates a chimney effect to the flame, focusing all the stove's heat directly into the bottom of the pot. Some models in the Trail Designs lineup have multifuel capabilities, including wood-burning and solid fuel (Esbit) options. Most of the cone models pack small enough to fit inside the dedicated pot for storage efficiency.

Trail Design's Caldera Cone is the most efficient way to conserve precious heat and fuel in an alcohol stove. The integrated windscreen also acts as a stable pot support.
Justin Lichter

I have not personally found much performance difference between alcohol stove designs, either from DIY homemade models or specialty designed models from established manufactures. The bottom line with alcohol stove use during winter is that they cater to a specific travel style. Where weight and reliability trump performance and gourmet cooking, alcohol stoves should definitely be considered. Interestingly, nearly every Iditarod musher uses an alcohol stove to tend to his or herself and dogs in some of the harshest conditions. Again, where weight and reliability are concerned, nothing tops an alcohol stove. Just be prepared to enjoy the confines of your sleeping bag for slightly longer before getting dinner, a hot drink, and/or a hot water bottle for the night's sleep; and be ready to create a cooking timeline that works efficiently with your nightly routine. For example, it may not make sense to make your tea or hot chocolate in your pot first, since you can pour off extra water from your dinner to make that.

Solid-Fuel Stoves

Esbit solid fuel tablets are an often-overlooked fuel source. Made from hexamine, these dense fuel tablets burn clean and smokeless and leave no ash or residue, although some folks complain of a waxy residue and fish-like odor from generic Esbit tablets. Similar to alcohol stoves, solid-fuel stoves are on the lower end of overall heat output and efficiency, but the tablets are easy to light and can be extinguished and then relighted as needed to conserve fuel. Each tablet is quoted as having a burn time of around 12 minutes and weighs about 0.5 ounce, so factor about a tablet per meal. The "stove" can be as simple as placing the fuel tab on top of a piece of aluminum foil. Other common fuel tab supports are fashioned from simple pop cans, akin to alcohol stoves. Best utilized as an emergency backup fuel source, the tablets also make for an ultralight fire starter in wet and otherwise unfavorable conditions. At only 0.5 ounce and extremely compact, their stable shelf life make fuel tabs a great tool to toss in your emergency kit.

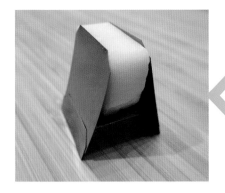

Trail Design's Gram Cracker "stove" is about as light as you can get. At 3 grams the stove base helps elevate the Esbit tablet off the ground for proper combustion. Esbit is a more efficient fuel than alcohol but can leave a tar-like residue on your cookware.
Shawn Forry

Wood-Burning

Fundamentally, the use of a stove is adding convenience to an otherwise already established cooking system. In most environs you'll travel, resources abound for the creation of fire, a true ultralighter's dream. Rarely will the aware traveler not pass or camp near a fuel source, typically found below timberline. Nothing is more primal than sitting around a campfire cooking your dinner—a lost art, typically discussed within survival manuals.

The truth is there are a lot of drawbacks to solitary wood-fire cooking. Collecting branches and twigs can be tedious and time-consuming. The accumulation of soot and sap on pots and cookware will seep into the contents of your entire backpack if cookware isn't carefully packed and quarantined, not to mention the lingering aroma of smoke that can percolate into food, water, and clothing. Travel and weather conditions can additionally thwart your efforts to collect dry fuel. The harshest days typically signal the highest demand for the warmth of fire; driving rains, bitter cold, and howling winds take mental fortitude and determination to overcome when daylight is dwindling as you arrive at camp.

Any skilled traveler should possess the basic skills required to build a wood fire as a backup emergency option. Scenarios abound of when cooking over a fire would be necessary: the loss or miscalculation of fuel, a temperamental or damaged stove, to name a few.

Cooking by wood fire can be done with or without a stove apparatus. A wood-burning stove like a Bushbuddy or Trail

Backcountry fires can be a multifunctional way to cook food, dry gear, and achieve temporary warmth. Fires should be used sparingly to conserve resources, and their lack of concentrated heat makes them challenging to properly cook on, not to mention the plethora of burn holes that will further lighten your gear!
Justin Lichter

Left: The Trekker Ultra 004 is the lightest offering by Bushbuddy yet weighs nearly twice as much as a similar offering from Trail Designs. The Bushbuddy requires less assembly, which is favorable with cold gloved hands. *Bushbuddy*
Right: Trail Design's Sidewinder Ti-Tri Caldera Cone stove shown in wood-burning mode. This versatile stove can also run on Esbit tablets and denatured alcohol to suit your cooking preferences. Wood-burning stoves eliminate the need to carry a fuel source when the surrounding environment has copious amounts of dead and down tinder. *Shawn Forry*

Designs Ti-Tri will use fuel sources more efficiently, but the weight of carrying the stove system should be considered versus an open fire where no stove is required. Comparatively, a Bushbuddy tips the scale at around 5 ounces; the Ti-Tri comes in a little lighter at 3.5 ounces, is notably more efficient due to the caldera cone, and is slightly less robust in durability. Both will stow inside certain cook pots, a boon for spatial efficiency, critical for fitting everything inside that ultralight pack. The sheer increase in efficiency in cook time and preparation is notable if you're considering whether to go sans stove or not. Once lit, both stove systems use very little fuel in the way of small sticks and twigs. They do require constant oversight to keep the stove fed, and it takes practice and patience to manage the flame height appropriately to simmer or reach an outright boil. That being said, wood

For large groups, an open fire is the quickest way to boil large volumes of water. Gallons of water can be processed in less than 5 minutes. A tripod such as this is effective at centering the pots over the large flames. While not the most LNT (Leave No Trace) approach, cutting green alder branches can substitute for the heavy steel legs, requiring only the drop chains to be carried.
Larry Mishkar

burning stoves really show their worth on extended expeditions where fuel weight is essentially eliminated.

For outright open-fire cooking, allowing time to establish a proper bed of coals will engender more controlled, even cooking and baking, while engulfing a suspended pot within a raging fire will provide the quickest boil times imaginable—and melted silicon handles. Having a means to suspend a pot over a fire not only minimizes the potential for seared fingers but also adds some adjustability to the heat source for a more controlled cooking system. A personal favorite when paired with a pot with a bail-style handle is to bring along a length of 10 to 15 feet of thin ⅛-inch gauge steel cable with a hook on the end that can be draped over a low-hanging branch. With a fire built conveniently under said low-hanging branch, you can not only achieve a more protected fire location against wind and rain, but the adjustability of the pot in proximity to the wire is nearly limitless.

As with any ultralight system, the compromise to save weight by eliminating a stove from your camp kit will warrant an increase in skill, time and patience. Best reserved as a backup cook system, wood-burning stoves have their time and place. It should go without saying that practicing proper Leave No Trace ethics is a basic expectation with backcountry fires. Fires put more strain on backcountry wilderness resources.

Windscreens and Base Plates

The best method for minimizing fuel weight and decreasing cook time is the use of a proper windscreen. Nothing is more frustrating than waiting for a pot to boil when conditions are windy. It's not unrealistic for boil time to double during unfavorable conditions. Windscreens not only help focus the precious heat coming off your stove into the pot but also prevent heat loss from external factors.

The simplest windscreens can be fashioned from a length of aluminum flashing wrapped around a pot; more elaborate designs can incorporate pot supports and adjustability. A roll of aluminum flashing can be easily acquired at any hardware store for cheap and then designed using scissors and a hole punch. Keep in mind that some flow of air is required to permeate the windscreen to make sure the stove is receiving oxygen to assist with proper combustion. Experimentation may be required in windscreen design and application to squeeze the most efficiency out of your stove. Significant improvements in cook times can be achieved by simply elevating the windscreen slightly off the ground, adjusting the gap around the pot, or adjusting the height between the stove and pot.

Windscreens are an essential component regardless of which stove system you are using. They funnel and direct heat, focusing every precious BTU toward the pot. Windscreens are simple enough to fashion from aluminum flashing purchased at a hardware store, or they can be well-designed systems like this one from Trail Designs. *Shawn Forry*

For folks with deeper pockets, sheets of thin 0.03-millimeter titanium can be purchased for twice the price, half the weight, but at the expense of lower durability. The cheapest, lightest option is to fashion a windscreen out of common household heavy-gauge aluminum foil. Again, practicality, durability, and rigidity will be minimal, sacrificed to the goal of shaving every possible gram.

One of the most overlooked requirements of wintertime cooking is the need to incorporate a stove base plate or something similar. When cooking atop snow, the heat from the stove will begin to soften and melt the underlying snow, eventually disrupting the stove's stability and potentially leading to a culinary catastrophe. At a minimum, any cook site should be prepped by consolidating and leveling the cooking platform. Still, disaster will lurk around the corner, especially if long cook times are anticipated to melt snow, cook group meals, and prepare water for the next day's travel. It's not uncommon for your stove to be going for more than an hour to accomplish all these evening chores.

Simple, homemade solutions include using a common pie pan or heavy-gauge aluminum foil under your stove. Another DIY solution is to cut a turkey pan to size. The platform can be further stabilized by lining a base of sticks under the foil to prevent the platform from sinking into the snow. The foil will prevent the sticks from catching fire, and by utilizing found resources in camp, this system further minimizes pack weight during the day.

Commercial variations are obviously available. MSR manufactures their Trillium Stove Base, which is easily integrated into any of their stove models. At 2.8 ounces it's not "break the bank" heavy, but the fact that it serves only a single purpose limits its appeal. If you're carrying an avalanche shovel, these can sometime be utilized as a stove base. Due to variations in curvature, type of paint, and design, some models are better suited than others for this multipurpose option.

SLEEP SYSTEMS

A sleeping bag is commonly referred to as the third leg in the "Big 3" considerations in outdoor gear purchases (in combination with a shelter and backpack of choice). For wintertime travel, a stand-alone sleeping bag will not suffice for nighttime temps that can dip well below freezing. We need to take a holistic look at all the variables and moving pieces that will link together the proper combination of sleeping bag, sleeping pad, liner, overbag, bivy, and specialty clothing. There are many myths and misinterpretations surrounding the dynamics of sleeping warm. While overnight warmth is obviously a focal point for overall comfort, the successful implementation of a proper sleep system contributes to a larger margin of safety in the scope of overall risk management. Proper rest will not only restore our energy reserves for the next day's travel and decrease the likelihood of injuries, but will also increase our body's overall metabolic efficiency. This will directly correlate to a feeling of overall greater warmth, smarter decision making, and increased enjoyment in our surroundings. Consider it the "anti–grumpy pants."

So much goes into ensuring a warm, restful night's sleep, further complicated by everyone's different physiology and preferences. Each component must work in concert based on the particular set of conditions faced. *Shawn Forry*

SLEEPING BAGS

Most conversations about sleeping bag selection first come down to the age-old debate of down versus synthetic. So why after years of technology and human survival are we whittled down to only two choices? For the purposes of backpacking, we're keenly aware of weight, bulk, cost, and comfort. We could just as easily stuff dry leaves into a trash bag at night or go the way of polar explorers and tote around 20-pound sealskin sleeping bags. Stylish, yes! Practical, not so much.

The reality is that only a few inches of feathers or fibers will separate you from the frigid outside temps. The dust of the debate is kicked up further when deciding which insulation type is better. The answer is simple: It depends. In simplest terms, down is lighter, compresses smaller, and lasts virtually forever. So why does the debate not end there? Moisture management is the biggest drawback to down insulation. When down gets wet, the plume, or "loft," of the feather collapses. Warmth has a direct correlation to the material's ability to trap YOUR heat. No gap, no heat. It is important to note here that the fabric or material itself does not create heat. A commonly overheard statement is that "this _____ is so warm!" The item itself is not creating its own magical heat source; it is merely highly efficient at trapping the heat your body is producing. The effect is that you are selfishly keeping yourself warm rather than generously heating the world around you.

The characteristics of synthetic insulation are quite literally the opposite of down: bulkier, heavier, cheaper, and will typically only last two to three seasons before the insulation begins to pack out. A subtle advantage is that synthetic insulation is naturally hypoallergenic, important for those with an aversion to duck and goose feathers. Where synthetic insulation shines is in its ability to remain warm(er) when wet. It is important to note that comfort is not lumped into this claim, and a wet synthetic bag will be significantly colder than its claimed (dry) temperature range. If you've ever slept in a wet sleeping bag, you'll know how uncomfortable it can be when your backcountry experience is pushed far into the survival category.

While synthetic insulation is engineered to mimic natural down, they are not created equal, and there are even tiers of quality within each type of insulation. Take synthetic insulation for instance. We've likely all seen a tag bearing the name Thinsulate on a pair of gloves. But how does this compare to the other popular name brands of synthetic insulation, such as Climashield, PrimaLoft, or Polarguard? The clutter of marketing spiels makes it hard to distinguish one from another. The important tidbit things to know are how they were created and their intended purposes. Insulation for a jacket is going to have much different priorities than insulation for a sleeping bag, for instance.

Synthetic insulation is nothing more than plastic that has been extruded under high pressure through a very fine jet. The resulting threadlike fibers can be overlaid to create a matrix that mirrors the randomized, lofty piles of down plumage. This can further be classified into long and short staple fibers. Because long staple fibers are more substantial and intertwined, they are more stable, which minimizes their tendency to shift, collapse, and create gaps. This, in turn, means a firmer feel, higher compression rates, and generally a more durable product. Polarguard and Climashield have been the gold standard in this type of insulation and the mainstay in synthetic insulation in sleeping bags.

PrimaLoft, on the other hand, specializes in short-staple filaments. This design more closely replicates down. With a very short fiber length, the resulting filament is lighter and freer to move around. This closer resemblance to natural down creates a loftier, softer nap. The resulting advantage is that PrimaLoft is currently as close as you can get to down's warmth-to-weight ratio. The downside is its tendency to shift and collapse over time. These characteristics are why you'll rarely see PrimaLoft utilized in sleeping bags. The lack of rigidity in the fiber also means it lacks durability, which contradicts its higher price tag.

This swatch of PrimaLoft insulation illustrates how synthetic insulation tries to mimic the loft of natural down. For a slight weight penalty, synthetic insulations like this excel in wet climates where down falls short.
Shawn Forry

The value of down is equally complicated to discern. What makes a boutique $600 sleeping bag any better than a generic $30 down comforter found at a box store? Both are filled with the by-product of "birds of feather." Like an exotic sports car, the difference lies in what's under the hood. For a goose or a duck, the horsepower lies not in the outer feathers but in the soft and lofty underplumage that is referred to as down. Most low-end "down" products likely contain a high percentage of feathers, not down. If you've ever had a quill poke through your sleeping bag, that is a cheap feather rearing its ugly head.

True down plumage looks like a puffed-up dandelion seed head, and the loftiest samples come from the breasts of mature female ducks or geese. Some will argue that even a duck's or goose's habitat can affect the quality of the down. Birds living and migrating through colder, harsher environments will naturally develop denser, loftier down plumes. The most prized down comes from the Eider duck and the Hungarian goose. The size of each individual plume can range from dime-size for lower quality down up to quarter-size for the best of the best. To extract the highest performance out of a single plume, it all comes down to how the plume is cleaned and refined. Who knew so much went in to getting the look of the "Michelin Man" jacket!

So how do we compare one batch of down with another? Like the measurement of horsepower, the comparative metric for down is "fill-power." Take 1 ounce of a down sample and put it into a graduated cylinder. The volume the down takes up in cubic inches is said to be its fill-power—600-fill represented as 600 cubic inches; 700-fill represented as 700 cubic inches, and so on. Fill-powers under 600 are generally considered low grade and the down used commercially for products like pillows and toys. The hallmark of ultralight backpacking in the realm of 750+ fill-power, with some claims as high as 1,000. There is an inherent qualifier that boosts fill-power numbers into the upper echelon of 900+, usually entailing obsession over plume selection, days lofting inside a tumble drier, and controlled amounts of humidity in the lab. The real world is a far cry from the lab, and even the highest end down is going to be more susceptible to collapsing under the weight of a humid summer night. That being said, by utilizing high-quality down, a weight saving of 4 to 8 ounces can be had just in the difference between 650 fill-power versus 800+ fill-power for the same warmth.

TIP

If you have a few feather quills poking through the shell of your sleeping bag, resist the temptation to pull the feather out. It could bring a few precious friends along with it! Instead pinch the sleeping bag fabric and pull the feather back in. Gently massaging the fabric where the quill hole was will seal the fabric back over.

Shawn Forry

COATINGS AND SHELLS

So-called "waterproof" down has been highly marketed over the past few years by companies like DriDown and DownTek. Although any "waterproof" claim should be scrutinized, there seems to be some merit to the hydrophobic claims companies like Sierra Designs, Big Agnes, Mountain Hardwear, and even cottage manufactures like ZPacks are making. While the exact science of the technology is proprietary, the basic principal is that a coating is applied to the individual down clusters to extend the time frame of absorption when they're exposed to moisture. How long these coating will last or how much weight (if any) is added to the down is yet to be determined. Adding any coating to a down cluster is likely going to "weigh" the cluster down, which is likely why there currently isn't a high fill-power offering of waterproof down. Plus, the added "weight" could impact durability and long-term performance and as with fabric coatings, probably will wear off with use.

Waterproof shell materials like Gore-Tex also seem like obvious solutions to minimize the catastrophic effects of a completely waterlogged sleeping bag. But similar to the limitations of "breathability" in these fabrics with rain jackets, the same internal condensation is noted when these fabrics are incorporated into a sleeping bag. Although far less moisture is produced and accumulated during the night while you're sleeping, it is important to consider these limitations when purchasing so-called "waterproof" sleeping bags. These bags are more challenging to wash and maintain due to their excessive dry times, challenging to remove excessive body oils, and add considerable cost. When thinking about minimizing the amount of moisture getting into a sleeping bag, we need to look at the bag holistically and think about moisture from both internal and external factors. Eliminating one side of the equation only exacerbates the other.

With full disclosure toward a personal bias for high-end ultralight down sleeping bags, buy the best bag that fits into your budget. With proper technique and care, down bags will function as intended, last longer, and carry lighter. My first sleeping bag was a $150 synthetic

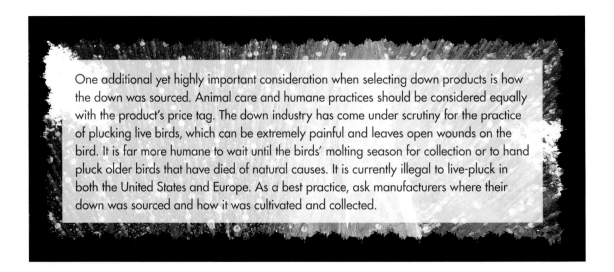

One additional yet highly important consideration when selecting down products is how the down was sourced. Animal care and humane practices should be considered equally with the product's price tag. The down industry has come under scrutiny for the practice of plucking live birds, which can be extremely painful and leaves open wounds on the bird. It is far more humane to wait until the birds' molting season for collection or to hand pluck older birds that have died of natural causes. It is currently illegal to live-pluck in both the United States and Europe. As a best practice, ask manufacturers where their down was sourced and how it was cultivated and collected.

North Face Cat's Meow sleeping bag—bulky, cheap, and plenty warm. If you can only afford one bag, one in the 15°F to 20°F range will cover a broad range of conditions.

QUILTS VS. MUMMY

When pushing ultralight to the extreme, everything carried comes under careful examination. By understanding the science of how insulation effectively regulates nighttime body heat, it is no wonder that inquisitive ultralighters finally critiqued the excessiveness and inefficiency of a traditional mummy bag. We will omit the discussion of semi-rectangular and other antiquated sleeping bag designs due to their assumed inefficiency and irrelevance to ultralight travel.

By design, literally half a traditional sleeping bags' materials lie compressed under the sleeper. This compressed insulation does little to bolster the claimed warmth of the overall sleep system. The sleeping pad is effectively maintaining and regulating the loss of warmth toward the ground. By eliminating this insulation and shell material from the bottom of a traditional sleeping bag, weight savings in excess of 8 to 10 ounces are easily achieved at very little compromise to overall comfort. Quilts, by design, can cater to a broader range of internal bulk and size due to their variable girth capabilities. If you want to utilize a bulky

Closure systems for quilts all serve the same function but can vary from Velcro to snaps to zippers to webbing. All systems prioritize minimizing drafts and sealing in warmth. The variable girth approach to quilts allows the bag's warmth to be customized to suit the conditions, even opening up fully to blanket mode.
Shawn Forry

Katabatic takes a unique approach to their closure system by integrating the quilt to the pad through the use of clever fasteners and thin cord ties. Enlightened Equipment simply uses an elastic band around the pad. Both are effective and highlight the overall attention put into the design.
Shawn Forry

puffy jacket under the quilt, you are not limited by the internal girth as defined by a zipper closure. Most quilt users also appreciate the additional comfort and mobility while sleeping under a quilt due to the adjustability inherent in the design.

The caveat with quilt design is the necessary adjustment in technique to minimize drafts and accommodate the lack of a hood. Ensuring that the quilt stays tucked under you at all times during the night is a factor in regulating warmth. While a traditional sleeping bag will move with you as you toss and turn without introducing a blast of cold air, care and technique are required to ensure that a quilt remains on top of you while you shift sleep positions. With extended use, this adjustment becomes second nature, and as with most ultralight techniques, a compromise in comfort and weight savings must be acknowledged.

The hood dilemma is easily overcome by the mantra of multiuse objectivity. Since most hikers carry some sort of camp jacket or puffy in addition to a warm beanie, these two items are integrated into the overall sleep system and a simple and elegant solution is achieved. The added

Insulated balaclavas like the Mountain Laurel Designs Apex not only solve the dilemma of hoodless quilts but also increase versatility in layering systems and move more effectively with the body while sleeping.
Justin Lichter

advantage of utilizing a jacket hood versus a sleeping bag hood is that the jacket will move with you as you adjust from back to side to stomach sleeping. No more suffocating into the hood of your sleeping bag.

Katabatic Gear makes some of the best quilts in the business due to their use of quality materials and attention to design detail. Their strap systems can attach directly to a sleeping pad or be used independently. The use of a light elastic band around the perimeter of the quilt opening further minimizes drafts because of the form-fitting, "hugging" nature of the elastic against the body.

To combat this perceived drawback from drafts, most quilt users incorporate a dedicated bivy sack to the equation. Keep in mind that by using a bivy, you are offsetting the overall weight saving gained by transitioning to quilt use, and bivies have their own inherent drawbacks (see "Bivies" in the Shelter section).

Quilts like the Mountain Laurel Designs Spirit offer the option of adding a head slot to convert the quilt into a poncho for additional warmth in camp. Creative alternatives like this weigh nothing and add more versatility to your layering and sleep systems.
Shawn Forry

Mummy versus Quilt

Mummy			Quilt			
Make/Model	Temp	Weight	Make/Model	Temp	Weight	Savings
Montbell Alpine Down Hugger	50	15.0 oz	Montbell Down Multi-Blanket	50	12.0 oz	-3 oz
Montbell Down Hugger 900	40	16.3 oz	ZPacks 900	40	13.6 oz	-2.7 oz
Western Mountaineering MegaLite	30	20.0 oz	Katabatic Palisade	30	17.5 oz	-2.5 oz
Western Mountaineering UltraLite	20	29.0 oz	Katabatic Alsak	22	21.0 oz	-8 oz
Feathered Friends Lark UL	10	32.0 oz	ZPacks 900	10	23.0 oz	-9 oz
Feathered Friends Snowbunting EX	0	45.0 oz	Enlightened Equipment Revelation	0	22.8 oz	-22.2 oz

SLEEPING BAG LINERS

Sleeping bag liners are not only a great way to extend the temperature range of an existing sleeping bag but can also serve as a stand-alone bag for hot summer nights or "European hostel"–type backpacking. Additionally, they are a convenient way to keep your bag clean longer. Body oils are one of the quickest ways to saturate and degrade a fluffy down bag. Sleeping bag liners come in a multitude of fabric and material choices and can boost night-time temps by 5 to 15 degrees. A simple silk liner has the highest warmth-to-weight ratio and feels luxurious next to the skin. Jagbags out of New Zealand (now distributed through Terre Vista Trails) has been a personal favorite for a cost-effective solution. They will do custom sizing and features at low to no cost. A simple hoodless mummy-shaped silk liner can come in under 3 to 4 ounces and can double as a town skirt when doing laundry in town or keeping the mosquitoes off your legs while in camp.

Silk liners like this 2.7-ounce (custom) version from Jagbags offer approximately 5 more degrees of warmth and silky smoothness against the skin and also extend the loft of a sleeping bag by preventing body oils from penetrating the insulation. Liners can also serve double garment duty as a sarong in camp or town and a scarf on colder days. *Shawn Forry*

Other common liners are made from heavier fleece or synthetic microfiber fabrics. With a weight increase upward of 8+ ounces, these types of liners are less favorable when doing a warmth-to-weight analysis. Their claimed performance boost of 15-plus degrees is optimistic at best. One perspective to consider is that 8 additional ounces of down in a sleeping bag will easily boost the internal temperature range of the bag by 20-plus degrees but add significant cost to the initial purchase.

Another simple solution is to utilize an ultrathin summer-rated down sleeping bag inside a traditional three-season bag. This provides you with effectively three independent sleeping bags to adjust to anticipated conditions ranging from extreme summer heat to the deep chill of fall and early winter. Montbell makes a 12-ounce down inner bag that is rated for 45°F to 50°F and would boost temps by 25-plus degrees. A simple equation for factoring the effective temperature when combining sleeping bags is:

$$[x - (70 - y)/2 = z]$$

In this equation "x" is the existing sleeping bag and "y" is the outer or inner bag you are going to add. For practical purposes in the above example, say you added the 45°F Montbell Down Multi-Blanket to an existing 20°F sleeping bag. With the two combined, your new effective temperature range would be -2.5°F. This route will always be slightly heavier than just purchasing a dedicated -2.5°F degree bag from the start, but the added versatility in bag combinations cannot be understated. Additionally, similar to modular mitten designs, the ability to separate an inner bag from an outer will decrease dry time in the event that moisture builds up within the bags.

One key consideration with this approach is to ensure that there is enough internal space to incorporate an inner liner. Knowing that warmth is a factor of dead air space, by "crushing" or compressing the inner sleeping bag against the outer bag, you are effectively limiting the maximum warmth potential of the combined bags. Some will argue that the density of the insulation will remain the same and that no effective loss of warmth will be noted. Regardless, it's a consideration, and this same principle applies to wearing puffy insulated clothing inside a sleeping bag.

OVERBAGS

In principle, using outer bags, or overbags, is effectively the same as incorporating inner liners, the end goal being to add additional warmth to an existing bag. Where outer bags shine is the additional consideration of shell fabric material in addition to insulation choice. If there is ever a place to "have your cake and eat it," it's in the ability to marry the pros of

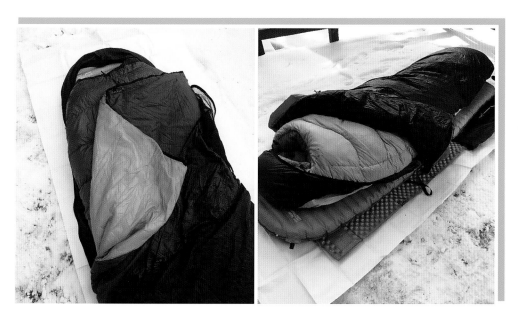

A synthetic overbag is a highly effective way to manage moisture and retain warmth in winter sleep systems on extended expeditions. The various combinations of down inner and synthetic outer bags create a versatile system to cater to nearly any condition. *Left:* Successfully used on our winter PCT traverse, this 30-degree Katabatic Palisade inner quilt and 38-degree Mountain Laurel Designs Spirit outer quilt couple for a combined weight of 34 ounces good to about -5°F. Pad and bivy add another 20 ounces for combined warmth down to -10°F. *Right:* For extreme temps, this North Face Momentum 0-degree inner and Enlightened Equipment Revelation Quilt 25-degree outer can be pushed down to -45°F with incorporating clothing layers (58 ounces combined). Note the addition of a three-quarter-length Therm-a-Rest Z-Rest (8 ounces) and backpack under the feet for additional ground insulation. Total system weighs 86 ounces.
Shawn Forry

down insulation with synthetic. When moisture management is of utmost concern, we can prioritize a shell that will shed spindrift and condensation more effectively, merged with synthetic insulation that will better manage the internal moisture coming off our bodies and damp clothing we are attempting to dry out.

As moisture moves from our bodies through the insulation to the external world, at some point it is going to cool and condense, which leads to the buildup of moisture within the insulation. In extreme cold environs, this moisture will condense all the way to the point of freezing into ice crystals. You'll note this phenomenon by the crispy, crunchy exterior of a frosted-over outer bag. The use of synthetic insulation at the point where this moisture will cool and condense minimizes the collapse that down would experience while simultaneously maintaining the warmth benefits of a double-bag system.

Quilts are by far the best design for an outer bag, given their inherent variable girth ability. The limitations of compressing the insulation between the two systems is greatly minimized or eliminated altogether. Like the benefits mentioned above with quilts versus traditional mummy bags, an overbag is effectively draping more warmth over an existing bag without the unnecessary bulk and weight of insulation on the bottom. Controlling the movement of both bags is a factor to consider. Most quilt-type overbags utilize various straps to keep both sleeping bags not only aligned with each other but also aligned with the sleeping pad.

This down inner, synthetic outer double-bag system was our system of choice for the PCT during winter and was derived from many winters operating in the frigid North Woods and on the Appalachian Trail during wintertime. There is no better system in terms of simplicity and effectiveness. Enlightened Equipment makes excellent custom overbags with a plethora of options, materials, and sizes to select from. Mountain Laurel Designs also makes quilts that can be oversized to work.

VAPOR BARRIER CLOTHING AND LINERS

One of the least understood applications within a sleep system is the use of vapor barrier clothing and sleep liners. A vapor barrier liner (VBL) is a fully waterproof membrane that restricts the transmission of moisture. It should be clearly stated that, by design, there are no claims of breathability with VBL use. The theory states that the human body has a preferred microclimate of humidity it is always trying to achieve. Once this microclimate is achieved, the body will reduce moisture output, defined here as sweat. Where this benefits a sleep system is that less moisture will be lost through perspiration, which means hydration will be further maintained, which directly correlates to sleeping warmer. The reduced transmission of moisture from our pores into the sleeping bag at night also means optimal loft over extended days during an expedition.

This all sounds great in principle, but the understated reality is that VBLs are commonly experienced as a clammy feeling throughout the night. Since the moisture coming off our body is no longer able to percolate through the insulation and away from the skin, we experience this effect as a noted dampness during our sleep cycle. If you perspire heavily, a less-insulated sleeping bag can likely be utilized to achieve the same warmth and comfort, further exploiting the weight-saving effects of VBLs.

Companies like RBH, Stephenson's Warmlite, Integral Designs, and 40 Below currently make commercially available vapor barrier liners and clothing. Most of these offerings are unnecessarily heavy for sleep use and are intended more for extended use during daytime activities. We strongly prefer vapor barrier clothing over a vapor barrier liner, since with the use of a liner, you essentially have to sleep naked to minimize dampening any clothing worn between the skin and liner. This negates the multiuse nature of isolative camp clothing into a sleep system. The options for dedicated VBL clothing for sleeping are currently under-represented in the market. Using DCF or silnylon rain gear is currently the best option, and even these are overbuilt and heavy for their intended use. A simple home solution is to make a jacket/pant combo using a Mylar space blanket. Using a simple pattern and some clear tape, a low-cost ultralight solution can be made for under $10 and an hour of time.

With better understanding of the use and application of VBL liners and clothing, you can maintain the optimum isolative characteristics of your sleep system over many days in unfavorable conditions. By compromising a bit of sleep comfort because of the clammy nature of VBLs, you can further push the ultralight envelop in extreme conditions. Keep in mind that, again, we must look at the entire sleep system as a whole. Vapor barriers prevent moisture from our bodies from entering the insulation, so now it becomes prevalent that we keep external moisture from entering our bags through the use of a waterproof bivy and waterproof shell

While not technically fully waterproof, the WP/B DCF rain jacket by ZPacks is backed with an eVent membrane, offering limited breathability in low-aerobic activities in cold conditions. Where this jacket shines is that for just over 5 ounces you get a fully weatherproof rain jacket that can double as a VBL jacket. We highly recommend opting for the pit zip option to increase ventilation and versatility.
ZPacks

The now lighter HotSac VBL liner by Western Mountaineering, weighing in at 4.5 ounces, prevents radiant heat loss and moisture buildup within the insulation of a sleeping bag. While not as versatile as VBL clothing, the use of VBLs is critical during extended time in cold climates.
Western Mountaineering

fabrics. Everything must work in concert, and a misunderstanding or misuse of one system can greatly compromise the margin of error that is ever present during extreme winter conditions.

CARE

Few things conjure up more fear than the need to wash a down sleeping bag. A quality sleeping bag is a huge investment, and with proper care it will last a lifetime, so fear not. The two biggest killers of a good sleeping bag are improper storage and poor hygiene.

Body oils will percolate through the inner shell fabric and collect on the down clusters. Storing a sleeping bag fully compressed will damage the plume, minimizing the natural warmth-retention characteristics. Proper care should include always storing a sleeping bag uncompressed in a cotton storage sack, away from sun and moisture. Bags should be routinely washed with dedicated detergents, such Gear Aid Down Wash or a similar product. Bags should be washed in a front-loading machine to avoid damage to the delicate baffles and then run through several rinse cycles to ensure that all the detergent has been removed. Not doing so can result in residual detergent preventing the down from fully lofting.

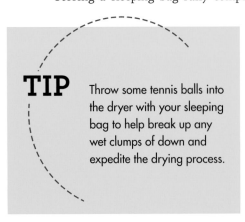

TIP Throw some tennis balls into the dryer with your sleeping bag to help break up any wet clumps of down and expedite the drying process.

Drying is one of the most important and often overlooked components of the wash regimen. Down takes a LONG time to fully dry. If in doubt, send the bag through another dry cycle; you won't regret it. Mold and mildew can set into down clusters within 24 hours if a bag's not properly dried. This is by far the quickest way to ruin that $600 boutique sleeping bag.

SLEEPING PADS

Probably one of the most overlooked components of a proper sleep system is a well-insulated sleeping pad. While comfort is an important consideration in a sleeping pad, warmth retention should be the gold standard when selecting a pad to use in winter. We lose far more heat through conduction sleeping on the cold ground than by radiational heat loss through our sleeping bags. As discussed above, any insulation in a sleeping bag that is between our body and the sleeping pad is being crushed and rendered ineffective. This leaves the pad itself as the sole barrier and guardian of heat between us and the ground.

Similar to home construction, the means by which we compare the warmth of one sleeping pad to another is through the language of R-value. The higher the value, the warmer the pad will be. R-value is the measurement of thermal resistance—in our application, the resistance of the cold ground to seep into your sleeping bag! For perspective, the R-value of air alone is 1.0. Sleeping pads like a Therm-a Rest NeoAir that lack any insulation materials outside of the face fabric will have an R-value just about that of air—great for mild summertime use, a miserable night's sleep if utilized for the winter.

In terms of options, we have two broad topics: inflatables and closed cell foam. Both have their advantages and disadvantages, and similar to the above discussion with sleeping bags, we want to consider both.

Inflatable pads are inherently more comfortable at the risk of puncturing. For winter use, our campsite for the night might be devoid of sharp rocks and roots, but snow and ice and can be equally lumpy and abrasive. Closed cell foam pads are bulkier but allow for more multiuse applications, like a sit pad during breaks and a kneel pad while doing camp chores. Planning on sitting next to a fire for the evening? You'll have less puncture anxiety from a rogue ember if you're sitting on a closed cell foam pad!

You might want to have both for extreme winter use. Pairing a über-thin foam pad like a Gossamer Gear ⅛-inch Thinlite pad with a light, thermally efficient inflatable like a Therm-a Rest Neo-Air X-Therm (R-value 5.7) is about as light and functional as you can get. The X-Therm achieves a ridiculously high R-value by using Mylar reflective panels. I was truly skeptical of its claimed warmth until I tried it myself—it ended up making a big difference.

Similar to sleeping pads, other insulators in inflatable pads include synthetic and down insulation, housed within the independent air chambers of the pad. The same pros and cons of sleeping bags apply to down-insulated mats. While lighter, they are prone to getting saturated by your breath. Since you need to blow up the pad and your breath contains A LOT of moisture, using a dedicated hand pump for all down mats is essential. Otherwise you

So many choices, but color isn't one! Sleeping pads can range in size and insulative materials, including air, closed-cell foam, and down and synthetic insulation. Comfort should come secondary to ensuring adequate warmth from the ground.
Shawn Forry

During extreme cold, the pad's release valve can freeze shut after coming into contact with your saliva. To prevent damage to the valve, thaw it in your mouth before attempting to turn it open.

TIP

Sleeping Pad Comparison*

Make	Model	Insulation	R-Value	Weight	R-Value / Weight Ratio**	Price
Therm-a-Rest	NeoAir XTherm	Air/Mylar	5.7	15 oz	0.38	$199
Exped	DownMat UL 7	Air/Down	5.9	20 oz	0.30	$249
Exped	DownMat Winterlite LW	Air/Down	7.0	24 oz	0.29	$249
Exped	SynMat Hyperlite	Air/Synthetic	3.3	12 oz	0.28	$169
Big Agnes	Q Core SLX	Air/Synthetic	4.5	16 oz	0.28	$159
Exped	DownMat XP 9	Air/Down	8.0	31 oz	0.26	$259
Klymit	Insulated Static V Lite	Air/Synthetic	4.4	19 oz	0.23	$94
Big Agnes	Insulated Air Core Ultra	Air/Synthetic	4.5	21 oz	0.21	$99
Therm-a-Rest	Z-Lite Sol	CCF	2.6	14 oz	0.19	$44
Gossamer Gear	Thinlite	CCF	0.5	2 oz	0.03	$18

*All mats are full-length 72-inch pads for comparative purposes.
**R-Value/Weight Ratio: The higher the number, the more efficient the pad.

quickly end up with damp down that is extremely hard to dry out given the limited access of air to the down. These hand pumps can weigh 2 to 5 ounces. Some manufacturers use lighter stuff sack–type inflators that can "roll" large volumes of air into the pad while doubling as a waterproof stuff sack during the day.

Whether it is warmer to have the foam pad on the bottom or top of the inflatable is a "hotly" debated topic. You will feel more warmth if the foam pad is on top, but we personally like to have the foam on the bottom to better protect the inflatable from punctures, and there's a little less slippage of the pads. If you ever have to sleep directly on the ground in winter due to a punctured inflatable sleeping pad, you'll learn rather quickly the importance of carrying a dedicated repair kit with you!

Stuff sack inflators like the Exped Schnozzel Pumpbag prevent moisture from freezing inside your sleeping pad and are the fastest means of inflating large-volume pads. This one also doubles as a waterproof dry bag.
Valerie DiPonio

SUMMARY

Bearing in mind personal preferences and styles, there is a lot to consider when selecting a sleep system. The most important concept to highlight is that everything is connected. You switch one thing out, it is likely to affect something else. As with all things, a compromise must be reached in order to find the right balance of warmth, weight, cost, and margin of error. After years of use and many sleepless nights of experimentation, here is our go-to sleep system for temps down to -20°F:

- Katabatic Sawatch 15-degree Quilt (24 oz) or Montbell Down Hugger 900 #2 (24.3 oz)

- Mountain Laurel Designs 38-degree Spirit Quilt, custom (16 oz)

- Therm-a-Rest NeoAir XTherm (16 oz)

- Gossamer Gear ThinLight (2 oz)

- Katabatic Bristlecone Bivy, custom (6 oz)**

**XTherm is positioned inside the bivy to minimize drafts and contain all the components.

WATER TREATMENT AND HYDRATION

When we look at the basic intent of water treatment and hydration, we're looking at the need to drink clean, safe water in a consistent and timely manner. When we view these requirements through the lens of ultralight travel, we also prioritize techniques and equipment that will accomplish this by the lightest and fastest means possible. Distance is a function of time and rate, so minimizing the superfluous facets of collecting and consuming water will directly correlate to not only covering more distance per day but also staying warmer by doing so.

Marketing efforts of many large water treatment companies have convinced us that the slightest drop of untreated water upon our lips will send us into uncontrollable bowel movements. The big G-word comes to mind for many people: giardia. While there are many disgusting backcountry water sources in the world, with a basic understanding of what causes a water source to become "contaminated," we can better choose sources that are cleaner to begin with (see "Staying Hydrated" in chapter 4).

There are several options for water purification, all of which have their drawbacks and advantages. We are all aware of what happens to water when the temps dip below freezing. This reality directly affects access to water during the winter months. Even our means of transporting water can be adversely affected without proper foresight. This section provides a broad overview of methods of treatment and considerations for streamlining the efficiency with which you use and carry water throughout your trip.

First let's provide a quick overview of the nasty critters that could be residing at a microscopic level within our water source.

- **Bacteria:** Bacteria are around us all the time. They are on your hands, within your mouth, and all around you as you read this. Paranoid? Fear not, there are many good types of bacteria that we rely upon to live healthy lives. Within your stomach there is a healthy plume of bacteria that is helping you digest that doughnut you just ate. The culprits we want to pay mind to and that occasionally make the headlines of newspapers are coliforms like *E. coli*. Fecal coliforms are more common coliforms. Did you wash your hands after that bathroom visit and before eating that doughnut? Our personal opinion is that this is the number-one culprit of hikers feeling ill in the back-country—a self-imposed ailment caused by poor hygiene, an unclean hand mining in your GORP, and/or poor Leave No Trace practices, not contaminated water sources.

- **Protozoa:** Here's where we mention the big guns: Giardia and Cryptosporidium. These single-celled parasitic organisms can cause intense intestinal problems, with symptoms appearing anywhere from two days to two weeks after ingestion. Crypto's hard exterior and ability to survive in cold temperatures can make it especially challenging to eradicate from our water sources. That is why you will find treatment times of up to 4 hours to effectively kill Crypto with conventional chemical treatments like iodine. Who has that kind of time to wait for drinkable water? In winter your water would refreeze while you were waiting.

- **Viruses:** The name alone conjures up fears of lifelong symptoms. The reality is that such viruses as Hepatitis A and Rotavirus are extremely rare in most wilderness water sources in North American. When traveling in countries where basic sewage treatment is primitive, your exposure can increase. Because viruses are extremely small, they cannot be effectively filtered out. The only effective means of treatment is purification (chemical treatment), which we will discuss below.

So what are our options? When perusing the aisles at your local outfitter, it can be overwhelming to differentiate between myriad options and, more important, which option is going to work best for your preferences and hiking style. At a basic level we can either try to remove, kill, or ignore these pathogens. Step into the world of filters, purifiers, and fingers crossed.

FILTERS

Size matters, and by size we'll speak the ultra-small language of microns. Traditional water filters work by passing untreated water through a series of porous filter elements. Common elements can be composed of fiberglass, silica, and ceramic. Some filters have a carbon element added to improve taste. These filters work well to remove larger pathogens like bacteria (0.5 to 2 microns) and protozoa (1 micron) but fail to kill or remove viruses (0.02 to 0.3 micron).

Filters tend to be the heaviest and most tedious method of water treatment. There are many variation to accomplish the same results. Ultra-traditional hand pumps like the MSR MiniWorks weigh in at 1 pound and take about 1 minute of hand-pumping to filter 1 liter of water. Again, a filter will not remove viruses; but once pumped, this water is effectively ready to drink.

Gravity filters like the Platypus GravityWorks can filter large volumes of water without the physical exertion of hand pumping. They work by utilizing two large droms (dromedaries) connected by an in-line filter. One drom should be designated clean water and one dirty water as to not confuse the two. Slightly lighter at around 11 ounces, these types of systems also have multipurpose capabilities since the "clean" drom can double as additional water storage capacity for longer carries. With filtration times being about 4 liters within 2.5 minutes, gravity filters truly shine in group camp settings, where multiple people can acquire water in a short amount of time. Setup can be cumbersome at first until you gain efficiency, but the hands-free design allows you to multitask with meals or camp setup while filtration is taking place.

The last commonly used filter system is the on-demand, in-line filter. The Sawyer Mini has quickly become the most popular of these types of filters. They can be integrated into any hydration system by simply cutting the hose and placing it in line and can be adapted to connect to popular drinking vessels with a 28-millimeter thread, like any Platypus or Sawyer

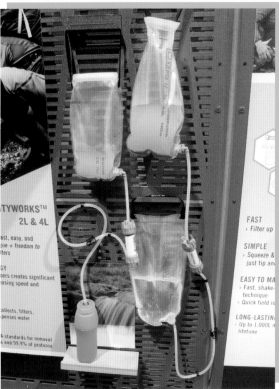

Left: Traditional water filters will quickly turn into 1-pound frozen bricks on winter expeditions because it is nearly impossible to expel every drop of water from the tiny filter membranes after use. Alternative water treatment methods should be considered.
Right: Gravity filters are a great solution to filter large volumes of water without the hassle of pumping. Bear in mind that even the tiny in-line filter element seen here will struggle to stay thawed enough to properly function, slowing your filter rate to a crawl.
Shawn Forry

drom bag and even a standard soda bottle. These filters may be tiny in size and weight (2 ounces), but they are advertised to filter more than 100,000 gallons before retiring.

The caveat to keep in mind with all filters is that the more water they filter, the slower they will operate due to accumulated particulates beginning to clog the filter elements. Some models can back-flush the filter to remove some of the accumulated particulate, restoring some of the original flow rate.

The largest consideration, especially as it relates to winter travel during extended periods of subfreezing temperatures, is the filter's tendency to freeze and occasionally burst once frozen. By design, it is nearly impossible to remove all the water from the tiny pores within the filtering element. Once these pores are clogged from frozen water, your frustration will quickly elevate as your expensive filter renders itself nonoperational. The only effective means to prevent these situations is to ensure that the pump remains above the freezing point at all times. This could entail hiking with the pump next to the warmth of your body. Not a convenient or comfortable solution. Due to this limitation, filters are NOT recommended for winter travel, and alternative methods should be utilized.

PURIFIERS

Purifiers are essentially the chemical warfare of treatment options against pathogens. Rather than removing these pathogens from the water source, everything from bacteria to protozoa to viruses are left intact but rendered harmless. You're left with a harmless microbe milk shake. Maybe there are even a few extra micro-calories to account for in your food rations!

Treatment options include iodine and chlorine-based products like Aquamira and even household bleach. UV treatment options like the SteriPEN technically fall under the purification banner since they do not remove pathogens but instead render them ineffective by scrambling their DNA; think neutered giardia cyst.

Purifiers are generally the cheapest and lightest options. While quick to implement treatment, most methods require upward of 20 to 30 minutes to reach full effectiveness in warm water. (Remember that 4-hour time frame for treating Cryptosporidium?) Solid pill form will have a higher potency than liquid droppers. All chemical methods add some level of foreign taste to the water, which can be a deal breaker for some compared to heavier filters. Additionally, at a chemical level, as temperatures decrease or water turbidity (fine sediment in the water) increases, reaction time and/or dosage will also increase.

Iodine

Cheap and light, iodine is one of the longest unchanged chemical treatments out there. Iodine tends to add the strongest taste to water and can be a bit of an acquired taste. Vitamin C can act as a neutralizer to help offset some of the "sweet" taste of iodine. Make sure to add the neutralizer only after the required treatment time. Adding the neutralizer prematurely can prevent the treatment from taking full effect, as the iodine molecules will bond to the neutralizer rather than the pathogen.

Iodine can commonly be found in both pill and dropper form, but because of the link between iodine and the manufacture of methamphetamines, liquid form iodine can be

Iodine tablets are much lighter than the liquid form but cost more and are prone to getting crushed. These Potable Aqua tablets have been repacked into a lighter non-glass container to further save weight.
Shawn Forry

harder to locate. Liquid iodine in large volume generally requires a doctor's prescription.

Potable Aqua iodine tablets are one of the most common versions of pill-form iodine. Potable Aqua also offers their PA Plus neutralizer, and the two items can be purchased as a set. Care must be taken if using Potable Aqua, since the pills are fragile and can crumble, altering the effective dose.

Chlorine-based Treatments

Aquamira is the most popular chlorine-based water treatment. Chemically different from bleach, both methods effectively work the same. Aquamira comes in both pill and dropper form; the latter is heavier but more cost-effective. In liquid form, the two-part dropper bottle method requires Part A to mix with Part B for 5 minutes, forming chlorine dioxide. Aquamira has a very short shelf life once mixed due to its off-gassing characteristics. Its half-life of around 90 minutes means that after 90 minutes your dosage will be 50 percent less affective. The temptation to premix should be avoided.

Common household bleach can also be used. A ratio of 2 drops to 1 liter of water with 30 minutes of reaction time is a common dosage. One key thing to note about bleach is that as it ages and mixes with air, its potency decreases. A good rule of thumb is that if your bleach doesn't have a strong "bleach" smell, it has probably neutralized to a point that it shouldn't be used to purify water.

Note: Both bleach and liquid Aquamira will freeze at around 15°F to 20°F. Even as temperatures approach that range, dosages can be affected as the liquid begins to congeal.

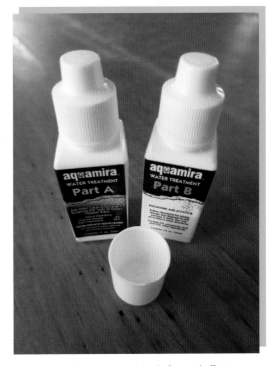

Aquamira, at 3 ounces, is relatively fast and effective, adding only a mild "chlorine" taste to the water.
Shawn Forry

UV Treatment

SteriPEN has effectively cornered the market in ultraviolet water treatment. Utilizing the same technology as large-scale wastewater treatment centers, SteriPEN is a portable version of what most major cities use to treat their wastewater. SteriPEN works by exposing a quantity of water to a concentrated dose of UV rays. As mentioned above, UV treatments

TIP

When you're filling your water bottle, contaminated water will come into contact with the lip of the bottle along the threads. This water will not come into contact with any chemical treatment you later add. To prevent cross-contamination, you must "burp" the bottle. After adding a chemical treatment, turn the bottle upside down and crack the threads until treated water washes over the lip of the bottle.

Quick and tasteless during treatment, the SteriPEN uses UV light to neutralize bacteria, protozoa, and viruses in your water. Since the device requires batteries, keeping them warm will help to maintain proper function. Be mindful of ice freezing to the sensors, which can cause the unit to temporarily malfunction.
Justin Lichter

will not filter out particulates but are highly effective at neutralizing all the major players in the water critter arena. Dosages are quick (90 seconds per liter) and do not add any foreign taste to the water.

SteriPEN relies on battery power, which can be adversely affected by cold temperatures. On models where the batteries can be removed, you can keep the batteries at a suitable temperature by carrying them in a pocket close to your body's natural heat. Some models, like the SteriPEN Journey, while the lightest at 3 ounces, rely on a USB port for charging, which can be inconvenient on extended trips, especially in cold weather. Similar to chemical treatments, the more turbid the water, the higher the chance the UV will not be able to "see" all the pathogens to render them inert. We recommend carrying a backup treatment if using a SteriPEN for winter use.

WATER STORAGE

There is an innate catch-22 in water carrying and water storage during winter. Due to the often inaccessible nature of natural water sources, there is a need to carry more capacity. More capacity takes longer to consume, usually at the expense of carrying around a fully frozen water bottle by the time you've consumed its contents. The other challenge is that once a bottle is frozen, it can be challenging to thaw without damaging the vessel, and you'll be carrying around dead weight. Soft-sided, Platypus-type dromedaries are notorious for puncturing once frozen if you're acting too forcefully. The trick is to prevent them from freezing in the first place.

Water bottle cozies are a common remedy for frozen water bottle syndrome. While not foolproof, they will greatly slow the progress of winter's tenacity at turning water into its solid form. There are many commercially available water bottles cozies; one of the most popular models is the Outdoor Research Water Bottle Parka. At a hefty approximately 5 ounces, it adds considerable weight to your gear. Equally effective models can be made from scratch using retired foam sleeping pads for a fraction of the cost and weight. Bear in mind that a proper lid, while more challenging to construct, will greatly increase the vessel's usable time before a complete freeze.

Hydration bladders can be too much of a nuisance for winter use. The exposure time and large surface area of the hose water exposed to the air creates the perfect environment for a fully frozen bite valve and hydration hose. As temps drop and the rubber bite valves become less flexible, they are susceptible to leaking as well. The neoprene "winterizing kits" that are commonly sold tend to sway toward the gimmicky end of the spectrum and do not warrant their weight when more winter-appropriate systems are available.

Another consideration for water bottle vessels is that wide-mouth bottles are far superior to their lighter, narrow-mouth cousins. After pouring precious hours into melting snow in the evening, the last thing you want to do is have half your now-liquid (and hot!) water run down the sides of the bottle as you transfer from pot to bottle. It's a great way to burn your hands and add inefficiency to your camp scene.

It is equally important to note that common summertime ultralight sports drink–type bottles do not withstand repeated use carrying hot liquids. The threads and cap of the bottle tend to warp over time, causing them to leak. If you're using your water bottle as a nightly hot water bottle, this is the last thing you want to discover in the middle of the night! Some of us found out the hard way about the limitations of ultralight sports drink bottles. You're welcome.

A traditional thermos is also a consideration for a water vessel. While they're not light by any means, being able to have a sip of hot drink during the middle of the day is a luxury to say the least—and will make your travel companions infinitely jealous. No plastic bottle and cozy combo will come anywhere close to the thermal efficiency of a proper vacuum-sealed thermos. The lightest model currently on the market is the über-expensive Snow Peak Titanium Kanpai bottle. While only available in a 350-milliliter capacity, at 5.7 ounces this thermos is nearly as light as some water bottle–cozy combos, with likely ten times more thermal efficiency.

An insulated thermos helps prevent your water from freezing throughout the course of the day. At only 5.7 ounces, this titanium thermos from Snow Peak is lighter than Nalgene yet is much more functional for winter travel. Hot water is not only more enjoyable to drink but can be a lifesaver in emergency situations—a small weight penalty to pay for safety. *Shawn Forry*

BACKPACKS

Let's boil a backpack down to the essential things it must do no matter what your intended use is. This glorified sack with straps must be comfortable, easy to use, and ideally last a long time. Sounds simple, right? But there are a lot of choices out there.

To help in the selection process, start by asking yourself a series of questions. What will the primary use of the pack be? How many consecutive days do I think I will utilize the pack? How long do I want this pack to last? Do I anticipate any international flying where nondescript equipment is advantageous and size restrictions are at play? How important is it that the pack doesn't clash with my swanky new Ray-Ban sunglasses?

When we take a look at how adding winter into the equation will affect our underlying product demands, we are faced with the following realities:

1. Winter loads are generally more bulky and slightly heavier, necessitating a slightly larger volume pack with a more substantial frame.

2. While in colder temps and wearing gloves or mittens, you will want things quickly accessible without the frustrational equivalent of trying to pick a dime up off the ground with oven mitts.

3. Snow is soft, but winter is harsh. Fabrics do strange things in subfreezing environments. Sparks from the fire, sharp and pokey things on your hands and feet, and branches weighed down by a fresh coating of white will all wreak havoc on a tissue-grade backpack.

VOLUME

Rather than starting with a pack and then trying to fit all your gear into it, let's start with the pile of gear you need to carry and then select the appropriate model to carry that gear in. As a general rule of thumb, winter capacities are going to be slightly larger than their summertime equivalent. All that fluffy downy goodness that is going to put a smile on your face at the end of the day has to go somewhere!

Pack volume will also indirectly dictate what you are planning to use the pack for. Übersmall >1,500 cubic inch packs are great for day hikes but maybe not realistic for extended forays. If you are looking for a single pack that can do it all, you'll want to err on the side of excess with a pack that has ample volume and the ability to compress down in size.

Another thing to consider is where the pack volume is distributed. In the summertime our preference is a simple frameless rucksack, where most items are stowed in the main pack compartment. In contrast, for winter there's a benefit from a more even distribution of pack volume through various side pockets. Winter is one of the few times when we will intentionally keep the lid of the pack attached. This allows quick, easy access to pertinent items like snacks, wind layers, and technical tools without the need to open the main pack body on a blustery day. This helps avoid the entire inside of my pack sponging up as many soggy snowflakes enter.

While pack design and technology have advanced over the years, one thing has remained constant: Carry all my stuff as comfortably as possible!
Justin Lichter

Plan on allocating 50 to 75 percent more pack volume than your summertime preferences. For example, for multiday treks, Pepper's go-to summertime pack is an approximately 30 liter pack like the Granite Gear Virga 26 or the Mountain Laurel Designs Prophet. Switching to his full winter kit, he bumps up to an approximately 55-liter pack like the Granite Gear Leopard AC 58.

FABRICS

Backpacks used to be constructed of cotton canvas and waterproofed with a heavy wax coating. Think Grandma Gatewood hiking the Appalachian Trail with her duffle bag slung over her shoulder or Earl Shaffer's World War II–era rucksack. While these packs exhibited exceptional waterproof characteristics, they were heavy, lacked durability, and were prone to rotting out when stored wet. In the half century since this cutting-edge technology first hit the trail, things have come a long way, to say the least.

What fabric a backpack is constructed from is going to have a direct correlation to weight and durability. Like the adage about "cost, quality and time . . . pick two," the same applies to backpack fabrics and construction; not all are created equal. Quality control between

With a wide array of outdoor fabrics to choose from, it can be overwhelming to decide which fabric will be best (and lightest) for a chosen application or activity. Understanding the basic pros and cons of each fabric can shine some light on this process.
Shawn Forry

manufacturers, brand-name versus generic fabric, and marketing mumbo jumbo can lead to discrepancies between models and manufacturers. We'll dive into the specifics of each fabric and its preferred applications and try to demystify the shopping experience at your local retailer.

Coated versus Uncoated

Adding a coating to a fabric drastically changes its properties and application. When a coating is applied, breathability generally decreases while durability and water resistance increase. Universally, the weight is also going to increase. Common coatings are silicone and polyurethane. Either can be applied before construction to each individual fiber or post construction. When individual fibers are coated and then woven together to make a fabric, the overall breathability will be reduced less and the longevity of the coating will be better. Coating a fabric after it's woven is generally a more cost-effective approach but more prone to peeling or delaminating.

Denier and Weights

To help speak apples to apples when discussing fabric "thickness," a common measurement is the fabric's denier. This formula was derived from how much 9,000 meters of a single strand of yarn weigh in grams; for example, if a 9,000-meter-long strand of nylon weighs 450 grams, then it is a 450D fabric. Who thinks up this stuff? Another common measure is a fabric's weight, commonly represented in ounces per square yard (oz/yd^2) or grams per square meter (g/m^2). Both of these measures help to define how "beefy" a fabric is, and thus how heavy it will be. For perspective, 1,000D pack cloth used to be the industry standard for backpack construction. Now Montbell makes a 7D wind jacket! When purchasing fabrics by the square yard, it is common that the "unfinished" weight of the fabric will be represented if it is a coated fabric. A common example is that silnylon is commonly sold in 1.1 oz/yd^2 varieties, but the true "finished" weight of the fabric is closer to 1.4 oz/yd^2.

Pack Cloth

Pack cloth is a cost-effective polyester alternative to nylon. While pack cloth does exhibit higher resistance to UV degradation, nylon is far superior in nearly every way. Pack cloth is what most price-point packs are constructed from and should generally be avoided unless cost-effectiveness is of upmost concern.

Ripstop

For all intents and purposes, we've omitted mentioning basic nylon and skipped straight to its bigger brother, ripstop. The downside of straight nylon is that once there is a tear or puncture in the fabric, the lack in tensile strength makes it prone to a continuous rip along the initial tear. If you've ever snagged a piece of thin non-ripstop nylon on a branch, it's frightening how quickly you'll end up looking like Raggedy Ann. Ripstop nylon is easily distinguished by its grid-like pattern utilizing heavier fibers woven into the warp and weft of the fabric. Simply, the heavier threads help the rip to stop running. Another advantage is that with ripstop nylon you will see less unraveling of the fabric over time if a rip should occur.

Dyneema

Dyneema is a specific brand of ripstop nylon on steroids. If you want to show off to your friends, refer to it as an ultra high molecular weight polyethylene. Simply, the "heavy fibers" of regular ripstop are replaced with a lightweight material that is stronger than steel, is more abrasion resistant than carbon steel, doesn't stretch or absorb water, and is distinguishable by its pure white appearance. 210D Dyneema has quickly become the gold standard in most cottage-industry packs and is making its way into mainstream use.

Cordura

The ultimate in balancing abrasion resistance with weight is Cordura brand fabric. As testament to its durability and utility, this fabric has solely been used by the military since the 1980s. Since Cordura comes in a wide range of fabric construction, weights, and textures, it can be adapted to almost any application. Denier weights can be as low as 30D and well over 1,000D, but most lightweight pack manufactures will utilize the 210D pack cloth.

Silnylon

All the rage several year ago when the ultralight movement first started taking off, silnylon is quickly falling out of favor for anything other than stuff sacks and shelters. It is nearly impossible to find a pack still constructed entirely of silnylon, and for good reason. Silnylon is a nylon blend where each strand is "impregnated" with silicone before it is woven. The hydrophobic nature of silicone makes it relatively waterproof, although air and moisture can push through the fabric under high pressure, like sitting down or pushing up against the fabric. The coating can begin to wear thin after experiencing much abrasion, and silnylon is simply not a great fabric for pack construction.

Dyneema Composite Fiber (DCF)

How often can you have your cake and eat it too? First introduced to the yacht racing community through ultra-light, high-tenacity sails in the 1990s, it only took a decade for the technology to trickle its way into backpacking applications. Remember the ultra high molecular weight polyethylene fibers of Dyneema ripstop nylon? Now take that ultra-strong, ultralight Dyneema grid and sandwich it between two layers of a thin transparent polyester membrane, aka Mylar. Think of the tensile strength of a space blanket, double it, and add in the properties of a Dyneema grid. By weight you'll have the most waterproof, rip-resistant, and lightweight material on the market. DCF does not absorb water, does not stretch, and there

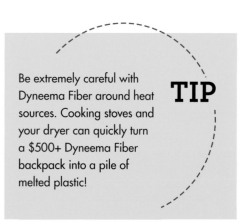

Be extremely careful with Dyneema Fiber around heat sources. Cooking stoves and your dryer can quickly turn a $500+ Dyneema Fiber backpack into a pile of melted plastic!

TIP

Be extremely careful with DCF around heat sources! Cooking stoves and your dryer can quickly turn a $500+ DCF backpack into a pile of melted plastic.
Justin Lichter

are literally thousands of variations to adapt to different applications. The downside is first and foremost the cost. Secondly, DCF lacks the abrasion-resistant properties of its heavier Cordura cousin. Over time DCF will become "fuzzy" as the fibers begin to fray. Unless shaving every ounce is your priority, for pack use it is best to utilize 2.9 oz/yd^2 hybrid DCF that has a layer of polyester laminated to the face fabric. There is even a variety of "waterproof breathable" DCF now being used in rainwear applications.

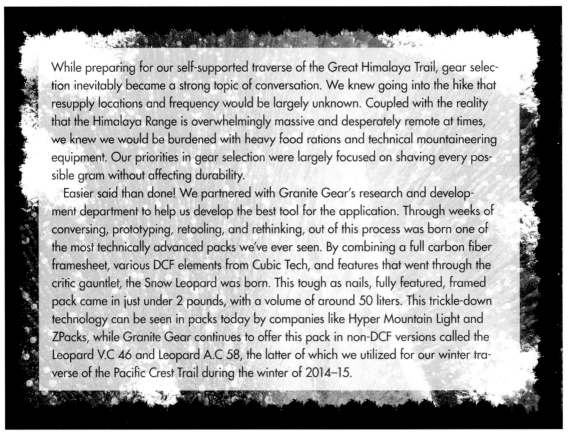

While preparing for our self-supported traverse of the Great Himalaya Trail, gear selection inevitably became a strong topic of conversation. We knew going into the hike that resupply locations and frequency would be largely unknown. Coupled with the reality that the Himalaya Range is overwhelmingly massive and desperately remote at times, we knew we would be burdened with heavy food rations and technical mountaineering equipment. Our priorities in gear selection were largely focused on shaving every possible gram without affecting durability.

Easier said than done! We partnered with Granite Gear's research and development department to help us develop the best tool for the application. Through weeks of conversing, prototyping, retooling, and rethinking, out of this process was born one of the most technically advanced packs we've ever seen. By combining a full carbon fiber framesheet, various DCF elements from Cubic Tech, and features that went through the critic gauntlet, the Snow Leopard was born. This tough as nails, fully featured, framed pack came in just under 2 pounds, with a volume of around 50 liters. This trickle-down technology can be seen in packs today by companies like Hyper Mountain Light and ZPacks, while Granite Gear continues to offer this pack in non-DCF versions called the Leopard V.C 46 and Leopard A.C 58, the latter of which we utilized for our winter traverse of the Pacific Crest Trail during the winter of 2014–15.

Granite Gear's R&D department pulled out all the stops when it designed the Snow Leopard pack for our traverse of the Great Himalaya Trail. Complete with proprietary DCF blends and carbon fiber framesheets, and stripped of all extraneous grams, this pack was one of the most advanced packs at the time.
Justin Lichter

FRAMES

In Western cultures, carrying heavy loads has placed the weight transfer predominately on the hips. Many other cultures around the world prefer to carry the load directly on the crown or brow of the skull. Regardless of where the load is carried, the end goal is to transfer the added weight of a rucksack off the body's soft tissue and onto its strong skeletal frame. While the history of pack frames is deeply rooted in external-framed packs, we'll exclude these packs from the conversation based on limited real-world experience and a general feeling of obsolescence, plus increased difficulty in carrying skis.

There are several different varieties of pack frames to choose from, each with its advantages and disadvantages. Some frames can be removed; others are hard fixed to the pack. The lightest of the light eschew frames altogether, instead incorporating other commonly carried equipment to stiffen the pack.

All frame designs try to achieve the same result: They need to be rigid enough to prevent the pack from slouching while on your back. If the pack can maintain its shape and remain rigid, the load will effectively be transferred through the pack onto the hips. There are two areas where this slouching can occur. The back panel of the pack itself can begin to crumple under its own weight and pressure. This can easily be addressed through a framesheet or the pack stay (see below). The other, more often overloaded, area is where the pack meets the hip belt. If this contact point is compromised, it will become an area where the pack has an opportunity to slouch, transferring the load off your hips and back onto your shoulders.

Regardless of which frame you opt for, know that everyone's preferences are slightly different in what feels comfortable to them. For perspective, you'll rarely see legendary hiker Scott Williamson use a framed pack, let alone a hip belt! If you can, try out various combinations of pack design, and find where the weight limitations are for you in each design. Factor in what style trip you will most commonly use this pack for. Depending on which frame design you choose, it can add 5 to 20 pounds of carrying capacity. We prefer to transition into a framed pack if total pack weight is consistently averaging more than 25 pounds. Anything beyond this and over an extended period, we will start to notice neck and shoulder pain and general discomfort.

Virtual Frame

Nine times out of ten, this is our preferred frame style for multiday summer trekking and short winter day hikes. The comfort in this frame design (or lack thereof) hinges solely on three key concepts: (1) a conscious effort to minimize extraneous pack weight, (2) seeking out multiuse opportunity within every piece of gear (in this case, your sleeping pad), and (3) a systematic approach to how the pack is packed.

There are two approaches to creating a virtual frame, but the end result will be the same. Since there will not be a dedicated frame to add rigidity to the pack, which will in turn transfer load, rigidity must jointly come from a tightly packed pack and the firmness of a sleeping pad. Obviously, closed cell foam pads are going to work better in this case over inflatable, but the same results can be had if the pack is packed correctly.

One style is the "tube" method, which utilizes a closed cell sleeping pad (three-quarter length is best) that lines the inside of the pack. All contents are then stuffed into the center of the "tube" that has been created. The cylindrical tube will add padding to your back for comfort and have the added advantage of further padding and protecting the contents inside. We personally find it hard to pack everything conveniently inside the tube and efficiently use up all corners and volume of the pack, and instead tend to gravitate toward the framesheet method.

The second method to create a virtual frame also uses the sleeping pad to create an impromptu framesheet. By folding a sleeping pad in half twice or in thirds, you usually end up close to the dimensions of the back panel in the pack. Either inflatable or close cell foam pads will work, with the caveat that closed cell is going to be more bulky but provide more cushion. If you're utilizing tent poles in your shelter system, these can double as mock "stays" in the pack. Just sandwich them into the folds of the sleeping pad or along the edges of the pack along the back panel.

The key to both these designs is to intentionally stuff the pack tightly and utilize the compression straps to cinch the pack down. This in turn will create a very dense pack that will resist the temptation to slouch or compress while on your back, which would result in more pressure over your shoulders instead of on your hips. The other caveat is that you will generally need to wear your hip belt slightly tighter than with a framed pack. This again is to minimize the opportunity for the pack to compress and slouch under its own weight.

Air Beams

A little-known trick for years in the ultralight community was to add a few breaths of air into your inflatable sleeping pad before creating a virtual frame with it. Doing so allowed a bit more comfort and rigidity at no additional weight. The only downside was that you would lose a bit more volume inside the pack.

Klymit saw the need to improve this practice and took it one step further with their Air Beam technology—essentially a mini sleeping pad that can be inflated to exceptionally high pressures with a hand pump. The air beam is then slotted into an internal sleeve along the back panel. For only a 3-ounce weight penalty, noticeable increases can be had to the carrying capacity of a standard frameless pack. Pepper used this system with great success during his unsupported speed hike of the Colorado Trail in 2012. With only a 6-pound base weight, he stuffed 37 pounds of food into a Granite Gear Crown pack and ate his way back down to 6 pounds of gear over the course of ten days and 450 miles. That's something he wouldn't dare try with solely a frameless pack!

Currently several manufacturers offer products designed to incorporate the Air Beam framesheet, including Mountain Laurel Designs, Granite Gear, and Gossamer Gear. Great in concept but poor in execution, a few design changes

The Air Beam by Klymit offers a lightweight solution for stiffening frameless packs to be more supportive. At only 3 ounces, this inflatable frame added stiffness and comfort during the day while doubling as a sleeping pad for the feet at night.
Shawn Forry

would make this a standout option. We've found the one-way air valves to be leaky over time and the hand pump cumbersome. Despite these shortcomings, the Air Beam does have the ability to mold to your back regardless of your movement or body positioning, something a rigid framesheet cannot do.

Framesheets

Regardless of the design, all framesheets are intended to bulk up the rigidity of a pack frame. You'll see all kinds of space age–looking designs, from swiss cheese cutouts and corrugated patterns to even vertebrae-looking apparatuses. While the stiffness can vary between designs, all will retain some level of torsional flex, which can be advantageous for the moving body. Removable framesheets are advantageous in that they can add flexibility to the use of the pack as well as skim approximately 6 ounces off the total pack weight. Framesheets also help prevent annoying pokes and prods coming through the back panel from hard-sided objects like cooking pots and bear canisters.

Left: Removable framesheets offer greater flexibility in a pack's design. Framesheet design can vary greatly, but all serve the same function: adding rigidity to transfer weight to the hips. Left: Granite Gear Crown 60 frame; right: Cilo Gear Worksack 45-liter frame with optional stay inserted.
Right: Mountain Laurel Designs Exodus FS ready for a PCT winter shakedown ski tour through the High Sierra. This 24-ounce pack comfortably carried a base weight of 14 pounds by incorporating a Klymit Air Beam framesheet and simple hooped carbon fiber rod. Ultralight doesn't have to skimp on comfort or function.
Shawn Forry

Pack Stays

Sometime used in conjunction with a framesheet or stand alone, pack stays are thin support rods that run the vertical length of the pack. They are commonly made from aluminum or composite material. Aluminum, while heavier, can be sculpted to match the curvature of the spine, increasing the overall comfort of the pack. A common stand-alone pack stay design creates a U-shape arc down the side of the pack that connects over the top. This design can be further improved by adding a subtle curve to the vertical stays in such a way that the pack is arched away from the back, creating more ventilation. This type of design detracts from the overall total capacity of the pack and pushes your center of gravity farther away from your spine.

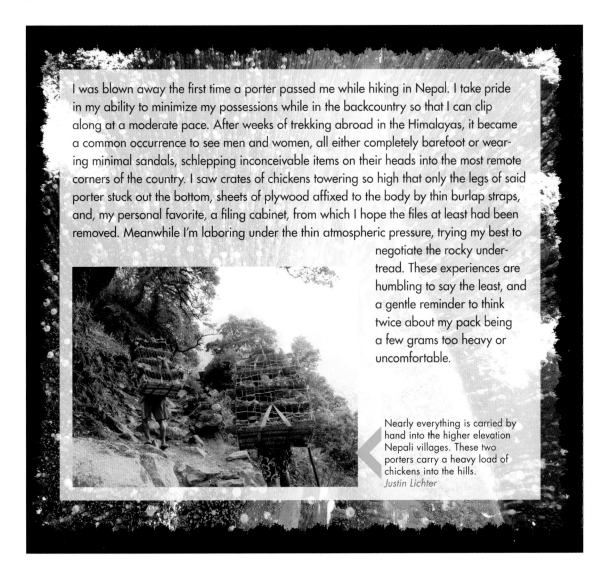

I was blown away the first time a porter passed me while hiking in Nepal. I take pride in my ability to minimize my possessions while in the backcountry so that I can clip along at a moderate pace. After weeks of trekking abroad in the Himalayas, it became a common occurrence to see men and women, all either completely barefoot or wearing minimal sandals, schlepping inconceivable items on their heads into the most remote corners of the country. I saw crates of chickens towering so high that only the legs of said porter stuck out the bottom, sheets of plywood affixed to the body by thin burlap straps, and, my personal favorite, a filing cabinet, from which I hope the files at least had been removed. Meanwhile I'm laboring under the thin atmospheric pressure, trying my best to negotiate the rocky under-tread. These experiences are humbling to say the least, and a gentle reminder to think twice about my pack being a few grams too heavy or uncomfortable.

Nearly everything is carried by hand into the higher elevation Nepali villages. These two porters carry a heavy load of chickens into the hills.
Justin Lichter

FEATURES

Winter will inevitably have a trickle-down effect to modify much of your traditional shoulder-season systems. Selecting a pack with the appropriate bells and whistles to suit your style of travel can mean the difference between a high mode of efficiency and spirit-dampening frustration. Not only do irrelevant features add undue weight to the pack, they can also increase your overall out-of-pocket costs. Having too little in the way of creature comforts can decrease your access and convenience while on the go. Access can have a direct correlation to your body heat and comfort during winter travel. The other key thing to consider is how your pack will interact with the inevitable accumulation of snow that will fall from the heavens. Convenient external water bottle pockets, for instance, can quickly turn into a slushy cooler if you're not mindful of their design and material choice.

External Pockets

Staying organized, no matter the season, is the perceived difference between a "green" weekend warrior and the hardened expeditionist. In keeping with the mentality that any time not moving is an opportunity for discomfort, having your organizational systems dialed in is a sure-fire way to success. Having external pockets with a well-designed closure system is preferred in winter. Your food intake will naturally adapt to grab-and-go snacks, and layers will constantly be coming on, off, and back on again.

Careful consideration should be made in the placement of these pockets. If travel will necessitate winter travel accessories like crampons, snowshoes, and skis, these large bulky items can quickly interfere with quick access to external pockets. The lid and hip belt are the most logical placement for universal external pockets. The hip belt is perfect for quick access to small items like cameras, water treatment, and lip balm, while the lid can fill the niche for larger items like shedding layers, repair kits, and snacks.

Material choice is harder to have a say in. During summer, mesh seems to be an obvious choice, despite typically weighing more than comparable fabrics, being prone to snagging, and being less durable. In wintertime it can quickly turn into a frozen mess as it collects snow and freezes into an unmalleable sheet. Pocket materials should be constructed either from similar pack fabrics

Anticipate snow covering your pack. Having everything stowed inside your pack will not only keep things drier but also prevent things from falling off your pack.
Justin Lichter

like Dyneema and pack cloth or from stretch-woven water-resistant fabrics like those made by Schoeller. These fabrics will both keep moisture at bay and add necessary durability at a minimal weight penalty.

The problems with side pockets like traditional water bottle holders are hard to resolve. During storms they will collect snow, and their elastic can lose its elasticity once frozen. One alternative is to mount an insulated water bottle holder to a shoulder strap or hip belt for quick access. These accessories will serve two purposes: slowing the rate at which your water freezes and adding quicker access, when it can be extra challenging to reach into side pockets while wearing gloves.

Compression Straps

Properly placed compression straps can drastically help control and stabilize the traditionally heavier and bulkier load while carrying winter equipment. This will be further appreciated when uncoordinated travel on snowshoes or skies causes you to bury yourself in the snow due to a top-heavy tumble. Compression straps can also work in coordination with external pockets to help secure items that benefit from quick access. An avalanche probe and shovel benefit immensely from quick retrieval in a time of need, but are worthless if they have fallen out of your side pocket because they were improperly stowed.

For as little as 1 ounce, insulated water bottle holders can extend the time before your water freezes. Storing water inside a pack wrapped in an insulated jacket will achieve the same thing but limit accessibility. Keeping water visible throughout the day is a good reminder to stay hydrated, which in turn will help the body maintain warmth.
Shawn Forry

These straps can also serve double duty to secure technical equipment if properly placed. It is most helpful to have a series of two parallel straps sewn into both the side and front panels of the pack. Straps that release by a buckle and can be threaded through items add convenience and adaptability, but they can also be limited by the holding power of the buckle, depending on the weight of the object they are required to hold. Also keep in mind that many three-season packs may not have enough of a tail on the webbing to fashion around snowshoes or larger items. Make sure the straps are long enough or you can tie them off to extend them if necessary.

Buckles and Fasteners

There is no perfect closure system during winter. Buckles with gloves are cumbersome, zippers can freeze shut, and Velcro ices over in no time. Drawcord cinch systems with appropriately sized cord locks tend to win over other systems but have limited applications. Whichever fastener you choose, first consider its use while wearing gloves or mittens. Überlight 10-millimeter buckles will be the bane of your existence with the limited dexterity afforded by bulky hand wear. It is highly recommended to add high-visibility zipper pulls to nearly everything in winter. We'll discuss this further in the clothing section, but once you've experienced the joy of opening a zipper with ease during a whiteout while your hands stay in a warm cocoon, you'll never look back.

Technical Equipment Compatibility

Inevitably, winter travel is going to dictate the assistance of technical equipment in your mode of travel. Skiing, ice climbing, and snowshoeing all require specialize equipment that will be cumbersome, sharp, or heavy—likely a combination of all three. As conditions dictate, you will likely need to stow this equipment on your backpack from time to time, even if it's just to get from your car to the trailhead.

While each of these modes of transportation is unique in its own right, having a pack that can quickly and easily adapt to all systems is achievable. The most obvious consideration is that these modes of transportation are heavy as well as bulky. If you've ever had to bushwhack with a pair of skis on your back, you'll understand how important placement and security are! When possible, it is much more preferable to keep the load narrow and centered. This is why the front panel of the pack has long been the standing tradition for technical gear placement. It allows for unrestricted arm and torso movement and, if placed high enough, adequate movement for the legs. Additionally, there is less of a chance for items to be ripped from the pack when you're navigating technical and narrow terrain.

Protecting the pack from these items is another consideration. It doesn't take long for ski edges, ice tools, and crampons to chew holes in ultralight fabrics. Careful packing and attachment can go a long way, but nothing replaces the durability of bomber fabrics like Hypalon and similar heavily coated and durable fabrics. Hypalon is the gold standard in products like rafts that will routinely be ramming into sharp rocks along the river, where a puncture would be catastrophic. Implementing selective placement based on where abrasion will likely occur adds minimal weight while greatly extending the life of the pack.

For attachment systems, Voile Straps are a favorite of ours. They are grippy due to their rubber-like construction, have great holding power, and are easy to adjust and secure. If removable from the pack, they also add a level of multiuse that carries over into repairs and shelter systems. Their size is also a good balance of weight and ease of use with gloved hands. On the opposite end of the spectrum is bungee or shock cord. While great for lightweight summer use, it is no match for the constructs of winter

Sometimes spring conditions and poor route selection dictate carrying your skis through uncharted territory. Having a secure way to affix your skis to your pack is essential to minimizing an already frustrating experience.
Shawn Forry

Voile Straps do an amazing job of securing even the most awkward items to a pack. Simple, lightweight, and versatile, they even work as an emergency fire starter.
Shawn Forry

attachment. A realistic limit of use would be to secure a pair of Yaktrax or temporarily stow a rain jacket.

FITTING

There is no greater feeling than donning your freshly packed backpack, stuffed to the gills with all your required equipment and multiple days of food, and have it settle on like the driver's seat of an Italian race car. Minimizing the weight that we carry is the first step in ensuring overall comfort. The next logical step it to ensure that the pack is sized AND adjusted correctly to our bodies.

We can modify this adjustment in several ways. The most obvious adjustment will be the overall size of the pack, NOT its volume. The standard approach to comparing pack sizes is to measure one's torso length. This is a measurement from the top of the hips to the base of the spine (cerebral vertebra 7; i.e., C-7). The current caveat with most ultralight packs is that they come in a narrow range of sizes (if any at all) and are generally gender neutral (read: male-centric).

With the addition of certain key pack features like load lifters, we can further adjust the shape of the pack to mold to our body's shape. Load lifters help arc the distribution of weight closer to your back. This is especially important for the towering backpack load, as it prevents the dreaded leveraging action as the weight of the pack tries to pry away from your back. Load lifter should angle up from the top of the shoulder to the pack at about

A side load lifter can easily be modified to create a simple lightweight alpine rack. A 5-inch length of ¼-inch vinyl tubing can be slipped over the webbing of the load lifter.
Shawn Forry

a 45-degree angle. While rarely needed for ultralight loads, even light bulky loads common with winter equipment can benefit from this added feature.

One often-overlooked feature in ultralight backpacks is having appropriately sized and shaped shoulder straps and hip belts. The quality in the foam alone in these features can mean the difference between pain and comfort at the end of a long day, especially after many years of use. An S-curve to a well-padded shoulder straps will help ensure that your neck is not pinched when the pack is on and that the straps comfortably wrap under your arms. Some poorly designed ultralight packs can have straight-cut shoulder straps. If you've ever seen a first-generation GoLite Breeze, you know what I'm talking about.

We are huge fans of broad hip belt wings and tend to eschew their über-light thin-webbing counterparts. Skipping on padding and foam in this region shaves merely an ounce or two from the overall pack weight but greatly increases the pressure placed on hipbones and simultaneously minimizes the effectiveness in the hip belt's ability to transfer a load. In the context of winter, proper padding in a hip belt will also help to retain heat.

The last piece of the fit puzzle is the use of load stabilizers. These adjustable pieces of webbing link the hip belt to the lower part of the pack frame. The intent is the same as the upper load lifters: Draw the pack closer to the back. While it is debatable whether they make a difference, these straps can also be helpful for attaching certain models of hip belt pockets. With the simple addition of a 4-inch length of ¼-inch tubular hose, these load lifters can be modified to incorporate a common alpine feature to rack draws, ice screws, and other rock climbing equipment.

ELECTRONICS

For the most part, electronics fall into the category of luxury items. The desire to disconnect from our connected lifestyles is one of the appeals of backcountry travel. A headlamp will likely be the sole mandatory winter electronic, regardless of your trip length, style, or pursuit.

There is an incredible array of headlamps to choose from these days. Regardless of which model you select, you'll be balancing brightness, weight, and battery life. You can't have your cake and eat it here. LEDs have long been the gold standard. I'm not even sure you can buy incandescent headlamps anymore. In winter, plan on using your headlamp for far more hours per day due to the limited daylight hours, and know that batteries do not last as long in the cold. An overall brighter headlamp is helpful, since peering through night flurries will limit visibility, similarly to winter night driving.

The cold will drain batteries far more quickly. Albeit expensive, lithium batteries preserve battery life over the more common alkaline style. Headlamps with remote battery packs are slightly heavier, but you can place the battery pack inside a warm jacket pocket to preserve battery life. Headlamp models with multiple brightness settings are helpful to cater to your needs without unduly wasting power and keeping your tent partner awake at night. Note that some headlamps are not recommended for use with lithium batteries, so check that out beforehand.

TIP

Plan on sleeping with all your battery-powered items in your sleeping bag to keep them warm. If possible, also keep battery-operated items near body heat throughout the day by keeping them in an internal pocket. Otherwise you may grab your camera for that once-in-a-lifetime picture, only to have it not power on.

OUTDOOR ATTIRE

There is a certain "look" to outdoor enthusiasts. Just as you can spot a doctor, firefighter, bullfighter, or ballet dancer from afar, the uniform of choice for any profession or activity is usually driven by "function follows form." Before there was an outdoor "industry," it took the creative sorts to adapt and pull together a hodgepodge of borrowed uniforms before the "outdoor" look could take shape. It's no wonder that at some point the cutting-edge style of cutoff jeans lent itself to zip-off nylon trekking pants and fully articulated soft-shell pants.

Today there is an almost dizzying array of outdoor attire to choose from. The outdoor industry is a multi-billion-dollar market chock-full of things you don't need and a handful of essentials. In today's market, when it comes to apparel it can be hard to separate the fashion from the function. In this section, we'll provide an overview of items to suit you from head to toe and separate the "musts" from the "wants"—all through the lens of the ultralight multiuse ethos.

LAYERING

"Layering" is a term commonly thrown around when selecting clothing. Cakes and haircuts aside, this key outdoor concept is akin to the construction of a house. While each layer is independently important, selected for its material and construction, the hallmark of proper layering is how everything works in concert in order to cater to a vast range of conditions, temperatures, and physical exertion.

In thinking of our home analogy, we want our innermost layer to be cozy and comfortable. This is the layer we will see most, much like how our "base layers" will be in direct contact with our skin. Next we have our insulative layers. Wall insulation will vary in thickness and location based on environment, much like our choice in insulating jackets, pants, and

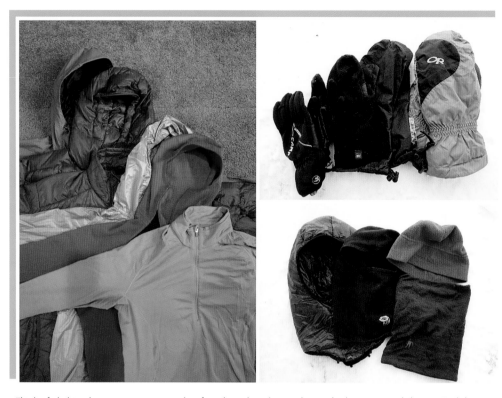

Think of clothing layers as a menu to select from based on the conditions, both pre-trip and during. Each layer should serve a unique function while working collectively to keep you warm, dry, and comfortable.
Shawn Forry

gloves—too little insulation and we're left frigid; too much and we constantly need to vent by opening a window, or zipper. Next we have our exterior siding. We want this to be durable and protective against the elements. Through the use of "hard" and "soft" shells, we can again cater to our needs based on the type of precipitation and abrasion we might encounter during our chosen activity.

Applying this concept through an ultralight filter, we want our house to be constructed adequately, but not excessively. Our choice in clothing should follow suit. By outfitting our closets with a few essential articles of apparel, we should have a wardrobe varied enough that we can head out and enjoy nearly any conditions we may face.

MATERIALS

Proper selection of materials in our garments will weed out the inappropriate and allow for fine-tuning depending on conditions. Materials can largely be split into two categories: synthetics and natural fibers. While marketing efforts might lead us to believe that "technology" has provided a far superior fabric than what nature has provided, the reality is that natural fibers usually outperform and out-sustain any petroleum-based textile.

The first Mallory-Irvine summit of Everest had them clad in layers of wool, silk, and even cotton. Studies have shown that not only was their clothing appropriate to make it to the summit, it may actually have outperformed some modern-day apparel. Ask any northern Inuit community what their fabric of choice is for the hardest conditions on Earth and nine out of ten won't give up their caribou-skin anorak.

Synthetics

Synthetic materials are largely made from petroleum-based products. Rayon was the first synthetic fiber developed, with the ever-versatile nylon coming shortly behind in 1938. Petroleum-based synthetics naturally repel water, thus dry quick, are highly durable and are typically cheaper than natural fibers. Synthetics are notorious for retaining odor, and their next-to-skin feel can be abrasive. Anyone who has experienced the "pins and needles" effect of dirty synthetic base layers will agree.

Things become greatly complicated by manufacturers who develop proprietary fabrics using blends of the fabrics described below, making it hard to distinguish one fabric from another. Knowing the underlying properties of a fabric will help you separate the marketing hype from true performance.

Polyester: One of the most commonly used fabrics in the outdoor industry, polyester has bred such outdoor staples as polypropylene, "polar fleece," and PrimaLoft. Relatively inexpensive to manufacture while offering great performance and value, polyester dries incredibly fast and has a great balance between stretch and durability. Polyester can be knit into very lightweight fabrics like polypropylene.

Malden Mills was the first to manufacture their polar fleece fabric known as Polartec. Fleece is nothing more than twisted polyester yarns that are knitted into a fabric, roughed up, and then sheered to create the soft fluffy feeling we are accustomed to with fleece. The properties of fleece can be modified in a plethora of ways to achieve a desired end result. So called bi-component fleeces offer two different types of yarns: the inner yarn, designed to transport moisture, and the outer yarn, designed to spread the moisture out on the surface for ease and expediency of evaporation. One such proprietary fabric is Polartec Power Dry. Fleece can further be exploited to highlight more loft, moisture transfer, or stretch or backed with a membrane to block wind. On the market for decades now, fleece is still one of the most versatile outdoor fabrics—and one that actually performs as marketed.

Soft shells are hard to quantify, as they are a hybrid category. The term has become a catch-all that describes fabrics that are highly wind and water resistant but not waterproof. For ultralight purposes they are generally overbuilt and heavy for their intended function. That being said, soft shells generally have wonderful stretch and durability properties. They are great for abrasive activities like alpine climbing and ski mountaineering, where fast-moving comfort and durability are of utmost concern.

Synthetic down products like 3M's Thinsulate and PrimaLoft try to replicate the qualities of natural down while addressing its shortcomings. Synthetic insulation is polyester filaments that have been extruded and intertwined to mimic the lofty clusters of down. Synthetic down is nearly as light and compressible as natural down yet retains nearly all its warmth when wet and dries notably faster.

Nylon: Nylon is an incredibly durable and versatile petroleum-based material. The tight weave is naturally wind resistant but limits breathability. Similar to polyester, nylon absorbs very little moisture and is commonly use for exterior face fabrics because of its high wear capabilities. In order for nylon to attain stretch qualities, it must be blended with Lycra, Spandex, or a similar stretchy fabric.

Natural Materials

Nature has a way of providing all the answers and resources we need. It is no wonder that some of the best outdoor materials are taken from nature's technology. Natural fibers can vary in their methods and ethic of source and sustainability and generally carry a higher price tag.

Wool: The stigma of scratchy rag wool has largely been removed thanks to the production of supple merino wool. Merino wool (the best is sourced from New Zealand) has an amazing ability to retain warmth and wonderfully repels odor. Wool falls short in terms of durability and dry times, but it does remain warm when wet. Wool will also be heavier than a comparative synthetic fiber. Better suited for cold climates, ultrathin superfine merino wool is also suitable for warmer climates. Wool comes in several grades—the lighter the grade, the softer and lighter the wool will be:

- 17.5 microns and less—ultrafine merino wool
- 18.5 microns—superfine merino wool
- 19.5 microns—extra fine merino wool
- 22.5 microns—medium merino wool
- 24 microns and greater—strong merino wool

Silk: Silk is a natural protein fiber spun from the raw silk fibers of silkworm (moth larva) cocoons. It is one of the strongest yet lightest natural fibers, making it a wonder that it is not more commonly used in outdoor apparel. Cost and durability can be issues, especially since silk loses up to 20 percent of its strength when wet. Having natural moisture-wicking properties, silk is best used as a base layer due to its supple next-to-skin feel, natural antimicrobial properties, and comfort throughout a range of temperatures. Since the larvae are killed in the process of harvesting the silk, it is not a truly renewable resource.

Bamboo: Far on the gimmick end of the spectrum, bamboo is a new "green" fabric to hit the market. A type of rayon, bamboo textiles are made from the raw cellulose of fast-growing bamboo. While slightly better than cotton, bamboo suffers from durability issues and generally has to be heavily subsidized with merino wool, cotton, and polyester to make a suitable proprietary fabric. Bamboo, while a fast-regenerating resource, has been cited due to caustic production methods.

Coconut: Using coconut shells from industrial food waste, companies like 37.5 (formally Cocona) are helping pioneer the "upcycling" model of sustainability in the outdoor industry. The activated carbon inherent in coconut fibers is perfect for neutralizing odor while having an enormous absorption rate. Fused into recycled polyester fabrics, when used as a base layer, the porous coconut fibers have the ability to increase the surface area of the skin up to 800 percent. This means you will stay dryer, cooler, and more comfortable over a range of conditions.

Coconut fibers also have the natural ability to transfer moisture without vapor pressure or high humidity differentials, an inherent limitation to current waterproof breathable fabrics like Gore-Tex. As this technology continues to develop and evolve, we could see increased breathability in rain shells and other waterproof-breathable apparel.

Note: In some trials for earlier prototypes of this base layer, we've experienced significant pilling and loss of the supple feel after some use.

Down: Down feathers are the underplumage of ducks and geese and have the highest warmth-to-weight ratio of any fiber on Earth. Down is amazingly compressible and long lasting. Properly taken care of, a down garment should last a lifetime and beyond. Down is expensive to source sustainably and does not retain its warmth when wet; dry times are excessively long. So-called "waterproof," or hydrophobic, down has entered the market, albeit with some skepticism. While independent lab results do show that treated down stays dry ten times longer, retains 170 percent more loft when exposed to moisture, and dries 30 percent faster, it remains to be seen if these treatments can retain their properties over time and how the coatings affect the down filaments over time and repeated use.

Fur: Hands down, fur is the warmest fabric on Earth. It is the sole source of warmth and protection for nearly every mammal that has adapted to extremely cold climates. Because fur is sourced from the hides of animals, it is also one of the least sustainable and cruelest fabrics to source. Fur is also much heavier than more sustainably sourced down. One of fur's greatest advantages is its ability to prevent ice from freezing to it. A fur ruff on the hood of an anorak or parka prevents the moisture in your exhalation from freezing to the perimeter of the hood. A fur ruff also blocks the wind and insulates from the cold. If you can source a coyote fur ruff from a hunter friend, it is a wonderful addition to an ultralight winter parka.

Fur ruffs do an exceptional job of sealing warmth in around the face, blocking the wind, and preventing frost from building up around the mouth. A simple coyote ruff can be sewn on to nearly any ultralight parka or puffy.
Calvin Croll

Cotton: Cotton is likely the most commercially produced fiber in the world. It is in nearly every common household good. We love cotton because of its amazing feel next to the skin. Despite the common belief that "cotton kills," it can actually be a great fabric for hot summertime hiking *because* of its shortcomings. Cotton is notoriously absorbent. Ever pull a pair of jeans out of the washing machine? The same occurs when cotton is used for active pursuits. Cotton takes forever to dry and does not retain warmth when wet. That is why it can actually be great for hot summer hiking. It will hold your sweat next to your skin for a long time, aiding in evaporative cooling. However, cotton should be avoided in any other condition, especially winter.

COST

With the price tags that accompany most high-end outdoor "performance" clothing, some might argue that any long-distance trail is nothing more than a thousand-mile-long fashion runway. Thumbing through any "extreme" backcountry magazine will surely inform you of the new "must-have" advances in technology. Truth be told, with proper technique and material selection, the margins of added performance are slim at best. Fashion statements aside, you could probably pull your dad's 1970s leisure suit (aka super duper fancy soft shell suit) out of the closet, have an incredibly pleasant day on the slopes, and still look good at the bar that evening.

If keeping costs down is a priority, the key concepts to grasp from this section are the applications of fabric and material. With this in mind, it's quite conceivable to source much of your outdoor attire at a fraction of the cost through military surplus stores, thrift stores, used-clothing vendors, online "seconds," and other discount retailers, although weights will typically be heavier.

So why the sticker shock? Simple. The fit is in the finish. There are a multitude of reasons that Item A from a name-brand company is ten times more expensive than Item B from your bargain box store. Higher end companies may be sourcing their materials in a more sustainable manner and/or have much higher quality control. It's amazing how something as universally used as ripstop nylon can have a huge range in quality. With so many things being manufactured overseas, the same factory might be sewing a backpack for one company one week and then switching patterns and stitching up a down jacket for another company the next week. Same employees, just higher quality inspection and higher quality materials.

When in a retail store, take the time to compare the fit and finish between a price-point base layer or soft shell jacket versus one from a high-end manufacturer. The differences can be stark. How this translates into real-world performance in the backcountry is that the price-point base layer could conceivably start chafing you an hour into your day or even constrict your circulation, leaving you cold and skeptical of what the fuss is over merino wool. The details in the high-end garment will be tailored precisely to your intended activity—bells and whistles applied where they are needed and stripped of excessive bulk and weight where required. Someone thought it would be a great idea to add that snot chamois to the thumb of those ski gloves. You know why? Because everyone's nose inevitably runs on a cold winter day. Do you need that chamois? No, but no one wants to sport a raw Rudolf nose either.

Most high-end companies also stand by their products through varying degrees of warranty programs. You may be hard pressed to return your waterproof hardshell from a big box store when it starts leaking and the zipper blows out after a few months of moderate use. But Gore-Tex, for instance, has a zero-questions-asked return policy for the lifetime of the garment. Lifetime! Customer service for established companies is generally up to snuff in the friendliness category; they might even ask you about your recent trip using their products.

It's expensive to innovate and invest in research and development, even more so to patent technologies to protect your products. If you must be the first person on your block to have the new silver woven, bamboo sustained, helium filled whatchamacallit, you're generally going to pay top dollar for it. Wait a few years, and the trickle-down of technology will usually lower the cost of those products substantially.

The bottom line is to shop within your budget. Cost should never be a barrier for getting out and enjoying the backcountry. With enough insight and patience, you should be able to fully outfit yourself without breaking the bank. Borrow from friends, look on Craigslist or into rental programs, beg, plead! Whatever it takes to get outside!

BASE LAYERS

A base layer is just that—the foundation all other layers will be stacked upon. It is the layer that will be in direct contact with our skin at all times, so it makes sense that fit, function, and comfort should be the hallmarks of this essential piece.

The base layer serves a few primary purposes. First, to maintain a satisfactory level of comfort, it must pull excess moisture, à la perspiration, from the surface of our skin, transport it through the fabric, and spread this moisture across the exterior of the fabric to expedite evaporation. Moving the evaporative process away from the surface of our skin greatly reduces the chilling effects of evaporative cooling. The fabric itself should be hydrophobic (water-hating) and have a quick dry time.

A base layer should simultaneously retain a small amount of insulative properties. It should be form fitting but not constrictive. The trim profile will minimize excess bulk to facilitate the addition of exterior layers without inhibiting movement. Seams should be placed away from pressure points like shoulders and hips to increase durability and prevent chafing while wearing a pack.

There are a few added niceties to look for in base layers to increase the overall comfort and functionality. Collars and quarter zips complement each other by facilitating venting during exertion and add an additional layer of warmth to the nape when temps drop or the wind picks up.

Thumb holes in sleeves help minimize the drafty gap between glove and sleeve. Ever have that annoying pocket of snow accumulate in this region and feel the chilling affects?

Hoods, while appealing in base layers, can add undue bulk if other exterior layers incorporate hoods as well. Too many hoods and you'll feel like you have an airplane pillow around

Wool base layers have a wide range of comfort and help stave off unwanted odor. Same shirt in each photo—only a 50+°F difference between the two environments. Features like one-quarter zips help vent excess heat when needed.
Shawn Forry

your neck. We find them best in moderation to prevent bunching. Refrain from anything more than a mid-layer hood and an outer layer hood.

INSULATION LAYERS

Insulation layers are designed to trap heat coming off our bodies, preventing it from expelling into the atmosphere. These layers are highly dictated by our physical output and are the layers we will typically be adjusting constantly throughout the day. This category can further be broken down into mid-layers and insulating "puffy jackets."

Mid-layers are typically composed of thin microfleece, mid-weight merino wool, or a thin synthetic puffy coat. They should be highly breathable and add just enough additional warmth when a base layer and wind shell alone do not suffice. Patagonia's waffle-knit R-series and Montbell's synthetic ThermaWrap jacket are great examples of versatile mid-layers. Some mid-layers incorporate stretch panels in select regions to improve breathability, mobility, and fit. The addition of a hood in this layer can be beneficial to add flexibility as winds and temps change throughout the day. Monitoring your head warmth, particularly the back of the neck and ears, is a quick measure to maintain overall comfort.

Down is generally frowned upon in this category, since mid-layers will most often be used when on the go. It is all too common for the back and shoulders to "wet out" from sweat if exertion is not closely monitored.

Insulating puffy coats are often our warmest layer and are predominately used for retaining heat while in camp or during breaks. The coat should be sized to fit over all our existing

The waffle knit of Patagonia's R4 insulation strikes a great balance in warmth retention and breathability. Proper layers for winter travel allow for comfort in a wide range of physical outputs.
Larry Mishkar

No one can argue with the versatility of a multifunctional mid-layer like the Montbell ThermaWrap. It traps heat, blocks wind, is warm when wet, packs down to 8 ounces, and looks good while hitching in a Santa hat.
Shawn Forry

layers and definitely incorporate a hood. When the mercury drops, this will be our go-to layer to stay sane and happy. Down is far superior in this category for warmth to weight. A parka with 2 to 3 ounces of premium 800+ fill down will yield ample warmth in all but the most extreme conditions when combined with all our other layers. Encapsulated in 7- to 10-denier ballistic nylon, these parkas can weigh as little as 8 to 12 ounces total. If conditions favor sustained inclement weather with warmer temps, switching to a synthetic puffy is encouraged to add an additional margin of safety and comfort. A synthetic puffy with comparable warmth to down will generally weigh about 30 percent more.

The addition of highly water- and wind-resistant membranes like Gore Windstopper or Pertex Endurance is generally reserved only for expedition-weight parkas used during extremely cold outings where the parka will commonly be used as the outermost layer. Otherwise this additional membrane is redundant with layers already in tote like wind and rain shells.

WIND LAYER

Probably one of the most underrated articles of clothing to incorporate into your layering system is the humble wind jacket. For less than the weight and bulk of an energy bar, you can drastically increase your overall warmth. Typically constructed of tightly knit nylon, the wind jacket strikes the perfect balance of deflecting much of the wind's convective cooling efforts without compromising breathability. Most wind jackets, or "windshirts," will also add a durable water-repellent (DWR) coating to stave off light precipitation.

No layering system is complete without a wind shell. At under 2 ounces, the Montbell Tachyon anorak sheds wind while offering just enough breathability to stay comfortable through a range of conditions.
Shawn Forry

Working in concert with a base layer or thin mid-layer microfleece, this combination provides a one-two punch to moisture transport, warmth retention, and breathability when active in temps hovering around freezing. Due to their extremely small size when packed, wind jackets can be stashed in an outside pocket and retrieved effortlessly when needed. A hood is an essential in a wind shell. The added weight and bulk are negligible compared to the versatility and warmth to be gained.

By incorporating wind shells into your sleep system, you can further trap heat coming off the body. Also, due to the tight weave of the fabric, wind shells are also perfect for warding off bites from mosquitoes and no-see-ums during bug season, eliminating the need for bug netting in your shelter.

There are very few situations where a windshirt will not be of use in winter; it is one of the few layers that are seldom removed. The lightest models tip the scales at less than 2 ounces. Durability is surprisingly remarkable in this weight range, but if you're engaging in activities that will cause more abrasion and abuse, a super-thin soft shell can achieve similar results for about three times the weight.

WATERPROOF LAYERS

It must first be stated that no other piece of outdoor clothing or equipment leaves more to be desired than the so-called "waterproof-breathable" category of apparel. Despite the marketing hype, there is no such thing as a truly waterproof AND breathable fabric. The reality is you will be overcome by dampness from either precipitation or perspiration. For the truly active, our basic movements will quickly overpower the current ability of these fabrics. This is especially exacerbated in winter, when temps expedite perspiration condensing to frost inside our jackets before the material has a chance to transport the moisture to the exterior of the garment. Until true advances occur, we are left with acknowledging and managing this reality.

The colder the ambient temperature, the less we should rely on waterproof fabrics. In temps consistently below 0°F, they should be avoided all together, instead leaning heavily toward highly breathable soft shell and natural fibers. Once temps reach this level, the air becomes extremely dry, minimizing the chances of snow saturating our clothing. True breathability and wind protection should be prioritized to minimize moisture condensing in our clothing layers. Plus, in most climates, especially in North America, when temperatures get below 0°F, there is little chance of significant snowfall. Such frigid conditions usually come on clear, cold nights or under a strong ridge of high pressure from the north.

The most challenging winter conditions are precipitation events occurring between 20°F and 40°F. Here hypothermia can rear its head at any time if we do not manage ourselves carefully. At these temperatures, the state of the snow, sleet, and rain is still very close to or at the liquid state. Humidity will generally be high, which further limits the transport of moisture through the garment due to the lack of temperature and moisture gradient between us and the outside world. The higher this gradient, the easier it is for the fabric to work as claimed. The irony is such that the optimal conditions are when it's not precipitating.

Our strategy in these situations should be to adopt full waterproof fabrics and assist them through manual ventilation. Fabrics like DCF or PVC are the lightest option in this category. Lowering our expectations of "comfort" should also follow suit. These conditions are miserable, no matter how you slice it.

Manual ventilation can occur through the use of large pit zips and vents in the garment. We want to increase physical airflow as much as possible to transport perspiration away from our bodies while still maintaining a watertight exterior to prevent our getting soaked. High-priority are the armpits, stomach, back, and thighs. Additionally, managing the layers under the jacket to prevent overheating goes a long way as well. Jackets with these features provide some reprieve from the dampening effects of sweat but can also be challenged by restricting precipitation from entering at these ventilation locations.

For traditional waterproof breathable jackets, features to seek above pit zips and other means of venting should be fully taped seams, waterproof zippers, and a hood that provides ample mobility and visibility when in full storm mode. These features will increase the overall effectiveness of the jacket. Avoid combo "ski" jackets that have fleece linings or other insulation materials sewn into the jacket. These types of jackets will limit the versatility of your layering system and increase drying times once saturated.

Here is where the incorporation of ponchos shines. At the far end of the style spectrum, ponchos do an incredible job of providing ample ventilation and complete water protection. Suited only for certain activities, ponchos would be quite restrictive if you're trying to alpine climb or ski in them. In basic activities like hiking and snowshoeing, however, they provide the added benefit of keeping your entire pack dry and provide a place to hunker down for a snack break. Their long coverage also provides ample overlapping protection for the lower extremities when paired with a pair of waterproof pants. Most ponchos can also serve dual purpose as a tarp, which can be handy in camp use as a cook shelter or expanding an existing tent vestibule.

Ponchos take an entirely different approach to WP/B fabrics, relying solely on ventilation for moisture management. Ponchos have limited coverage in the arms and are prone to flapping around in storms. Staying 100 percent dry is not possible with high-humidity/high-output conditions like this.
Justin Lichter

When dexterity in movement and durability are priorities, ponchos are not your best option. In these scenarios, select a traditional waterproof breathable fabric. Over time make sure to keep up on restoring the DWR qualities of the jacket, and tightly manage your mid-layers underneath.

When it comes to waterproof protection for the lower extremities, the same concepts apply. Waterproof breathable fabrics respond better around the legs, since they tend to be a much less sweaty region and aren't being compressed by your pack and pack straps. High wear areas where "wetting out" will be most common are the butt,

Claimed WP/B fabrics try to keep us from getting wet both from the inside and the outside. Regardless if using a proprietary fabric or an industry standard like Gore-Tex, all WP/B fabrics will fail at some point. To extend their effectiveness, use products to maintain their DWR finish, and wear only in conditions where you need them.
Shawn Forry

thighs, and knees. Full-length waterproof side zips may seem excessive, but in winter they are very handy. They greatly help with venting, going to the bathroom, and getting boots on and off.

Consider instep crampon patches a must along the lower inseam of the pant leg. During winter, when sharp objects like skis, snowshoes, or crampons will be underfoot, the resulting change in stride will inevitably create holes and rips.

Internal gaiters can be helpful in sealing out unwanted snow between boot and ankle. This is a much lighter approach than dedicated gaiters.

HEAD, HANDS, AND TOES

The extremities can be one of the hardest areas of the body to properly regulate. Being far from the warmth of our core, they take longer to circulate warm blood and are constantly exposed to the elements by handling snowy objects and sloshing through deep snow; coincidentally, they are one of the sweatiest parts of our body. That all suffices to say that properly regulating warmth in the hands, feet, and head can seem a Sisyphean task.

Tailoring a system that works for each individual takes time and patience. Hopefully we can lay a fact-based foundation upon which to begin the process of determining your individual preferences. Staying uniform with the concept of layering, we want to take a similar approach to how we regulate the head, hands, and feet to better cater to the range of physical exertion we will see.

TIP

Add a short length of thin, brightly colored 2-millimeter accessory cord to all frequently used external zippers for ease in locating and opening zippers with gloved hands—especially helpful when thick mittens are required to keep hands warm. The marginal gain in grams will pay dividends in efficiency.

BEANIES, BALACLAVAS, AND NECK GAITERS

The adage goes that we lose 50 percent of our heat through our head. This reason for ensuring our head is covered is only partially true. While regulating the thermal comfort of our head gives us a greater perception of warmth, the head actually loses an amount of heat proportional to the total surface area of skin exposed, or about 7 percent.

Materials of choice will be very similar to other articles of clothing, addressing the same pros and cons to the conditions and our preferences. The key to effective head wear is flexibility. Having a system that can suit a range of conditions and exertion will best serve your purposes. For ultralight, multipurpose tactics, we should also plan on incorporating hoods on wind shells and jackets into our overall head warmth plan.

A slightly oversized beanie can be pulled down to adequately cover the nape or doubled over to better insulate the forehead and ears. Similarly, the hat can be tipped back to vent the forehead as needed. This type of flexibility is required for all active winter pursuits. Products like Buff highlight the versatility a hat can offer.

For bitter cold and windy conditions, we also want to make sure we have ample coverage for the cheeks, chin, and neck. It can be hard to prevent the accumulation of frost around our mouth without also inhibiting breathing. Neck gaiters are a great way to add an additional layer of warmth around the neck while also preventing heat loss from our collar. They can be pulled up to the chin or nose to better protect the face. Keep in mind that covering the mouth will reap the benefit of pre-warming our breath, but all moisture from our exhalation will accumulate in the form of frost over the fabric covering the mouth.

Balaclavas are equally effective, as they can be used as a hat, neck gaiter, face shield, or complete coverage. Avoid gimmicks like neoprene breathing ports. A simple thin fleece or merino wool balaclava is both light and effective

Incorporate any parka hoods into your overall layering warmth for sleeping and taking breaks. Be mindful of how many jackets have hoods on them to minimize excess bulk.
Justin Lichter

TIP

To regulate the amount of frost building up on a scarf, neck gaiter, or balaclava, routinely rotate the frosty section to the back of your head. The warmth from the back of your head will thaw out the frozen section while you are on the move.

For around 1 ounce, balaclavas offer unparalleled versatility in warmth retention and are a great addition to your sleep system. Cheeks and noses are two of the easiest areas to forget about on blustery days, resulting in frostnip. Balaclavas allow you to dial in the level of protection you need.
Justin Lichter

and should weigh only around 1 ounce. A very versatile system can be created by layering your head gear with a balaclava, then a brimmed hat, then a beanie. This helps keep you warm and keeps the snow out of your face.

MITTENS, GLOVES, AND OVERMITTS

Let's put this out there from the start. There is no Holy Grail of hand wear that is going to maintain 100 percent dryness and warmth at all times. Let that sink in. Similar to the limitations of rainwear, all gloves will eventually soak through; likely at a faster rate than a rain jacket because of the exposure time our hands have against the elements. Nearly everything we touch in the wintertime will have some residual moisture. Combine that with the fact that our hands sweat more than we think, it is no wonder that hand wear is an often hotly debated topic.

All hand wear is going to be balancing weight, durability, warmth, and dexterity. Super warm gloves struggle with zippers and toggles. Ultralight gloves cannot stand up to the abuse or abrasion of simple tasks, nor are they very warm. Understanding the activities you will be doing with your hands can help narrow down the features and priorities in the gloves you select.

Mittens are, hands down, warmer than gloves. Since the entire warmth of your hand is being captured in the same "room," all fingers share the warmth equally. In gloves it's an "everyone fend for yourself mentality." Anyone who has used mittens knows how limiting your dexterity is. Even buckling your pack can take longer.

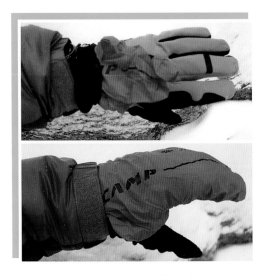

Keeping the convective cooling effects of winds off hands can significantly retain warmth. These stowable wind mitts in the Camp G-Comp glove are a clever and lightweight solution without adding undue bulk.
Shawn Forry

TIP An extra pair of socks can serve as an emergency pair of mittens when the mercury takes an unexpected plunge.

Shawn Forry

This updated version of the classic mitten-minder doesn't require your mom's help getting dressed to venture outside. The greatest sin with winter gloves is laying them down in the snow. Instead stow them in a pocket or inside your jacket, or rely on mitten-minders like these.
Shawn Forry

A good compromise is to layer a thin mitten over a glove, providing the best of both worlds. Mittens will keep your hands toasty warm while on the go; and any time you need to complete a task with your hands, you simply pop the mittens off, complete the task, and put your still warm mittens back on. Remember to keep your gloves out of the snow and put them inside a pocket when you remove them. This will keep your gloves warm and help keep your hands warm when you put the gloves back on. Cold gloves can provide the initial shock that sends your hands into a chilly downhill spiral. Some mittens convert into gloves, and some gloves have mitten covers that stow in the cuff of the glove. The later seems to work better for function and weight.

For durability, look for a glove that at least has reinforced patches over the index finger and thumb. These are the highest wear areas in a glove. Reinforcement patches can be nylon, leather, or a synthetic siliconized material.

They may feel reminiscent of the 1980s, but mitten minders, or a similar concept, serve a useful purpose. Since our gloves are constantly coming on and off to do simple tasks, a mitten minder helps keep them out of the snow and, more importantly, from being left behind at a break.

Material choice in a glove can play a big part in its overall performance and function. Fleece is extremely warm for the weight, but snow has an annoying tendency to stick to pile fleece. Leather is extremely durable and slightly water resistant, but it takes forever to dry out and can even shrink when wet.

How a glove fits will directly correlate to the feeling of overall warmth it provides. Gloves that are too tight restrict adequate blood flow to the hand, and big floppy gloves can be annoying. Remember, we're trying to trap small pockets of warm air

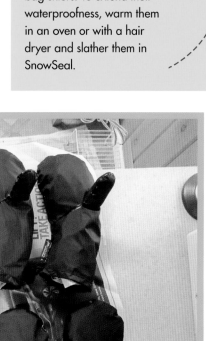

TIP

Ski patrollers love the warmth and durability of the classic Kinco, and they are priced perfectly for dirt bag skiers! To extend their waterproofness, warm them in an oven or with a hair dryer and slather them in SnowSeal.

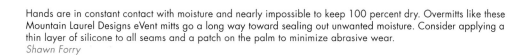

Hands are in constant contact with moisture and nearly impossible to keep 100 percent dry. Overmitts like these Mountain Laurel Designs eVent mitts go a long way toward sealing out unwanted moisture. Consider applying a thin layer of silicone to all seams and a patch on the palm to minimize abrasive wear.
Shawn Forry

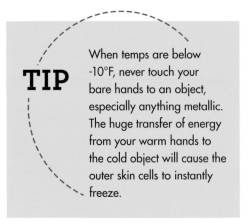

TIP

When temps are below -10°F, never touch your bare hands to an object, especially anything metallic. The huge transfer of energy from your warm hands to the cold object will cause the outer skin cells to instantly freeze.

around our hands. You'll pay a premium for gloves that are articulated in their construction, but the fit and finish of these higher end gloves are worth it. Some gloves minimize insulation in the tips of the fingers to address limited dexterity. Keeping the back of your hands warm will lead to an overall greater sensation of warmth versus function. The wrist is an area of significant heat loss. A glove that has adequate wrist cover will feel infinitely warmer and will seal out that annoying pocket of snow that likes to accumulate right next to the wrist.

An overmitt serves best to address waterproofness. A modular glove system is far easier to dry out than an all-in-one glove. A simple Gore-Tex or eVent overmitt can jointly retain the warmth of a mitten and seal out unwanted moisture and wind. Avoid fabrics like neoprene in the hopes of finding a truly waterproof glove. Neoprene works great to retain warmth when you are active, but it becomes cold and clammy the moment your activity level drops.

SOCKS AND DOWN BOOTIES

Foot warmth needs to work in conjunction with the proper footwear (as discussed in the Modes of Travel chapter). Without this, your feet will be a heat sieve. Socks therefore must work in collaboration with the shoe. Yes, thicker socks will be warmer, but they must fit inside the shoe so as to not constrict the foot. It's not uncommon to oversize a shoe by half a size to accommodate thicker socks. Double-check the fit of the shoe to the foot, since thicker socks can also interfere with fit, causing more slippage at the heel. Layering multiple socks has good intentions but usually results in a colder foot due to restricted blood flow. At most,

layer a medium- to heavyweight sock over a liner. Wool socks are by far the warmest and most commonly used in winter.

Most of our foot warmth is lost as conductive heat loss through the ground. If

Women's hose actually make for an incredibly thin, warm, and light sock liner. They offer just enough friction reduction to combat those pesky ski boot heel blisters that are bound to creep in. Experiment with wearing them over and under your preferred insulating wool socks, as personal preferences may vary.
Justin Lichter

your shoe can accommodate a thicker insole, it will make a huge difference in the sensation of warmth. At minimum, you may want to consider gluing a piece of Mylar below the insole.

Vapor barrier liners (VBLs) in footwear are on one of the more common applications. Keeping the foot dry goes a long way toward the feeling of warmth. VBLs prevent not only the sock but also any insulation layers in the footwear from becoming saturated.

Camp booties are amazing to slip into at the end of a long winter day's travel. They are a lightweight way to make sure your feet maintain warmth in camp while also giving them a break from the confines of ski boots and other winter footwear. Camp booties can be slipped inside overboots or ski shells to keep them dry while you're tending to camp chores and nightly bathroom breaks. As tempting as it may be to incorporate booties into a sleep system, feet often tend to get sweaty and thus colder when you're sleeping in down or synthetic camp booties—at least in our experience. Others, however, rave about their warmth.

The ZPacks Goose Sock is one of the lightest, warmest, and least-durable camp bootie, weighing in at a scant 1.9 ounces for the pair. For folks needing more utility in their

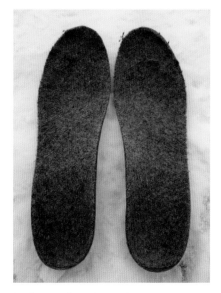

Insoles can play a huge role in minimizing conductive heat loss through the ground. Wool-lined insoles like these from Superfeet provided a slight amount of heat without undue bulk. Some liners may even have a layer of Mylar to reflect heat back to the foot. Avoid gimmicky electric heated insoles, and keep in mind that you may need to size up footwear to accommodate thicker insoles.
Shawn Forry

Insulated sleep socks are a wonderful addition to a sleep system and for doing camp chores. Camp booties try to balance weight, durability, and warmth. From left to right: ZPacks Goose Down Socks, Big Agnes Milner Mall Mountain Booties, Integral Designs Hot Socks.
Shawn Forry

camp bootie, offerings from Integral Designs and Big Agnes have a durable nylon sole and slightly heavier face fabrics.

VAPOR BARRIER CLOTHING

As alluded to throughout this book, the concept of vapor barrier technology is commonly misunderstood. On extended outings in extreme cold, our dependency on insulation layers

RBH Designs is one of the few companies that take advantage of VBL technology. VBLs not only prevent insulative layers from saturating with perspiration but also minimize dehydration once the body senses a "microclimate" of humidity has been established against the skin. Their use can be invaluable during extended cold-weather expeditions. *RBH Designs*

TIP Simple VBL liners can be made from bread bags or ziplock bags if you're in a pinch for foot or hand warmth.

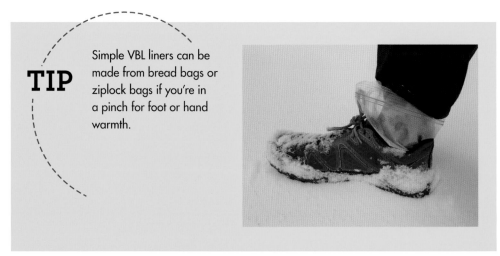

is invaluable to the success of our trip. Regardless of our activity, we want to prevent outside moisture and perspiration from entering this precious layer. VBL clothing is a means to prevent our sweat from unduly saturating our insulation clothing. Knowing that our hands, feet, back, and forehead are some of the sweatiest areas of our body during high exertion, it makes sense to address this through the application of VBLs.

Whether wearing a VBL jacket, glove, or sock, having a thin moisture-wicking layer between us and the VBL fabric will help to minimize that clammy sensation. Keep in mind that if we are incorporating VBL technology, it is appropriate for our outer layers to be 100 percent waterproof, eliminating the need for breathability since, in theory, there should be no moisture that needs to transport through the garment away from our bodies.

VBLs are an extremely niche market and confined to only a few manufacturers. Stephenson's Warmlite has been preaching the merits of VBL technology since the 1970s, providing a line of apparel, tents, and sleeping bags. RBH is newer on the market and puts a more modern spin on the Warmlite products, providing more ultralight offerings in jacket, hand, and footwear. VBLs take some experimentation to dial in and may not be for everyone.

Hands and feet are among the most challenging parts of the body to keep warm—and, coincidentally, among the sweatiest. VBL mitts are exceptionally warm due to their ability to prevent the insulation from wetting out and to share collective warmth throughout the fingers.
RBH Designs

CHAPTER 3

MODES OF TRAVEL

HOW WE CHOOSE TO TRAVEL IN THE BACKCOUNTRY CAN RANGE FROM JOYFUL RECREATION TO STRICTLY UTILITARIAN TO DOWNRIGHT MISERABLE. The nature of moving through an ever-changing medium such as snow means that some days are effortless bliss while others are best defined as an arduous slog. While not all winter environments are snow-bound, this chapter will cover the possible methods and options for things you can strap to your feet to expedite travel and diminish effort. Each method has its definitive advantages and equal limitations. There is no perfect system that spans the range of conditions you could encounter in the backcountry, so a "lesser of all evils" approach should be applied.

Within each mode of travel is an opportunity to broaden your skill set and experience the solitude of winter in its own unique way. As with anything new, it's best to take things in a logical progression. Rather than diving straight into a multiday kite-skiing expedition across Greenland having never even heard the term "off-piste," it's best to tackle each new skill one at a time until competency is reached. Taking on too much too soon is a surefire way to get discouraged, injured, or worse. The views and opinions within this chapter will be slanted toward multiday excursions to highlight the pros and cons of each chosen mode of travel. That being said, the foundation of each overview will apply equally to day excursions.

HIKING

Sometimes the simplest way to get out and enjoy winter is by doing what we already know. Adapting general walking and hiking to winter conditions when trails are still free, or lightly covered in snow, can be a great gateway to enjoying the experience and an opportunity to shake down basic camping and navigation skills. Depending on your geographic location, winter may be mild or fleeting. Even so, hiking in snow can be a pleasurable experience. With hard-packed trails or less than a foot of unconsolidated snow, only a few minor tweaks to footwear need apply.

The priority here is to ensure that footwear provides adequate traction and warmth. Common summertime trail runners can work seamlessly in winter conditions depending on how we meet the above requirements. Adapting light hikers and full-grain leather boots can similarly follow suit. Sometimes simply stepping up to a thicker wool sock and some simple gaiters is all that is needed to enjoy a wintery trail run.

Whichever hiking footwear you choose will also strike a balance in comfort and dry times. So-called "waterproof" boots will eventually soak through and take longer to dry than a non-waterproof equivalent. This can be more problematic on multiday excursions than on a

Winter does not always mean snow. Historically dry Sierra winters have allowed winter hiking—seen here, crossing a frozen lake along the Tahoe Rim Trail in January.
Shawn Forry

casual day hike. A surprising amount of foot warmth is dictated by overall foot movement. Shoes and boots that do away with shanks are easier to flex, which translates to better circulation and comfort. There is a delicate balance to strike with ensuring the foot has proper circulation, protection, and movement when considering the right footwear for the occasion.

SOCKS

Additional means to adapt summer footwear for winter include the use of Gore-Tex or neoprene socks. Both increase foot warmth by limiting the foot's exposure to icy cold socks and shoes. Shoes should be sized to accommodate the extra bulk to prevent constricting the feet. Gore-Tex socks are great for your favorite pair of non-waterproof running shoes, but they tend to bunch and are prone to wearing out prematurely due to the high abrasion that occurs in footwear. Neoprene socks are usually worn over a thin liner sock, with a warmer wool sock worn over, if desired. Since neoprene is non-breathable it will act as a VBL of sorts. The liner sock is essential to wick moisture away to prevent clammy feeling and to help prevent blistering from macerated feet. Both sock systems have been met with limited success and personal preference.

Neoprene socks have mixed results in providing additional warmth in cold, wet conditions. Best to wear them over a thin liner sock, making sure there is adequate space in your footwear to accommodate the added bulk. If the neoprene sock is overly constrictive, it will make your foot colder. Be mindful of seam location to minimize chafe-induced blisters.
Shawn Forry

TRACTION DEVICES

When trails are icy or increased traction is desired, the addition of simple traction devices like micro-spikes or instep crampons can greatly increase purchase and confidence. Most attach to the shoe via elastic bungees and/or straps and range in weight from 2 to 10 ounces. Traction is gained through metal coils or small crampon-like spikes. Their point of contact to the ground will dictate their overall grip in the snow. Small instep crampons make purchase with snow or ice only when the arch of the shoe is in direct contact with the snow. This can leave the foot vulnerable to a slip when pushing off with the forefoot while climbing or landing heel first upon descent. Traction devices that span the whole foot have more consistent traction, but usually at a cost of more weight. Vargo's titanium model is very light and can be effective in many conditions, despite lacking heel traction. Overall, strap-on traction devices are a great middle ground between nothing and full-on twelve-point crampons. They pack small, are inexpensive, and are effective for their intended use.

A simple instep crampon like the Vargo Titanium Pocket Cleats weigh just over 2 ounces, pack down to nothing, yet provide just enough traction for casual hiking/running on icy trails. The lack of any heel traction requires attentive care on steeper descents.
Shawn Forry

At 11 ounces, Katoola's Microspikes offer full foot traction and work with a range of footwear options. They are compact to pack and are a good solution for icy trail runs and hikes.
Kenneth J Hamilton Photography, LLC

Shawn Forry

TIP

Adapt an old pair of running shoes into dedicated winter trail runners by inserting metal machine screws into the tread. They can easily be removed if desired, cost only a few bucks, and can be installed with a simple screwdriver.

GAITERS

Depending on the depth of snow or the height of the shoe, adding a simple gaiter can go a long way to prevent unwanted snow from entering the shoe. Gaiters can range in size from ankle to knee height and differ in material choice depending on whether waterproofness is desired. Common materials, ranging from most breathable to most waterproof, are Schoeller and Gore-Tex, respectively. Gaiters can add a surprising amount of warmth to the lower legs and help prevent the icing-up and saturation of pant legs, enabling them to be "quarantined" in order to keep sleep clothes dry while in the shelter at night. It can help to place these wet items underneath your sleeping pad to prevent them from freezing.

The topic of whether to wear gaiters over or under pants is hotly debated. For most winter excursions, they will be more effective over the pant leg. Their tight fit helps keep bulky pant cuffs out of harm's way of skis and crampons, minimizing trip hazards. The only time it makes sense to wear pants over gaiters is during extended downpours where rain would run down the leg, under the gaiter, and directly into the boot. This is why internal gaiters in ski pants tend to be the best of both worlds. They have an external crampon patch sewn in and prevent snow from going up and over the boot cuff.

Montbell Spats gaiters are made from super-stretchy Schoeller soft-shell material, which means they are highly breathable and water resistant. Gaiters like these can be used in winter for high-aerobic activities like trail running to prevent snow from balling up inside the shoe without being too restrictive or sweaty.
Justin Lichter

For under 2 ounces, simple waterproof eVent gaiters like these from Mountain Laurel Designs help seal out snow without adding much weight or bulk. Gaiters like these can work with a wide range of footwear, and their short height minimizes perspiration buildup.
Justin Lichter

Most ski pants offer internal gaiters to prevent snow from entering ski boots and external crampon patches to minimize cuts and abrasion from sharp ski edges and crampons. For ski touring boots, consideration of how the walk/ski mode integrates with the gaiter will increase dryness to the liner and efficiency in transitions. With these Dynafit Vulcan boots, the gaiter must be lifted each time to transition.
Shawn Forry

INSULATED PACK BOOTS AND MUKLUKS

With a finite amount of additional warmth and adaptability in traditional hiking and running shoes, stepping up to an overall warmer design and approach is sometime required. Insulated boots provide an additional layer of warmth for the foot through an internal lining of a synthetic like PrimaLoft, Thinsulate, Climashield, or fleece or of felted wool. This lining can either be removable or sewn into the boot. The advantage to removable liners is their ease in drying at night and the ability to use them as camp and/or sleep booties. Most boots in this category have a waterproof upper by incorporating Gore-Tex or a similar proprietary membrane, rubber, or full-grain leather. Gore-Tex and full-grain leather have a narrow window of effectiveness but provide some breathability. Rubber, while completely waterproof, provides zero breathability.

Common hiking boot designs that incorporate a sewn-in liner are relatively lightweight and provide decent comfort. Due to the challenges in drying them out, they are better suited for day trips and shorter excursions. To keep the insulation liner dry and extend its effectiveness, VBL socks should be highly considered.

Modular systems are preferred for extended trips. The most common example of these is a Sorel-type pack boot. The Sorel pack boot, with its full rubber rand and water-resistant leather upper, has a removable liner and provides ample warmth. The boots' overbuilt design is not the lightest option out there, but they are easy to source. The leather uppers are prone to soaking through, causing the felt liners to become saturated. Felt liners, while amazingly light and warm, take a long time to dry out and are prone to mildew if not thoroughly dried in a timely manner.

Borrowing antiquated but proven technology from the military, "Mickey Mouse" boots were designed during the Korean War and require ultra-low maintenance. Their full rubber inner and outer shells have a layer of fully encased felted wool sandwiched between. This system ensures the insulation will stay dry at all times, making these boots perfect for multiday trips. Best worn with a thin to medium-weight wool sock, these boots are designed for temps down to -20°F to -40°F. They come in two versions, the warmer white and the lighter black. Tipping the scale at just under 3 pounds, they are not the lightest option available, but their low maintenance and proven design make them extremely user-friendly with minimal opportunities for user error.

As they are no longer produced, these boots must be sourced at military surplus and online vendors. Take the time to inspect them before purchase, as the rubber can be prone to dry rot, causing leaks into the felt lining. Problematic areas are most commonly found on

The classic Sorel pack boots are great for comfy day hikes, but their overbuilt design and excessive dry times make them less suitable for extended trips. The removable felt liner and full rubber lower help address some of these limitations.
Shawn Forry

Military-issue "Mickey Mouse" boots are a carryover from WW II but provide exceptional warmth while requiring very little maintenance. A felt liner is sealed between two layers of fully waterproof rubber. These boots haven't been manufactured since the 1980s, so inspect them for dry rot before buying from a military surplus shop.
Shawn Forry

TIP

"Mickey Mouse" boots can take a while to warm in the morning. To get a head start, preheat them by pouring boiling water directly into the boot. Crazy as it sounds, once they are warmed, just pour the water out and you're good to go. Since the entire boot is made of rubber, there is nothing to absorb water. Slipping your foot into a preheated boot in the morning is a surefire way to start the day off on the right foot.

the crease in the forefoot. There is also an air valve in the heel of the boot to account for the changes in air pressure as troops flew and parachuted out of planes. Make sure this valve is tightly closed to prevent water from entering and saturating the felt lining. If this occurs, it is nearly impossible to fully dry out the boot. The Bata brand tends to be the higher quality model. An added bonus is that since they were utilized by the 10th Mountain Division, they integrate into military-style ski bindings.

For extremely cold conditions, the design of the mukluk is hard to beat for warmth, weight, comfort, and maintenance. Based on traditional Inuit footwear, mukluks were historically made from moose or caribou hide and lined with beaver fur. The modern approach incorporates breathable canvas, leather, and felted wool liners. Proven on many polar expeditions, the concept for their success is like the approach to clothing in extreme cold. Since snow will be extremely dry in conditions at or below 0°F, breathability and foot articulation take precedence over waterproofness. Impressively lightweight, their comfort is unmatched, feeling more akin to slippers than winter footwear. Steger mukluks are probably the most common design. The discontinued Empire Canvas Works model took a slightly more modern approach to their design by adding a quick-lace system and durable hard-rubber sole. Liners can be pulled out of all models for drying.

Another model worth mentioning is Cabela's Trans-Alaska. A hybrid in technology, the Trans-Alaska incorporates a waterproof outer, removable felt liner and a quick-lace system. They're probably the most common boots worn during the Iditarod

A modern mukluk is best suited for extended trip in subzero conditions. This lightweight modular system includes a wool felt bootie, double wool insoles, and a quick-lace system for gloved hands. The emphasis on breathability and foot articulation is the best way to maintain warmth and dryness in extreme conditions.
Shawn Forry

Cabela's rugged Trans-Alaska boots have been worn by more first-place Iditarod mushers than any other boot. With a waterproof membrane, they are suited for a wider range of conditions than a mukluk while still being warm in temps down to -50°F. The modular system addresses the reduced breathability caused by the membrane. Quick-lace systems are a must when wearing thick mittens. Note the use of three insoles, highlighting the importance of insulating your foot from the ground.
Shawn Forry

because of their exceptional warm. Their incredibly thick sole protects feet from conductive heat loss with two layers of removable footbeds. The size of the boot can limit access to snow-shoes and provide a high center of gravity, which can take a while to get used to.

OVERBOOTS

In keeping with the modular theme, one approach is to incorporate an overboot into your overall footwear system. Overboots can provide an additional layer of waterproofness and/or warmth. NEOS are by far the most common overboots and work over nearly any footwear of choice. A common approach is to wear comfortable trail runners inside the overboot, striking an overall balance in comfort, warmth, and maintenance. Since NEOS utilize 100 percent waterproof, non-breathable polyurethane-coated fabric, zero moisture will enter or exit the boot. Depending on what footwear you decide to wear inside the overboot, it may get wet or damp from sweat, since NEOS overboots don't breathe. A VBL sock can be used to decrease the maintenance in keeping the entire system dry. The lightest model, the Villager,

Overboots like NEOS can suit a variety of conditions and footwear. It is simple to convert them to a mukluk-style boot for colder temps, or simply slip in a running shoe for quick winter access. NEOS come in a range of models; this particular insulated model has sheet-metal screws in the sole for better grip on ice.
Shawn Forry

weighs in at around 1.5 pounds. Heavier models include insulated versions and those with removable sheet metal screws installed to facilitate better traction in icy conditions.

A hybrid mukluk that accounts for a broader range of temperatures and conditions can be modified to suit. By utilizing a VBL sock and slipping a simple felted wool liner inside the NEOS, you have effectively created an extremely lightweight mukluk that can slosh though icy slop all day, has slipper-like comfort, and is good down to temperatures of -20°F. The VBL will encourage the liner to maintain dryness, and a Superfeet-type footbed can be inserted to add structure to the boot.

Yet another overboot to consider is the 40 Below neoprene overboot. These boots come in a range of designs and models to suit anything from a trail runner to ski and mountaineering boots. They lack a proper sole, which renders them inappropriate as a stand-alone system without some sort of traction device underfoot. This makes them best suited for snowshoes or mountaineering boots that will incorporate a full crampon. The lightest model comes in at around 12 ounces, and a VBL sock should be utilized to manage any foot moisture. Since the neoprene will maintain good flexibility in the footwear, comfort is maintained when it is used over a trail runner. Keep in mind that the bottom of these overboots does not have a solid sole, so any metal grippers on the top of the snowshoes will eventually cut into the overboots.

MOUNTAINEERING BOOTS

A more robust version of insulated hiking boots, mountaineering boots are specifically targeted for the application of technical equipment and travel. When extended travel in icy, vertical terrain is to be encountered, this style of footwear allows for proper technique in footwork where traditional footwear would be limited. Unless your travel dictates the incorporation of semi-rigid technical crampons, the use of a stiff full-shank sole will be unnecessarily uncomfortable and unneeded. Foot fatigue will be pronounced, and the rigid sole will further limit movement and circulation. When these factors are deemed necessary, it is still possible to travel the mountains in a fast and light manner.

The world of technical mountaineering boots has made substantial advancements in the past decade. Boots in this category will range in warmth, function, and weight depending on the desired application and conditions. Most boots will favor the use of a synthetic upper to promote lower moisture saturation and reduced dry time. Leather uppers will provide moderate increases in durability if desired. Like nontechnical insulated footwear, this category can be broken down into subcategories, each with its advantages and considerations. Variables are largely narrowed down to removable (or not) liners and the incorporation of integrated gaiters.

Single Boots

Single boots are essentially hiking boots on steroids. They will have a full or three-quarter–length shank and incorporate some level of internal insulation, best suited to warmer conditions above 0°F. They are the lightest offering in this category and are best for done-in-a-day activities, since the liners are not removable.

Boots with a three-quarter-length shank have more forefoot flex and are slightly more comfortable. They are best for non-vertical travel when moving fast through nontechnical terrain is a priority. Full-length shanks and toe welts are best suited for the incorporation of rigid or semi-rigid crampons for ice and mixed climbing activities.

Double Boots

When colder conditions or extended travel is anticipated, stepping up to a removable-liner double boot is desired. With slightly thicker liners, these boots are best in temps at or below 0°F and have the user-friendly convenience of removable liners to facilitate quicker drying. They come at the expense of heavier weight and cost. Clunky plastic boots fall in this category, but due to advancements in technology, they have nearly become extinct. Modern double boots offer greater warmth, range of motion, and dexterity.

Super-Gaiter Boots

In each of the above examples, an external gaiter must be incorporated into the overall system to ensure that unwanted moisture does not enter the boot. Super-gaiter boots improve and streamline this demand by integrating an internal gaiter, reducing bulk and weight. While waterproofness, warmth, and durability will increase, the downside is that dry time will unsatisfactorily increase as well. In general, an improvement over single boots, their lack of multiday practicality and warmth still make double boots a better contender.

Mountaineering boots should only be considered if technical travel is required, including kicking steps and the use of crampons. Their stiff sole prevents proper foot circulation and a natural stride, leading to colder feet and foot fatigue. Mountaineering boots can range from beefed-up backpacking boots to fully insulated boots with integrated super-gaiters.
Shawn Forry

SNOWSHOEING

As the saying goes, if you can walk, you can snowshoe. A bit tongue-in-cheek perhaps, but with the accessibility that snowshoes afford, it is no wonder they are commonly peoples' first experience into winter travel. With appropriately warm footwear in tow, by simply tightening a few straps and widening your stride, you are off to explore untrammeled virgin powder. Snowshoes are likely one of the oldest methods of improving efficiency in snow travel.

Modeled after broad, oversize animal prints, the earliest snowshoes were nothing more than sculpted "beavertail" timbered frames overlaid with a latticework of rawhide. They follow the same principal of distributing your weight across the snow. Today's snowshoes have near the same design, incorporating upgraded materials and ergonomic features.

Snowshoes excel over any other form of winter travel when snow conditions and coverage are not uniform and depths do not dictate something with more float and surface area. The ease with which snowshoes can be taken on and off and conveniently stowed on one's pack make them well suited for both early- and late-season conditions that dictate being on and off snow consistently. If you anticipate being above and below snow levels or in and out of snow, snowshoes will be easier to manage and lighter than skis. You will not really feel the benefits of snowshoes until snow depth exceeds 6 to 8 inches, and they will quickly be overwhelmed once snow depth exceeds past the shins to the knees. The lack of floatation will make your efforts exponentially harder in deep conditions, as snow will tend to fill in over the top of the snowshoe with each stride, adding pounds of lift with each step.

The type of snowshoe that will be best suited for the selected terrain will be dictated by how "extreme" the terrain you want to cover is. Simply walking down a level packed trail necessitates the most basic of snowshoes. Once you start traversing steeper slopes that are hard packed and icy, a more robust (heavy) snowshoe will be required. Similarly, if you need to rely on snowshoes for hundreds of miles of travel, durability should be prioritized over the pinching of grams. Snowshoes dedicated for racing are on the market now, with refined frame shapes and utmost attention to weight. Design considerations to help you find the shoe that serves your needs will fall into size, frame, decking material, and binding.

Taking snowshoeing to the next level. If you can walk, you can snowshoe . . . and if you can snowshoe, why not extreme snowshoe?
Justin Lichter

SIZE

Obviously, the larger the snowshoe the more float it will be capable of. Adequate float will be quantified based on body weight and snow depth. There is a point of diminishing returns, as at a certain point the length will begin to adversely affect stride and maneuverability around obstacles. Some models come in different widths, with wider snowshoes again having more float and narrower models better suited toward a natural stride. Some models allow for the addition of clip-on "tails" to increase their length to suit the conditions you will encounter.

Use the size chart below to get a ballpark idea of the size shoe you will need. Keep in mind that these weights include body and pack weight.

[20 in]	80–150 lbs; or best suited for racing and hard-packed trails
[25 in]	120–200 lbs
[30 in]	170–250 lbs
[36 in]	220–300 lbs

TIP Women's branded snowshoes are generally slightly narrower and lighter than regular snowshoes. We've found these models to be preferable, lending themselves to a more natural stride and minimizing the "bowleg" effect.

ASCENT SNOWSHOES

Flat rail snowshoe frames are stronger and offer more "bite" into the snow on steep terrain. The MSR Lightning Ascent frames have serrated edges all the way around the perimeter and should be considered mandatory if heading into steep terrain with hard snowpack.
Shawn Forry

FRAME

The frame is the foundation of the snowshoe and will determine its overall strength and use. Rarely will you find modern snowshoes made of wood, that material having been almost exclusively replaced by metal, composite plastic, or ultralight carbon fiber. Aluminum is the best all-around frame material, adequately durable and lightweight. Composite plastic snowshoes are comparable in strength and weight to aluminum. While metal frames are prone to bending, plastic frames will more commonly crack under extreme use and can be slightly louder to walk in. Carbon fiber frames, while enticing in their low claimed weights, are fragile and suited only for light use or racing applications. Their heightened expense is an additional turnoff.

Frames can be tubular, rail, or hybrid "all-in-one" in formation. Tubular frames are likely the most common, keeping cost and weight down but better suited for softer, flatter conditions. The round design is prone to slipping on hard-packed surfaces unless metal crampon-like rails are added to the perimeter of the frame. Flat rail designs are superiorly strong and enable a natural serrated edge to be carved into the perimeter. These frames can take a beating and are well suited to steeper, icy terrain. Most composite hybrid frames have the frame and decking material integrated into one form. This design adds stiffness to the frame, but the lack of malleability makes the shoe prone to slipping or skating out on the slightest bulge or obtrusion in the snow.

DECKING

Working in collaboration with the frame, the deck is the flat surface that spans the frame, creating additional surface area for the snowshoe. This material should be waterproof and extremely durable to prevent punctures and rips in the decking platform. Most commonly plastic, composite materials with PVC-coated polyester, urethane-impregnated nylon, thermoplastic urethane, Hypalon, or similar synthetic materials are used. Decking material that wraps around tubular frames can be prone to fraying if used on rough and rocky surfaces, but then again, these types of frames should be avoided on this terrain.

BINDINGS

How the snowshoe attaches to the foot can range from slick and sleek to fickle and fussy. The job of the binding is to center the foot over the deck and provide a secure and stable connection between the snowshoe and the foot. The binding should be easy to secure and have the ability to quickly adjust the tension without being overly complicated with too many moving parts. Some bindings will rely on straps, while others will form a pocket of sorts that engulfs the foot to better distribute pressure. Ratchet-style bindings borrow similar looking snowboard-style binding to secure the foot. The BOA system is even starting to show up on bindings. Keep in mind that this style of binding system, while quick to adjust and remove, is notoriously prone to freezing up. Similarly, nylon fabric webbing straps should be avoided at all costs, since these are equally prone to freezing up.

If you are already confused or frustrated when you try on your snowshoes in the store, it's likely best to move on to another model—things will only get worse when you use them in the real world. Once your hands are gloved and materials become stiff with cold, a poor binding design will be the first thing to make you regret the purchase.

CRAMPONS

Consider an underfoot crampon a requirement no matter which model snowshoe you select. Like traction devices for hiking, unless there is a mechanism to gain purchase underfoot, you'll be slipping all over the place. Lightweight aluminum crampons should be avoided in favor of hardened steel if you expect to encounter any sort of steep or rocky terrain. For light use, the lighter weight aluminum crampons should be fine. For increased grip on descents, look for a row of additional teeth placed behind the crampon situated under the foot. These, along with rail crampons around the frame perimeter, go a long way in rounding out the all-around traction of the snowshoe.

Snowshoe Comparison Chart*

Make	Model	Construction	Size	Weight/pr	Price
Northern Lights	Timber Wolf	Tubular	9.5" × 32"	4 lbs 3 oz	$239
MSR	Lightning Ascent	Frame	8" × 30"	4 lbs 9oz	$289
Tubbs	Flex Alp	Frame	8" × 28"	5 lbs 0 oz	$269
Atlas	Serrate 30	Tubular	Teardrop	5 lbs 8 oz	$329
Crescent Moon	Gold 10	Tubular	10" × 32"	4 lbs 11 oz	$269
Fimbulvetr	Hikr	Hybrid	10" × 24"	4 lbs 11 oz	$270
Louis Garneau	Black Everest	Hybrid	8" × 27"	4 lbs 6 oz	$184

*Most suitable for steep and deep

HEEL RISERS

To minimize strain on the calf during steep ascents, some models include an adjustable heel riser. Usually this comprises nothing more than a bar that can be raised and lowered under the heel section of the decking material. Unless dexterity in your ankle is limited due to footwear choice, this feature is frivolous and just adds unneeded weight.

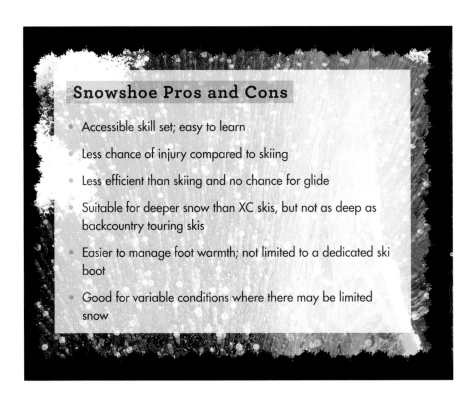

Snowshoe Pros and Cons

- Accessible skill set; easy to learn

- Less chance of injury compared to skiing

- Less efficient than skiing and no chance for glide

- Suitable for deeper snow than XC skis, but not as deep as backcountry touring skis

- Easier to manage foot warmth; not limited to a dedicated ski boot

- Good for variable conditions where there may be limited snow

SKIING

As conditions and skill sets allow, skiing opens up yet another realm of efficiencies and aesthetics in winter travel. The mechanical advantages of skiing are nearly unparalleled compared to the aforementioned modes of travel. Our vast distribution of weight across the snowpack is unified with minimal impedance to our stride. With gravity on our side, slipping around on snow can be as exhilarating as it is economical to our energy output.

It should be stated that with much freedom, comes much responsibility. The speeds generated during skiing greatly exacerbate the potential for injury, with contributing factors directly linked to variable snow conditions and general coordination. The thrill of the descent can blindside our objectivity when it comes to unfavorable avalanche conditions. In skiing, for every up there is a down, and the stark reality is there is usually a far-reaching expanse of flat between the two.

Skiing opens up all sorts of potential backcountry fun and exploration. Skiing also requires more astute know-how and competencies, as you can quickly get in over your head.
Justin Lichter

With regard to long-distance travel, priority should be central to efficiency in rolling terrain over up- and downhill performance. If maximizing control and stability in the steeps is a must, our gear requirements will follow suit. In both camps, it is easy to cater a ski setup to meet most needs with few compromises. With the bulk of the ski industry focused on day tripping in either steep or flat terrain, our greatest margin of compromise will be focused on ultralight multiday expeditions through ever-changing terrain and conditions.

As we dive into the myriad potential modes of travel within the ski realm, it will be important to define our priorities in relation to weight, performance, and cost. As with most things in life, pick two of the three. Where the confusion lies within the ski catalog is that there is a blurring and borrowing of technologies, nearly eliminating clean, clearly defined categories. This holds true as an advantage with regard to the selection of skis, boots, and bindings. It is quite possible to "Frankenstein" a ski setup, borrowing systems and technology from the cross-country, downhill, touring, and racing categories. By doing so, we can often better meet the needs of a given trip or style of travel.

Skis can be advantageous in many conditions, but if you think you will constantly be moving in and out of snowline or out of locations with decent snow coverage, they can be more of a hassle and a burden than worthwhile. The systems with bindings are typically heavier than snowshoes and need devoted boots, which you won't want to hike in, so you'll likely be adding an extra set of shoes or additional equipment to carry. Consider this when deciding what mode of travel to use on a particular trip or section.

CROSS-COUNTRY SKIS

Likely one of the original methods of distance travel on skis, cross-country (XC) skiing offers many nods to ultralight travel with respect to clean, simple equipment rooted in technique. The associated lower entry costs into the sport generally position in well as a gateway to other types of skiing. The versatility in application can range from leisurely strolls down groomed trails to off-trail exploration to outright speed and racing. Within the world of XC skiing, subcategories diverge among skate, classic (sometimes called Nordic or diagonal striding), and touring (BC).

Classic vs. Skate vs. Touring vs. XCD

Skate skiing largely falls outside the realm of appropriate winter travel and is an easy category to rule out without delving into too much detail. While one of our favorite methods of recreation, skate skiing relies exclusively on well-manicured, groomed trails and a narrow window of optimal conditions in the backcountry. With a technique closely akin to ice-skating, skate skiing is a highly aerobic activity where huge distances can be covered in a short time frame. Gear and equipment aside, the technique of "skating" can be applied to Nordic, touring, and downhills skis, albeit awkwardly, a fun and restful way to switch up technique throughout the day when conditions allow.

Similarly, Nordic or classic skis rely on groomed trails with a defined "track" to optimize technique and performance. One of the easier techniques to pick up, traditional Nordic skiing is closely akin to sliding your feet while walking and can range from scooting and shuffling your feet to mastering the art of the "kick and glide." This grossly simplified analogy highlights the accessibility in the predominant style and the skill set required for distance touring, making it a good one to master to optimize ergonomics. Classic skis are similarly skinny in width as skate skis, up to 70 millimeter to fit within the groomed track, and a straight profile to facilitate glide and straight touring. Their application is similarly limited due to the need for groomed trails. Unless your area of use affords miles of groomed trails to explore, traditional classic skis will likely not fit the bill either. Both skate and classic skis prioritize longer, narrower skis to maximize glide. For comparison, skis in this category typically range from 44 to 55 millimeters in width.

Touring or backcountry (BC) skis are specifically designed for off-track, non-groomed exploration on steeper terrain. These skis upgrade to metal edges to facilitate grip on icy terrain and help to initiate downhill turns. They are typically shorter for better maneuverability and wider for stability. While heavier than skate or classic skis, these design considerations afford more versatility and suitability across a range of conditions. Ski widths usually range from 65 to 70 millimeters.

A note about camber should be made here as it relates to this concept of "kick and glide." Camber relates to the "bow" a ski has underfoot, which dictates when and where the points of contract the ski with have with the snow. Traditional double-camber cross-country skis have a pronounced arch underfoot when the ski is unweighted. This arch emphasizes the lone points of contact at the tip and tail of the ski to minimize friction, maximizing glide. Forward movement is achieved by weighting the center arched section of the ski to activate the "kick" zone. This kick zone achieves grip with the snow through wax or special notches called fishscales on the base of the ski within the range of the kick zone. Through the mechanics of our stride, we alternate between weighting and unweighting the ski to engage either the kick zone for grip or the glide for forward movement—an intentional and complicated design that achieves effortless grace when mastered. The downside to traditional double-camber skis is that they lack the control to initiate turns due to minimal contact with the snow through sidecut underfoot, "sidecut" referring to the hourglass shape of a ski versus a parallel shapeless ski.

In an effort to have your cake and eat it, Karhu launched the venerable Karhu Guide ski nearly forty years ago that merged the versatility and lightweight design of a touring ski with the performance of a downhill ski. This XCD (or cross-country downhill) category is still one of the most evolving categories of backcountry skiing today. By widening the ski to a voluptuous 78 millimeters underfoot, eliminating the traditional double-camber design in favor of a single downhill-oriented camber, and maintaining a metal-edge profile, the Karhu Guide offers a killer balance in all-around, do-anything performance. The potential in this category as it relates today will be discussed in more detail, as the design principles are the hallmark of efficient ultralight ski touring.

Wax vs. Waxless

As previously stated, the manner in which a cross-country ski achieves grip for forward propulsion is dictated either by technique (skate skiing) or by mechanical means (Nordic). With regard to mechanical grip, this classification is categorized as either waxable or waxless (patterned) skis. Counterintuitive to general skiing principles, regardless of which style you choose, you want grip! There is nothing more frustrating than slipping out like Bambi on ice when initiating your kick!

While in the kick phase of the "kick and glide," there will be a finite area under the ski designated as the kick zone. On waxable skis, this area will have a thin layer of kick wax applied to achieve grip. Kick wax, sometimes called grip wax, comes in a variety of temperature ranges to cater to varying degrees of snow consistency. The colder the snow, the drier the snow, and thus a harder wax will be required. Conversely, the warmer the snow, the wetter the snow, and a stickier and thus softer wax will need to be applied. A perfectly waxed pair of skis will outperform a waxless pair nine times out of ten. The challenge is that the optimum range of peak performance can be very narrow, sometimes within 5 to 10 degrees before the wax begins to be too hard or soft for the conditions. For expeditioning this means carrying a wax kit consisting of a scraper, four to five waxes in varying degrees, and a small cork to buff in the wax. And with the changing conditions throughout the day, you'll likely have to stop to re-wax multiple times. Not the most ultralight approach.

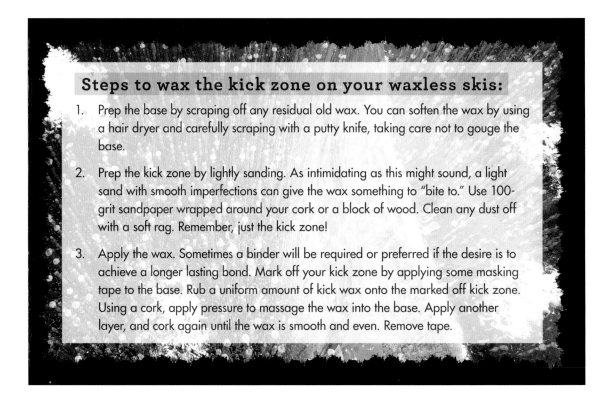

Steps to wax the kick zone on your waxless skis:

1. Prep the base by scraping off any residual old wax. You can soften the wax by using a hair dryer and carefully scraping with a putty knife, taking care not to gouge the base.

2. Prep the kick zone by lightly sanding. As intimidating as this might sound, a light sand with smooth imperfections can give the wax something to "bite to." Use 100-grit sandpaper wrapped around your cork or a block of wood. Clean any dust off with a soft rag. Remember, just the kick zone!

3. Apply the wax. Sometimes a binder will be required or preferred if the desire is to achieve a longer lasting bond. Mark off your kick zone by applying some masking tape to the base. Rub a uniform amount of kick wax onto the marked off kick zone. Using a cork, apply pressure to massage the wax into the base. Apply another layer, and cork again until the wax is smooth and even. Remove tape.

In terms of convenience and practicality, a comparative analogy would be a vinyl record versus an mp3. The vinyl is always going to sound superior, but in order to achieve this level of performance, the turntable must be calibrated and balanced, the pitch adjusted, and the record meticulously cleaned and brushed. This is all fine and good, but sometimes you just want to hit play on the iPod and enjoy some music. Enter the world of waxless skis.

TIP

1. If you need to re-wax or adjust wax temps while on the go, remember the analogy of PB&J. You can apply jelly on top of peanut butter, but not vice versa without making a mess. Similarly you can apply warmer (softer) waxes on top of harder (colder) waxes without fully scraping.
2. Multiple thin layers of wax are better than one thick blob.
3. Fresh snow right at the freezing point is near impossible to wax for.
4. Klister. Some love it, some hate it. By far the stickiest wax out there, it can be quite the mess, but it's the only thing that will grip when kick wax won't. Ideal for very warm or icy conditions, it's best applied when warmed. Just be prepared for it to get on everything it touches!

Waxless, sometimes called patterned or fishscale bases, have omnidirectional patterns etched into the base of the ski, in line with the traditional kick zone. While running your fingers along the base, this pattern is very smooth in one direction and grippy in the other, achieving the same effects of kick wax. The idea is maximum grip on the kick that does not interfere with glide as we stride forward. The term "waxless" is a slight misnomer, since all skis will benefit from glide wax. Waxless skis just eliminate the need for dedicated kick wax. A waxless ski still needs to be waxed periodically in the glide zones.

Waxless skis afford nearly zero maintenance and work under a large range of conditions. While never the fastest ski, their flexibility is perfectly suited to people who don't want to deal with waxing and to outings that will see variable conditions.

Like the Karhu Guide ski mentioned above, the application of patterned bases on traditional downhill skis is the signature combination of technology to achieve a well-versed touring ski. By minimizing the time committed to transitioning from the "up" to the "down," patterned bases optimize grip and efficiency through rolling terrain. In ideal conditions,

Wax & Waxless Ski Pros and Cons

- The lightest and fastest ski set up
- Narrow range of use. Only suited for groomed and/or consolidated snow conditions
- More affordable than touring skis but a steeper learning curve than snowshoes

patterned bases can maintain grip on slopes up to 35 to 40 degrees. While not as grippy as skins, the lack of friction works in favor to optimize the glide potential. Overall you'll maintain a quicker pace through rolling terrain compared to a similar ski with skins underfoot. Minimizing the overall weight of the boot, ski, and skin goes a long way toward minimizing energy use and fatigue, as we'll cover more at length.

BACKCOUNTRY SKIS

Backcountry skis are a subset within the overarching and hugely complicated world of downhill skis. Commonly called Alpine Touring, or simply "AT," these skis best cater to our needs of ultralight, ultra-distance snow travel. Before diving in, we'll lay a foundation of what makes these skis unique and stand out.

Skis have come a long way since the hand-carved hickory planks of yesteryear, yet most advances in ski design have come in the past two decades. With such a menu of design parameters and applications, a ski's signature characteristics can be refined through construction materials, dimensions, and shape. Within each of these categories, you'll find variables in speed, stability, floatation, and durability. As with most things, a compromise and balance will need to be achieved.

Ten or fifteen years ago, companies made skis that were telemark specific. Today you can telemark on any alpine ski if you mount telemark bindings on them. Any ski will work, but the mount point may be slightly different. As they learn to telemark, some people like either soft or stiff skis. Others like a standard mount and others prefer it over core center; there are other variations. Your preference can slightly depend on how you'll primarily be using the skis. If you'll mainly be touring and not shredding powder, you may want a different mount point and a different stiffness.

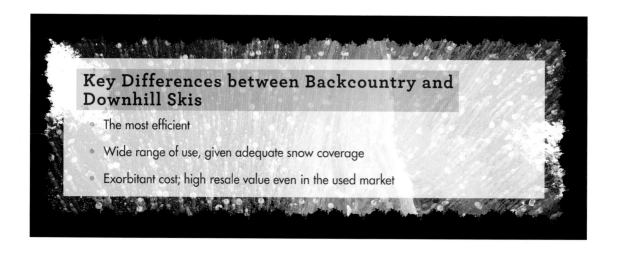

Key Differences between Backcountry and Downhill Skis

- The most efficient

- Wide range of use, given adequate snow coverage

- Exorbitant cost; high resale value even in the used market

SKI DIMENSIONS

Length

In general, the longer the ski the more stable it will be at high speeds. Shorter skis are nimbler under foot and easier to initiate turns. Taller, heavier, and more experienced skiers tend to favor a longer ski for the added control through leverage the ski offers. Shorter skis are favorable in forested glade skiing, where quick tight turns will be required.

Things get complicated when we start talking about effective edge. The ski profile is largely dictated by the overall length in conjunction with where the tip and tail contact the snow. Skis that feature "early rise" camber result in an effective shorter length ski, since the point of contact with the tip and snow has been moved back, or closer to the skier. Early rise lowers the ski's stability at high speeds but offers more float in deeper snow, since the tip will resist diving under the snow surface.

For a quick dirty on figuring out the best ski length for you, take your height and convert it to centimeters. This length will be the midrange of suitable ski length plus or minus 15 centimeters. For instance, a 5'9" skier is 175 centimeters tall. The ski range would translate to 160 to 190 centimeters. Beginner skiers should err on the shorter end of the spectrum; more advanced skiers, the longer end.

Ski Size Chart

Ski Size	140 cm	145 cm	150 cm	155 cm	160 cm	165 cm	175 cm	185 cm	195 cm
Height	Under 58 in (under 147 cm)	58–60 in (147–152 cm)	60–62in (152–157 cm)	62–64 in (157–162 cm)	64–66 in (162–167 cm)	66–68 in (167–172 cm)	68–70 in (172–177 cm)	70–74 in (177–188 cm)	Over 74 in (over 188 cm)
Weight	Under 100 lbs (under 45 kg)	100–110 lbs (45–49 kg)	105–115 lbs (47–52 kg)	115–125 lbs (52–56 kg)	125–135 lbs (56–61 kg)	130–140 lbs (59–63 kg)	140–160 lbs (63–72 kg)	160–180 lbs (72–81 kg)	170–200 lbs (77–90 kg)

Width

Simply put, the wider the ski, the more float it will have. The more we can spread out our weight across the snow, the higher we will ride along the snow's surface. Wider skis are also more capable of smoothing out variable ski conditions, allowing for a more stable and predictable experience. The downside of wider skis, besides the obvious weight gain, is the additional leverage they require to initiate a turn. Since the center of our foot is farther from the ski's edge, more force is required to filter into that edge.

Ski width is universally communicated by the width underfoot. A string of common measurements, such as 123 / 95 / 108, express the width (in millimeters) measured at the tip, waist, and tail, respectively. While 78 millimeters underfoot used to be the universal width for a backcountry ski, the past decade has seen the birth of the fat ski phenomenon, with planks more akin to mini snowboards underfoot. Thankfully this "more is better" mentality is waning, and more reasonable-width "powder skis" have normalized the category.

Recommended Ski Waist Width by Condition

Condition	Ice, Hardpack, Racing	Groomed Packed Powder	Ungroomed Packed Powder	Variable	Deep Powder
Waist Width	60–75 mm	75–90 mm	85–105 mm	100–115 mm	110+ mm

SKI SHAPE

It makes sense that more experimentation has been applied to a ski's overall shape, since it is the direct connection to how a ski will react in relation to the snow. While length and width are very easy to conceptualize for comparison, the subtle cues in shape and additional layer of technical terms can seem dizzying at times.

While challenging to equate in written form, a ski's shape is best defined on the slope. Here is where demoing as many skis as possible through a range of conditions will help define which style of ski is best suited to your abilities and local snow conditions. While terms like "all-mountain," "freeride," and "backcountry" may be tossed around to categorize and quantify characteristics, understanding the underlying rationale is a better approach for comparison's sake.

Sidecut

Best equated to an hourglass shape when viewing the ski from above, sidecut is predominately responsible for

With a wide array of ski shapes, construction methods, and binding choices, the selection process can feel overwhelming. Having the right tool for the trade not only increases your efficiency but maximizes your enjoyment.
Shawn Forry

Note: Ski tips are to the right; tails are to the left.

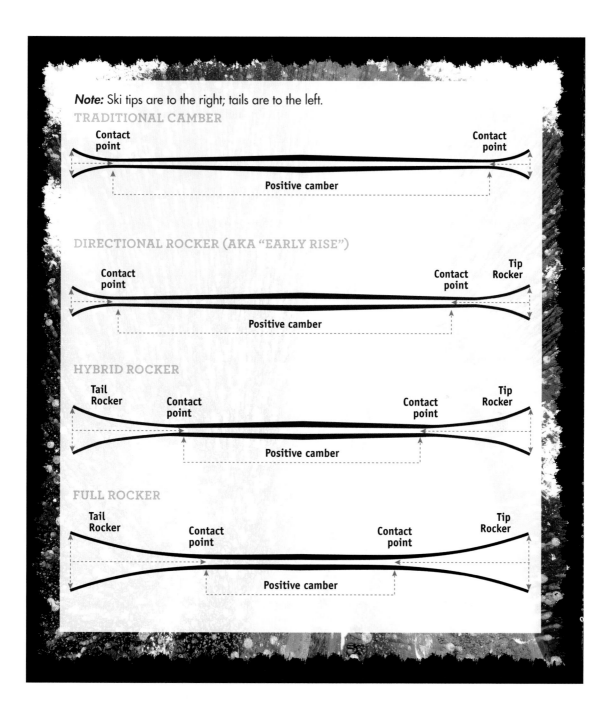

TRADITIONAL CAMBER

Contact point

Contact point

Positive camber

DIRECTIONAL ROCKER (AKA "EARLY RISE")

Contact point

Contact point

Tip Rocker

Positive camber

HYBRID ROCKER

Tail Rocker

Contact point

Contact point

Tip Rocker

Positive camber

FULL ROCKER

Tail Rocker

Contact point

Contact point

Tip Rocker

Positive camber

initiating turns. The more dramatic the hourglass shape, the more responsive the ski will be. While all skis will require some level of sidecut, a quick way to measure for comparison is to tip the ski on edge and measure the gap (in millimeters) at the waist of the ski.

Taking sidecut a step further, if we imagine the arch of the ski's edge extending to create a full circle, we come up with another measurement of turn radius. Typically measured in meters, turn radius is more commonly used when comparing one ski to another. The most responsive, "turn on a dime" skis will have a turn radius as low as 12 meters, while super-stable GS skis traditionally have a turn radius around 33 meters.

Camber and Rocker

A ski's shape when viewed from the side profile will be defined by camber, which describes the bow or arch in the ski's base. Camber is the downward arch under the waist of the ski and dictates where the point of contacts in the tip and tail will be between the ski and snow. The wider apart these distances, the more edgy and grabby the ski will feel; the closer these dimensions, the smoother and more float-like the ski will behave. Too little camber and the ski will feel slow and unresponsive.

Rocker is the upward curve to the tip and tail. The more pronounced, or "banana-like," this curve, the more float will be felt underfoot, at the expense of difficulty in initiating turns in hardpack conditions. As with most things, there is a compromise; but as a whole, rocker technology has become a mainstay in ski profiles since 2012.

The most desired ski profile for backcountry use is directional, or "early rise," rocker. The pronouncedly elevated tip will smooth out variable conditions without adversely limiting the ski's overall edginess, and afford a little more forgiveness against hooking a tip while trying to negotiate obstacles. The traditional "flat-like" rocker at the tail will better serve the application of skins, since grip is predominantly generated by the surface area and pressure underfoot through the tail.

SKI MATERIALS

With so many variables setting apart the characteristics of one set of skis from another, the hidden ingredient is what lies beneath the fancy graphics. What makes one pair of skis snappy and responsive while another pair of planks feel like wet noodles when pushed on edge? How can one pair of skis weigh less than half of another while having the same dimensions and outward appearance? Does core construction really make that much of a difference?

In broad strokes, we'll dive into the considerations and compromises required when trying to pare down every gram from our skis. Any chosen ski must work together with the selected boots and bindings while addressing ski ability and objectives. As technology continues to advance, the gap between all-around performance and compromise is beginning to narrow.

Core Construction

By far, core material and construction methods are the most defining elements of a ski's overall characteristics and specifications. With considerations geared toward minimizing weight, our emphasis will be to prioritize a ski that can handle a variety of conditions.

Operating at this level usually dictates a decrease in durability and performance, yet with care and attention, the chosen skis can serve our purposes effortlessly.

The purpose of the core is to be rigid enough to hold an edge, responsive enough to dampen vibrations, and flexible enough to store and release energy. Wood cores continue to be the gold standard in performance, but not all wood is created equally. When weight reduction is a priority, seek out poplar/paulownia blends or 100 percent paulownia. Poplar is stronger; paulownia is lighter. Wood cores always come at the expense of high retail shock, but they provide a much more stable platform than other core materials and will give you many years of use, minimizing degradation and loss of camber and stiffness.

To address the limitations of ultralight wood cores, composite materials will almost always be incorporated to increase stiffness and response. Carbon is the lightest composite material, but it is so stiff and resists flexing that only moderate amounts need to be incorporated into the overall composition of the core. Terms like carbon "stingers" refer to this precise application. Fiberglass is by far the most common composite material, encompassing nearly 90 percent of the ski market. While not nearly as light as carbon applications, it is a trusted material. Less expensive than carbon but lighter than fiberglass, Kevlar excels at dampening vibration and absorbing impact.

> **TIP**
>
> Scrapes, gouges, and punctures are all part of the reality that our precious skis will endure at one point or another in their lifetime. While most impact damage can be repaired, don't delay in getting a reputable ski shop to diagnose the problem. For damage that has extended into the core of the ski, the more water that gets sponged up and freezes inside the core, the more long-term damage your ski will experience. Get it looked at ASAP!

Base Material

The base material plays a critical role, as it is the material that is in direct contact with the snow surface. The good news is that nearly every manufacture uses the same material: ultra-high-molecular-weight polyethylene (UHMW-PE, for short). That's a fancy way of saying a material that can take a ton of abuse, can be reconditioned as needed, and slides well on snow. Sintered bases are superior to extruded due to their ability to hold and retain wax for a much longer time frame. Thickness can vary from 1 to 1.5 millimeters, and dedicated manufactures will shave grams by making the base material as thin as possible. This will come at the expense of much less durability and the risk of core shots. Being attuned to this limitation and skiing with intention can go a long way toward preventing damage to the core.

Top Sheet and Sidewalls

The top sheet plays a more critical role than just displaying the sickest new graphics. To protect the ski's fragile inner components, a protective outer shell encapsulates the core. Most top sheets are made exclusively of plastic with a variety of properties. Their job is to resist chipping and abuse from impact.

Having the lightest ski setup is a moot point when you have half a pound of snow sticking to the top sheet. Proactively wax the top, or try spray-on products like Pam or Pledge. A quick scrape at each break gives a fresh start.
Justin Lichter

TIP

Some top sheet materials tend to allow snow to stick to them, especially if they have little bumps or a matte finish. In warm, moist snow conditions, that added weight with each step can sap valuable energy over the course of a day. Take the time to wax the top sheet of your skis to prevent heavy snow buildup. Some folks have success with Pam cooking spray or Pledge furniture polish; common glide wax also works well. For good measure, scrape off any accumulated snow at each break.

Sidewall construction can be cap, hybrid, or true sidewall. Cap construction is just that, one entire piece of ABS sandwiching the core with the base material. This process is cheaper to manufacture and less durable, but is overall lighter.

Sidewall construction used to be only reserved for high-end skis. The three-piece construction incorporates the top and two sidewall pieces. The dense piece of ABS running the length of the ski is torsionally stiffer and creates more "pop" and acceleration out of the turn. Edging ability will be noticeably higher as well. The higher weight makes this construction slightly less favorable for ultra-light backcountry skis unless durability and absolute stiffness are a priority.

Hybrid construction can give you the best of both worlds. These skis incorporate sidewall construction where it matters—along the edge—and taper to cap construction in the tip and tail to save weight.

Ultralight Backcountry Ski Comparison Chart*

Make	Model	Dimensions	Weight	Construction
La Sportiva	Vapor Nano	130 / 103 / 120	1,342 g	Carbon, Kevlar
Movement	Response	128 / 89 / 116	1,195 g	Paulownia, Poplar
Ski Trab	Magico	116 / 84 / 104	1,010 g	Carbon, Aramid
Voile	Objective	115 / 82 / 99	1,005 g	Carbon, Paulownia
Dynafit	Dhaulagiri	130 / 99 / 114	1,400 g	Poplar, Paulownia
DPS	Wailer 99 Tour1	125 / 99 / 111	1,410 g	Carbon, Balsa
Goode	95	125 / 95 / 113	1,225 g	Carbon

*Based on surface area to weight

Ultralight Skimo Ski Comparison Chart

Make	Model	Dimensions	Weight	Price
Fischer	Alp Attack	99 / 65 / 81	650 g	$699
Movement	Rise Pro X	96 / 66 / 80	670 g	$899
La Sportiva	RSR	97 / 65 / 77	680 g	$899
Dynafit	DNA	99 / 65 / 80	690 g	$999
Voile	Wasatch Speed Project	84 / 63 / 72	790 g	$699
Ski Trab	Gara Aero World Cup Flex 60	91 / 64 / 80	1,005 g	$999

HYBRID SKIS

When snowshoes are too slow and full-on touring skis are too complicated and expensive, companies like Marquette Backcountry and Altai have formulated a functional blend of both worlds. The Marquette namesake backcountry ski is a shortened patterned-based touring ski with maneuverability more akin a snowshoe. At only 140 centimeters in length, the Marquette Backcountry ski offers unprecedented access to moderately deep snow conditions. Best suited for modest rolling terrain, the Marquette skis will maneuver effortlessly through dense trees but have limited control and grip on inclines and descents.

So-called "skishoeing," hybrid skis like the Altai Hok are great if covering ground is a priority over getting face shots on steep descents. Their embedded skins in the base material eliminate time-consuming transitions, and they can charge up moderate grades.
Nils Larsen/Altai Skis

The Altai Hok ski has a similar take, but instead of a patterned base, an integrated climbing skin is embedded into the base of the ski. With a size range of 125, 145, and 99 centimeters (the kid's version), the Hok functions similarly to the Marquette, with potentially more grip at the expense of less glide. With construction methods similar to traditional skis, the Hoks weigh nearly half the Marquette skis and costing about 20 percent more.

Easily adaptable to a range of binding options, both the Marquette and Altai skis offer entry-level fun for folks making the jump from snowshoeing to skis, but their construction has them tipping the scale at more than 2 kilograms each for the Marquette and 1 kilogram for the Hoks. While not quite advantageous enough to warrant ultralight enthusiasm, they do have benefits. It will be interesting to watch this concept evolve as market interest increases.

BOOTS AND BINDINGS

It's hard not to mention boots and bindings in the same breath. While independent in manufacture and function, even interchangeable in design, they work in collaboration to drive the ski forward. It is easy to correlate the Big 3 of skiing (boots, bindings, skis) to the Big 3 of hiking (shelter, sleeping bag, pack), yet even more so, since the combination of boots, bindings, and skis work together to sculpt the overall skiing experience. Beyond efforts to streamline base weights and shave extraneous ounces, the chosen ski system will dictate comfort, safety, efficiency, and performance.

Backcountry touring has a distinct challenge in that it must perform equally on the uphill as on the downhill. In principal, this necessitates a boot and binding system that caters to normal stride mechanics while enabling rock-steady stability akin to a traditional downhill ski setup. Additionally, this setup needs to be as light as possible. So we are asking a traditional downhill setup not only to operate more complex tasks but also to shed weight in the process. While in concept it is feasible to adapt any downhill ski boot for touring capabilities, a dedicated touring binding must be in place. This statement will segue into the great telemark versus alpine touring debate.

ALPINE TOURING VS. TELEMARK

As we discuss the different modes of backcountry touring, two distinct schools of thought will emerge: AT versus telemark. With a preference toward objectivity, a slant toward one mode will emerge based on the current market offerings, but personal preferences will always prevail.

Telemark skiing can claim to be the pioneer in backcountry skiing. Essentially a carry-over from cross-country skiing, with a "free heel" model, telemark boots and bindings rely heavily on "drop knee" technique to perform. With flex bellows in the boots and a hinged binding, telemark setups afford a very comfortable and natural stride that minimizes the need for transitioning between uphill and downhill skiing. It is fair to say that the feel and fluidity of cutting telemark turns is the largest appeal for traditionalists. Known downsides are limited comfort on steep exposed terrain, limited confidence in jump turns, a cap to advancements in technology, and the inefficiency of lunging hundreds of times, leading to thigh-burning fatigue. It should also be noted that most telemark bindings don't release, a huge consideration during falls and especially if caught in an avalanche.

Alpine touring setups have come a long way since first being introduced two decades ago. In comparison to telemark, the "Randonee Racing" subcategory truly highlights how far advancements in AT technology have come. It is not uncommon to find boots that weigh less than traditional hiking boots and bindings that weigh as much as a couple Cliff bars. Alpine touring relies on a releasable binding that can lock in for traditional downhill parallel turn technique and release into a walk mode. Similarly, the boots have a release mechanism that locks the boot for stiff downhill stability and pivots for more natural and unobstructed walk capabilities. All things being equal, AT gear is much lighter and energy efficient than telemark while also having the ability to release in the event of a fall. Some will argue that the process to transition from ski to walk mode is a bit clunkier than for telemark, since the ski must be removed from the boot to switch the binding back to walk mode.

For the sake of argument, AT is lighter and more efficient than telemark, especially over the course of multiday expeditions. With the facts stated, your choice of mode will be based solely on personal preference and familiarity, if not a little stubbornness. Regardless of which mode you choose, you'll have an amazing time exploring the backcountry. Ultimately it will be better to prioritize your budget and ability over facts and numbers.

BINDINGS

Through the lens of ultralight ski touring, there is one standout winner for binding choice. So-called "tech bindings" were first introduced by Dynafit and have been the gold standard for ultralight touring. Once their patent expired in the mid-2000s, an explosion of copycat tech bindings hit the market, testament to how effective and revered these bindings are in the backcountry touring market.

Before going into the specifics of tech bindings, it is worth noting what else is currently on the market. Frame-style bindings like the classic Fritschi Diamir Freeride are best suited to hard-charging skiers who want zero compromise on downhill performance. They are a good one-quiver crossover option for folks who spend the same amount of time at the resort as they do in the backcountry. Frame bindings excel at strength, elastic boot retention, and predictable release values. Offerings from Marker, Fritschi, and Tyrolia are largely similar. Unless you plan on hucking steep cliff bands and aggressively skiing extreme couloirs, frame bindings are going to be excessively heavy, weighing more than five to six times as much as a tech binding. That's like shaving nearly 2 pounds per foot!

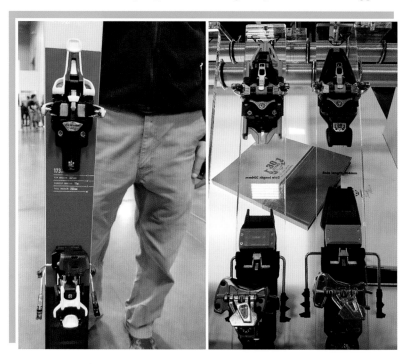

Hybrid bindings like the Fritschi Vipec (left) and Dynafit Radical ST (right) strike a good balance in weight, releasability, and high release values for skiing the steepest terrain. Depending on your objective, they may be overkill.
Shawn Forry

Heavy frame bindings are becoming even more obsolete with the advent of hybrid bindings like the Dynafit Beast, Fritschi Diamir Vipec, and Marker Kingpin. These bindings address the limitations of tech bindings while still shaving ounces off traditional framed bindings. Tech bindings, while technically "releasable," can be prone to not release under extreme conditions or, conversely, pre-releasing when you least want them to— namely under "no fall zone" steep descents. This problem can be grossly exacerbated, since many skiers "lock out" their tech bindings so that a pre-release cannot happen, further preventing them from releasing when desired. These hybrid bindings offer DIN-certified release values while still tipping the scales at nearly half the weight of antiquated heavy framed bindings. For skiers who need the utmost confidence of a DIN-certified binding and are willing to sacrifice in the overall weight category, these are the bindings of choice.

True tech bindings have been around since the 1980s and were originally designed for moderate terrain in a lightweight package as a priority. Since then they have been pushed

Hybrid/Light Frame Bindings

Make	Model	Weight	DIN
Dynafit	Beast 14	830 g	5–14
Dynafit	Beast 16	950 g	6–16
Dynafit	TLT Radical ST 2.0	599 g	4–10
Marker	Kingpin 10	730 g	5–10
Marker	Kingpin 13	730 g	6–13
Fritschi	Diamir Vipec 12	545 g	3–12
G3	Ion 12	585 g	5–12

into steeper terrain and stiffer demands, resulting in refinements in design. Tech bindings rely on a pin system for the heel and toe connection and only work with tech-compatible boots, easily identified by metal dimpled "tech" inserts in the toe and a slotted groove in the heel. They are elegantly minimalist in design and place a premium on weight reduction and stride efficiency. Most have a preset, nonadjustable release value (RV) for the toe piece; only some models offer an adjustable RV in the heel. They offer an appropriate balance of ski performance and dependability, and are what you will find on 90 percent of backcountry skiers.

For first-time users, tech bindings can seem a bit finicky to get into and out of, but they become effortless with practice. Most designs require the boot to fully release from the binding when transitioning from ski to walk mode. Again, with practice this will become second nature.

Despite the plethora of designs and manufacturers to choose from, all bindings function essentially the same. Minor differences to highlight include heel riser options, BSL (boot sole length) adjustability, RV adjustable heel pieces, crampon and brake compatibility, and material choice. The lightest options use lighter aluminum over hardened steel at the expense of durability. That being said, tech bindings have been known to last decades, and most are field serviceable.

Bindings that have adjustable BSL are handy to accommodate multiple boot styles, allowing you to tailor your ski objectives

Tech bindings can feel a bit finicky to get into and out of, but with practice they become effortless.
Shawn Forry

Same mondo size and about 1 inch difference in length! Scarpa Alien skimo boot (left) and Dynafit Vulcan Touring boot (right). Both of these boots won't fit into the same ski/binding combo unless the binding has some adjustability.
Shawn Forry

without needing a dedicated ski/binding combo for each outing. You could use your lightest race boots when efficiency is essential (which will likely have a shorter BSL) and switch to a burlier, stiffer boot when downhill performance is a priority simply by making an adjustment to the binding. Nonadjustable bindings can be altered with the use of base plates, at the expense of adding weight.

The option to go brakeless on your bindings is a matter of personal preference and comfort. With intentional awareness and practice, it is quite conceivable to go without brakes entirely. Some bindings allow for removable brakes, which typically tip the scales at around 100 grams. This added weight can provide peace of mind when losing a ski down a face could have dire consequences. A common middle ground is to incorporate leashes in the event of a pre-release or to provide peace of mind while transitioning in steep icy and/or windy conditions. While light in design, they can be finicky to take on and off and can become a head-bashing tomahawk in the event of a ragdoll-type fall. The best on the market seem to be the B&D ski leashes. At 85 grams for a pair, their coiled design provides enough length for easy transition while staying out of the way when skiing. They are designed to break away at around 40 to 60 pounds of force, which will further minimize the dreaded tomahawk effect.

Tech Bindings

Make	Model	Weight	RV	BSL	Crampon/Brake Compatible
Dynafit	TLT Speed Radical	370 g	4–10	22 mm	Yes/Leash Only
Dynafit	TLT Superlite 2.0	175 g	5–10	Fixed	Yes/Yes
Plum	Guide	341 g	5.5–12	30 mm	Yes/Yes
Plum	WEPA	270 g	5–10	18 mm	Yes/No
Kreuzspitze	GT	161 g	5–10	Fixed	Yes/Yes
ATK	Raider 12	335 g	5–12	25 mm	Yes/Yes
ATK	Haute Route	175 g	5–10	Fixed	Yes/No

Randonee race bindings are stripped of all nonessentials and embody pure dedication to touring. They're void of brakes, risers, adjustability, and, most important, weight.
Shawn Forry

When every gram must be shaved to maximize efficiency and minimize weight, nothing compares to the sheer minimalist design of dedicated race bindings. Race, or randonee, bindings prioritize the lightest materials at the expense of creature comforts like heel risers, adjustable RVs, ski brakes, and crampon compatibility. The lack of an adjustable RV is important to note, since the effectiveness of these binding largely falls on the competence and control of the skier using them. While they will release under extreme load, it is hard to guarantee which will fail quicker—your tibia or the binding. If that isn't shocking enough for you, a glance at the exorbitant price tag of any model will surely have you second-guessing your purchase.

Randonee Bindings

Make	Model	Weight	Crampon/Brake Compatible	Cost
Dynafit	Low Tech Race 2.0	110 g	Yes/No	$799
Dynafit	DNA / RC 1	75 g	No/No	$899
Plum	Race 99	99 g	No/No	$599
Plum	Race 150	150 g	Yes/No	$479
Hagan	ZR	116 g	Yes/No	$649
Kreuzspitze	SCTT	140 g	Yes/Yes	$499
Fischer	Tour Race 2.0	127 g	Yes/No	$699
Ski Trab	Gara Titan	105 g	Yes/No	$529

The evolution of these bindings is largely because of the emerging ski mountaineering, or "skimo," race category. These bindings are deceivingly strong when the ski mentality is to go up and down as quickly as possible with disregard to style and "huck" factor. Most will prioritize softer aluminum construction and a lack of auto-locking toe pieces. As with most things swung far on the ultralight spectrum, familiarity with the limitations of the equipment is of utmost importance to optimize their effectiveness and safety. If covering distance is your primary objective, these bindings should not be overlooked.

Telemark Bindings

Telemark bindings come in a variety of styles and designs. The beauty of telemark skiing in the backcountry is that you already have a free heel. This saves a lot of time and hassle on rolling terrain and on transitions. You never have to adjust your binding system from ski or downhill mode to walk mode. On the other hand, the advancement of telemark equipment for backcountry use has really lagged over the past five to ten years. Manufacturers have focused on heavier step-in telemark binding technology for resort skiing, while the AT boots and binding systems have been getting lighter and lighter. It is unfortunate that the industry has taken this direction, since there's a huge advantage to a free heel and inherent pivot point in the boot. Current equipment is efficient and usable, but it will undoubtedly be heavier than lightweight AT equipment. There are a few binding options, depending on what the goals of the trip are and what terrain will be like.

3-Pin Bindings (with or without heel bail)

The 3-pin binding is the age-old staple. Hardly changed in years, it's a simple metal plate with three pins that protrude and lock into the bottom of the boot. It's so simple it could be

a lot lighter, but unfortunately there are no titanium models currently available. That said, the binding has remained unchanged for so long because it works and works well, with minimal pieces to break, and is so straightforward that not much can go wrong. A mismount can allow them to rip out of the ski, but this is highly unlikely, since you'll likely be putting even less torque on these bindings. The heel bail could break, but it's not even a must-have piece, since you can just run with the 3-pin toe attachment. Overall, these are nearly foolproof, but snow can build up on the metal plate of the binding and in the three pin holes, which can be a pain to chisel away when you put your skis back on after boot packing.

If you are on a trip with a lot of downhills and challenging terrain, or icy conditions, you probably won't want a 3-pin binding. There's not a lot of support and

Lightweight and simple 3-pin telemark bindings
Shawn Forry

control, and it can be hard to engage your edges and hold sidehills. If you are touring on relatively flat or rolling terrain, however, these are great.

You can use any variety of telemark boot with these bindings as long as it has the three pin holes in the sole, called a 75 millimeter Nordic Norm toe piece (which most do). You can also add a spring and heel bail to the 3-pin to add a little more control on downhills and an ability to edge, though still not as much as with a full telemark binding.

The weight for the 3-pin bindings with cables is 1 pound, 13 ounces, and just a hair shy of a pound without the cables. These remain one of the most cost-effective binding options available.

Standard Telemark Binding

A normal telemark binding is basically a more robust 3-pin binding. Instead of locking the boot in by clamping down on the three pins, it locks the boot in by spring tension from the heel to the front. This maintains the ability to flex the boot at the bellows, which are at the ball of your foot, unlike AT boots, where the fulcrum point when touring becomes the front of your toes. When touring, the telemark system creates a more natural extension of normal walking technique. These bindings also continue to be heavier than many AT bindings, though. They will give you much more control on downhills and in varying conditions than the 3-pin. They are a little more complex but also relatively maintenance free and have the same advantages of not having to go back and forth between tour and ski modes for rolling terrain.

As you become a more proficient telemark skier, you can gain more control and precision by using a stiffer cartridge or setting on your bindings. This will make touring a bit more difficult, as there will be resistance pulling your heel back to the ski as you kick and take a step. Depending on your use and goal for the skis, you may want to mount them with different bindings or spring stiffnesses.

You can also buy heel riser bars for the heel plate. These add a little bit of weight, but if you are dealing with steeper uphills, they can help save your calves from getting tired. You'll be able to weight the ski so that your skins will grab but save a couple of inches on how far you bring your heel below your toes to save on some fatigue. These are best to add if you're regularly dealing with ascending steep terrain.

Telemark Tech System
Mark Lengel

Some models have the ability to switch into touring mode. This creates a free pivot point around the toe of the boot, like an AT binding, so that you can completely unlock your heel and not have any counter pressure from the spring system. If you are in the backcountry to make turns and are ascending steeper terrain and using stiffer springs (which will give you better control), you may need this feature to avoid increased fatigue. If you're just out for a tour, then this is probably not necessary.

Olympic Mountain Gear has patented the Telemark Tech System (TTS). This system has a Tech binding front, with the two pins inserting into the side of the toe area and a

Telemark Bindings

Make	Model	Weight	Cost
Voile	Switchback	3 lb	$279
Voile	3-Pin w/ cable 3-Pin w/o cable	1 lb, 13 oz 1 lb	$95 $60
22 Designs	Axl	3 lb, 9 oz	$340
22 Designs	Vice	3 lb, 2 oz	$220
G3	Targa Ascent	3 lb	$299
G3	Targa	2 lb, 10 oz	$199
G3	Targa T/9	2 lb, 4 oz	$219
Black Diamond	O1 (discontinued but can still be found online)	3 lb, 14 oz	$299
Olympus Mountain Gear	Telemark Tech System (TTS)	2 lb	$499

heel bail to create tension like a standard telemark binding. The problem is that only New Telemark Norm (NTN)–style boots have Tech inserts right now, so the use is limited and the boots are heavy. The current model weighs 2 pounds, plus 4 pounds for an NTN boot—still very heavy compared to AT setups.

We are purposefully not going into detail about the bindings that meet the NTN. These bindings are step-in, step-out and releasable, but they are just too heavy for more than day-trip touring. The boots are also on the heavier side. The bindings alone weigh 3.5 to just under 4 pounds, and many of the boots are in the 3-pound 12-ounce range. That would add a leg fatiguing 7+ pounds to your system—a nonstarter for us for more than a day trip.

BOOTS

Similar to summertime hiking boots, fit is going to reign king over gram counting for whichever ski boot you opt for. Beyond comfort and minimizing blisters, well-fitting ski boots will be warmer, eliminate annoying pressure points, and perform at a much higher ski level.

No matter which boot you select, the reality will be that your foot is engulfed in rigid plastic. The sheer idea of comfort seems a bit tongue-in-cheek. The good news is that boot liners can be custom molded, and the shell can be modified by a reputable boot fitter to better mirror your foot's natural shape from the start. The downside is that most ultra-light manufacturers skimp on adequate volume in the boot's last to engender lower claimed weights. Folks with broad feet will be most affected. The other contributing factor is that it can be infinitely challenging to find retail shops that carry niche touring boots. Especially problematic is knowing that getting a great fit is nearly impossible when buying from online outlets, and almost all boots will require some modification, sometimes beyond just heat-molding the liners.

AT AND RANDONEE BOOTS

Finding a manufacturer that best fits your foot will limit your options for which type of boot to choose. Whichever brand ends up fitting the best will still be a compromise of weight, downhill ski performance, and uphill walkability. Thankfully, as advances in technology trickle down, the gaps between these compromises are greatly narrowing.

Common categories of applicable ultralight ski boots are dedicated AT boots and ski mountaineering (skimo) boots, sometimes referred to as randonee racing boots. The former tends to be middle of the road in the AT category, and also tends to strike an equal balance between downhill performance and weight. While not entirely suited for aggressive downhill exploits, they won't fatigue your thighs or your wallet compared to full-on racing boots.

Randonee boots are basically ultralight, high-performance slippers—minus the comfort. Most boots in this category are lighter than most summertime hiking boots. Yes, that is not a typo. When uphill efficiency and weight reduction are of upmost importance, randonee boots fill the bill with top-notch carbon or Grilamid construction, and total disregard as to cost and features. Race boots are only compatible with tech bindings, which makes sense on many levels. Why ski the lightest boot only to click them into a portly frame binding? When the need to cover distance quickly is combined with conservative descents, randonee boots will be the clear winner.

One consideration for any boot is that most have been designed for "done-in-a-day" pursuits. In efforts to make ski boots as light as possible, some designs leave the liner exposed to moisture. This is especially true for race boots, when getting the liners damp is a small price

> **TIP**
>
> Regardless of which boot you select, plan on taking them to a competent fitter to get fine-tuned. It is incredible the amount of custom work that can be done to a ski boot to make them more comfortable, which will have a direct effect on warmth, enjoyment, and control.

Lightweight AT Boots

Make	Model	Weight	Materials	Articulation	Cost
Dynafit	TLT7 Performance	1,010 g	Grilamid	60	$849
Scarpa	F1	1,230 g	HPA/Carbon	62	$699
Scarpa	Maestrale	1,520 g	Pebax	39	$629
La Sportiva	Spitfire 2.0	1,130 g	Grilamid/Carbon	68	$799
La Sportiva	Spectre 2.0	1,445 g	Grilamid/Pebax	60	$679
Arc'teryx	Procline	1,240 g	Grilamid	75	$649
Movement	Alps Tracks	1,210 g	Grilamid/Pebax	62	$579
Hagan	Core TF	1,210 g	Grilamid	60	$749
Atomic	Backland Carbon	1,155 g	Grilamid/Carbon	74	$749

Ultralight Randonee Boots

Make	Model	Weight	Materials	Articulation	Cost
Dynafit	PDG	830 g	Grilamid	62	$849
Dynafit	DNA EVO	733 g	Grilamid/Carbon	62	$1,399
Dynafit	DNA	510 g	Full Carbon	75	$2,499
Scarpa	Alien	850 g	Polyamide/Carbon	60	$799
Scarpa	Alien 1.0	700 g	Polyamide/Carbon	58	$1,799
Scarpa	Alien 3.0	575 g	Carbon/Pebax	71	$2,999
La Sportiva	Stratos Hi-Cube	450 g	Full Carbon	76	$2,500
La Sportiva	Syborg	825 g	Grilamid/Carbon	75	$749

to pay for getting to the podium. Some manufactures have experimented with incorporating Gore-Tex membranes into their liners with limited success. Until the market realizes the need for ergonomic, ultralight multiday expeditioning boots, users will be left to their own devices to resolve this limitation. A common route is to modify a pair of ultralight gaiters, which seal out unwanted snow from saturating the liner without adding too much weight to the boot.

Walk/Ski Mode

This is the distinguishing difference between alpine and alpine touring boots. For folks who have experienced the walk from the car to the chairlift in traditional ski boots, you can imagine how tiring and impractical this experience would be on an all-day tour. The walk/ski mechanism enables the ski cuff to release and pivot, akin to the natural articulation of the ankle while walking. The best designs not only hinge the cuff but also release the topmost buckle to further facilitate comfort and dexterity, and reduce shin bang. As designs continue to improve, ultralight ski-touring boots are becoming nearly as stiff as alpine boots and have cuff articulation that far exceeds the human range. Any boot with a cuff articulation of 45 to 60 degrees will provide ample comfort while skinning.

Telemark fans will chime in here and state that all telemark boots are inherently crafted to both naturally walk and ski. While true, even the lightest leather or plastic telemark boot will be much heavier than the latest AT boot. Like the AT versus Telemark binding debate, telemark fans are always going to be a few turns behind the most advanced AT boot.

TELEMARK BOOTS

Telemark boots also come in a few varieties from the simple, old school leather boots, to basically an insulated hiking boots with a duckbill, to a full plastic boot with varying stiffness. Depending on the goal of the trip these each have pros and cons.

Telemark Boots

Make	Model	Weight	Materials	Cost
Scarpa	T1	4 lb, 4 oz	Pebax shell, Intuition moldable liner, four-buckle	$699
Scarpa	T2 ECO	3 lb, 11 oz	Pebax Rnew, Intuition moldable liner, three-buckle	$599
Scarpa	T4	2 lb, 15 oz	Pebax, Intuition liner, two-buckle	$399
Scott	Synergy	4 lb	Pebax, moldable liner, four-buckle	$680
Scott	Voodoo	4 lb	Pebax, moldable liner, three-buckle	$699
Crispi	XP	3 lb, 14 oz	Pebax, moldable liner, three-buckle	$425
Crispi	XR	4 lb	Pebax, moldable liner, four-buckle	$475

Leather Boots

I won't get rid of mine because they can be hard to find now. They are basically hiking boots with a duck bill. When broken in, they are very comfortable and flexible, not that warm (which can be both a pro and a con), and are fairly lightweight for ski equipment. They are also terrible at controlling a ski on steep terrain or in less-than-ideal conditions. Over time you'll also need to treat the leather to maintain waterproofing. Leather boots partner well with 3-pin bindings and fairly narrow skis for a touring-based trip without much elevation gain or loss. Other than that, they are less than ideal.

Synthetic Boots

Synthetic boots are basically updated leather boots. They usually have a synthetic exterior and some synthetic insulation for warmth. They are also best with 3-pin bindings on relatively flat or rolling terrain—and can be flat-out dangerous on other terrain or in bad conditions. Another downside of synthetic boots is that they are not entirely waterproof. You will have to seal the stitching with Freesole or ShoeGu to help, and on wet days water will still get in over time—and once it does, these boots will take FOREVER to

Synthetic telemark boots take a very long time to dry once they get wet.
Justin Lichter

Rando-race ski boots are intended for done-in-a-day activities. This simple modification to a Mountain Laurel Designs eVent gaiter better seals out moisture and snow for extended multiday function.
Shawn Forry

dry. This is not ideal for a multi-night or multi-week trip where there is a chance of hitting less-than-ideal conditions or even wet spring snowpack. They are comfortable, warmer, and take less time to break in than leather boots, though, so may be best for some climates and trips.

One advantage that 3-pin synthetic boots have that no other ski boot can claim is their ability to travel in extreme cold. Companies like Baffin have seen the need for extremely warm boots that integrate with ski bindings, commonly required for ski expeditions in the extreme cold. Boots like these are rated to nearly -100°F, which you will find in no other ski boot option.

Power straps can easily be removed to save about 1 ounce per boot without much sacrifice to performance while also expediting transitions.
Shawn Forry

Plastic Boots

Plastic boots are heavier but have much better control in bad conditions and steeper terrain. The more buckles on the boot, the heavier the boot but the better control. Many people use a two- or three-buckle telemark boot in the backcountry. These plastic boots have removable liners, which help with drying them and preventing them from freezing at night. These telemark plastic boots are much heavier than lightweight AT boots. If you really want to telemark and don't want to deal with transitioning into uphill and downhill modes, a decent compromise might be to choose a two- or three-buckle boot. With the three-buckle boot, you should still be able to enjoy the downhills and have the decent control of a typical wider ski that's 90 millimeters underfoot.

A common misconception in today's boot market is that the more buckles a boot has, the stiffer it will be. With advancements in shell materials, two-buckle boots can be just as stiff as four-buckle boots from a few years ago. Most AT boots and

Far lighter than traditional buckles, BOA laces are extremely fast and light, yet prone to icing and fraying—the inherent compromises of ultralight skimo boots.
Shawn Forry

Unrestricted motion while in tour mode will increase comfort, agility, and warmth while on the go. Ultralight rando-race boots have the highest range of motion. Both of these boots claim 60 degrees of cuff articulation, while it is easy to see which one truly offers more mobility.
Valerie DiPonio

TIP

Be mindful of how the walk/ski lever interacts with your ski pants and/or gaiters. Some require the ski cuff to ride high above the ski boot. A simple consideration, but when overlooked it can be annoying and require unwanted futzing during transitions and allow snow to enter the top of the boot.

telemark boots feature a removable "power strap." This strap is commonly removed to save weight and can be annoying to tighten and loosen during transitions. The small decline in downhill performance is made up tenfold in convenience.

Some ultralight boots incorporate racket-style BOA laces into the forefoot. While further reducing weight, this lacing system is quick to tighten and remove, yet prone to icing and having the cables fray.

Shell Materials

Polyurethane (PU): The heaviest, cheapest, and thus, most commonly used material for alpine ski boot construction, PU tends to "feel" the most like a ski boot because of its uniform flex pattern. The downside is that PU is highly affected by temperature, becoming stiffer when it's cold and softer on those warm spring days.

Pebax: While much lighter than PU, it can be hard to achieve suitable stiffness with Pebax without incorporating other materials. Overall a higher caliber material than PU, Pebax is far less affected by temperature swings.

Grilamid: Fast becoming the ski boot material of choice for high-end alpine touring boots, Grilamid is a relatively new shell material, most commonly prioritized in randonee racing and ski mountaineering. Grilamid is incredibly stiff, requiring less material. Cost will be higher, and some skiers feel the flex pattern is less predictable.

Carbon Fiber: This lightest and stiffest shell material is incredibly expensive and difficult to manufacture. It's most commonly utilized in key shell components like the cuff and tongue to balance cost while reducing weight. Full carbon boots barely tip the scale at 1 pound per boot. Beyond cost, it is nearly impossible to heavily modify the fit and volume of the shell.

Soles

Almost all AT boots and telemark boots feature a rubber lugged sole to help facilitate walking on difficult terrain. Consider this a must. Some boot designs even incorporate a subtle rockered sole that better facilitates natural walking.

Skins

In conjunction with backcountry touring binding, skins are the other critical component to define and separate backcountry skiing from its downhill counterpart. With the absence of chairlifts, they are the grip for the up. When functioning properly, skins act as a "magic rug" that grips the snow. On the worst of days, they are a frustrating icy mess that slips and slides with every step, if you can even manage to keep them attached to the bottom of your skis.

Like the patterned bases previously discussed, skins also work by providing omnidirectional grip. Using directional fibers attached to an adhesive backing, the fibers are oriented in a way that they lie flat with forward movement and perk up for grip to resist backward movement, similar to petting an animal's fur. Unlike patterned bases, skins are removable and can span the entire length of the ski, whereas patterned bases cover only the kick zone. This duality provides maximum grip on the up and maximum glide on the down. The downside is that they are yet another piece of equipment to manage to maintain optimum function, and without practice they can require precious time to transition from skiing to skinning.

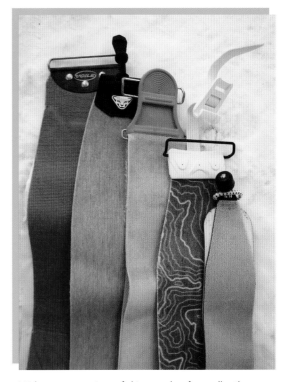

With so many options of skins to select from, all strike a compromise between glide and grip. When selecting which skin is right for you, also consider the ergonomics of the attachment system and the dry time of the fabric.
Shawn Forry

Styles

Weight can vary depending on the skin material you select. There can be drastic weight differences between styles of skin. All skins will be most effective if there is maximum grip from beneath the foot to the tail of the ski for forward traction and edge to edge to prevent washing out while sidehilling.

Kicker Skins: Kicker skins are the most minimal in design and cover only the "kick zone" of the ski. They are best for very moderate rolling terrain and are the lightest option for those "just in case" scenarios. Since both the front and back are attached with straps under the binding, they are prone to getting snow balled up between the skin and ski.

Full-length Skins: The most popular skin design, these skins stretch from the tip to tail and attach via proprietary clips or straps. Since the skins curve up off the ground toward the tip of the ski, they are less prone to getting snow balled up between the skin and ski. You will get wall-to-wall coverage for maximum grip. Alternatively, when you trim your skins to match the skis, you can cut them narrower to get a bit more glide on flat and rolling terrain.

Split Skins: For über-wide powder skis above 110 millimeters underfoot, the overall surface area of the skin can reach a point of diminishing return, adding unnecessary bulk and weight. To combat this, some manufactures have developed a split skin that will either split entirely down the middle, creating a gap, or eliminate the skin fibers, leaving just the adhesive backing.

The former will be the lightest option, but with four exposed edges to the snow, they are more prone to peeling and getting snow accumulated on the skin glue. The latter option eliminates this burden at the expense of being slightly heavier.

Materials

Once upon a time, skins were actually made from seal skins, hence the name. Today's materials of choice are natural mohair, synthetic nylon, or a blend. Fischer has even introduced all-plastic "patterned base" skins, further complicating a standout choice.

Nylon: Nylon is the cheapest option; it provides the best grip uphill but the worst glide on the flats. The synthetic material resists water absorption slightly better than mohair but is still susceptible to freezing. Nylon requires the least maintenance and is the most durable option.

Split skin designs like these Camp Contour skins reduce weight without limiting upward traction. With proper technique this style skin will stay adequately attached and reduce weight by around 15 percent. They can be a bit more time-consuming to get on and off.
Shawn Forry

Mohair: This natural fiber, sourced from Angora goats, excels in glide and packs super small. No other fabric will restrict your natural forward movement less than mohair. Slightly more prone to abrasion and wear than nylon, mohair also does not excel in all snow conditions and requires slightly more upkeep to prevent them from absorbing undesired moisture. Cost can also be a deterrent, as they are the most expensive option.

Hybrid Blends: A mohair-nylon blend is the best of both worlds and the most common skin purchased. Well balanced in glide versus grip and cost versus durability, mohair-nylon blends provide well-rounded performance with very little compromise.

When speed and weight are of utmost concern, choose mohair. When durability is paramount and extended variable conditions are predicted, lean more toward full nylon.

Plastic: Fischer has introduced fully plastic Profoil skins that mimic removable patterned bases. These skins excel at zero water absorption and maintenance, but struggle with the same limitations as patterned-base skis. They struggle for grip in icy hardpack conditions and are prone to washing out while sidehilling. While not a clear standout in many categories when considering cost, weight, and performance, here's a tip of the hat to Fischer's thinking outside the box.

Glues

Each manufacture has its proprietary glue formula. And each company is balancing the same conundrum: making the skins as sticky as possible so as to adhere to the ski through a range of conditions while not being so sticky that they are impossible to separate from each other while in storage or to remove from the base of the ski. Carrying the dedicated skin savers that come attached to the skins during purchase combats this problem, but they are time intensive and finicky to apply and add unnecessary bulk and weight.

So-called "glueless" skins are a bit of a misnomer. Rather than relying on traditional solvent-based glues, they simply use a different formula that incorporates silicone. These skins adhere using pressure and "suction" rather than outright tackiness. Far easier to manage than the brute force needed to separate traditional glue skins, they can have limited success in wet snow conditions, where any moisture on the skin prevents sufficient suction. With the removal of the glue layer, these skins can be expected to last longer, pack smaller and weigh less, and they are nearly impervious to debris sticking to them.

Left: Stow skins inside a jacket pocket during descents to keep the glue dry and sticky. The waist belt of your pack will prevent them from falling out of the bottom of your jacket while skiing.
Right: Removing skins on windy days can be a test in patience and technique. To prevent them from flapping in the wind and collecting snow on the glue, use the half-fold technique. Remove one-half of the skin and fold into the middle. Next, with a quick motion, rip the rest of the skin from the ski and fold the second half of the skin into the middle. Fold skins in half again, and stow inside a jacket pocket. This technique is much easier than wielding full-length sticky skins.
Justin Lichter

Tips for Skin Management:

1. Do not drag the glue edge through the snow! Immediately brush off any moisture or powder that comes in contact with the skin glue. Brush with a glove, or scrape lightly with the edge of a ski.

2. Melt tenacious snow patches stuck to the glue by blowing warm air on the skin, and then wipe away any moisture.

3. Scrape any snow off the base of your ski before applying a skin. Wipe with the back of your glove to further dry out the skin.

4. Keep skins tucked inside a jacket next to the body while on the descent or after transitions. Your body heat with go a long way toward keeping the skin glue tacky for the next ascent.

5. If skins become saturated and begin to glob up with snow, rub skin wax into the base. A common candle will work in a pinch.

6. Thoroughly dry out skins at every opportunity. Hang them in a place where they can fully open without encountering contaminants and debris.

7. Store skins in a cool dry place and attached to the skin savers to preserve the glue.

Regardless of which skin type you choose, proper care is paramount to optimize their effectiveness and lifespan. The importance of keeping the skins as dry as possible may seem counterintuitive given that they are in constant contact with a water source. That being said, the worst thing you can do is drag the adhesive side through powdery snow!

Attachment

When the adhesive backing is new, any skin will stick perfectly to a ski at the retailer or the trailhead. While most skin glues are sufficient to hold the skin to the ski under optimal conditions, the rigors of sliding the skin along the ground will demand a more robust attachment system. It is paramount that the skin glue seals out any snow moisture along the edge of the skin, while the attachment at tip and tail similarly prevents the skin from rolling off and exposing the skin glue to fresh powder and moisture. Proper technique is important to maintaining the tackiness of the skin. The foot should glide along the snow, unlike the

Dynafit offers a well-thought-out attachment system for skins. The notch at the tip of the ski not only minimizes the chance of the skins coming off but also makes removal much easier without having to remove the ski. With heel released, simply flip the ski toward you to reach the skin toggle and rip the skin off.
Shawn Forry

TIP

Black Diamond tail clips are one of the most common designs but also one of the biggest offenders for tail clips detaching from the ski. Once this happens, it's only a matter of time until the tail of the skin peels, flips, and gets dragged through the snow. A quick DIY improvement is the "rat tail" method: sewing a short length of half-inch flat grosgrain webbing to the butt end of the skin to create a long tail-like feature. A simple loop of bungee cord can be affixed to the end of the webbing, which will wrap around to the top sheet of the ski. Partially screw in a small panhead screw 10 centimeters from the rear of the tail for the bungee loop to hook around. No more tails coming off, with a minimal weight penalty!

common stomping akin to walking. Just think, every step in a ski setup is like lifting 5 to 15 pounds per foot!

So-called "standard style" skins are void of a tail clip altogether. While lighter by design, they are more prone to adhesive failure. Euro-style skins have both a tip and tail attachment, but not all designs are created equal. The best designs have some sort of elastic component incorporated into the clips to help prevent them from coming off. Better still, proprietary skins like Dynafit skis and skins have a notch in the tip and tail to accept the clip mechanism, preventing most premature detachment.

Regardless of how foolproof you make your attachment system, at some point in the backcountry you're going to have to deal with a temperamental skin not sticking. Having a stash of Voile Straps can do wonders when combating a skin that is too far done to revive in the field and you need to get out before dark. Simply strapping the skin on at all the problematic areas will not only get you out but also sap all your glide—a small price to pay. Zip-ties can also be used, especially to replace busted or bent tail clips.

CRAMPONS AND ICE AXES

Regardless of our chosen mode of travel, at some point, as terrain steepens and conditions become hard packed, traction will suffer. This can be as unnerving as it is dangerous. Crampons can resolve a multitude of limitations across the spectrum of travel modes and are a proactive measure to ensure proper footing at all times.

Traction devices like the micro-spikes mentioned earlier will have limited applicant in these conditions, especially as objective hazards increase. This is the time for crampons. Whether you are wearing mountaineering boots, ski boots, or overshoes, there is a crampon to fit your needs.

Left: Full automatic crampons provide the lightest attachment system but work with a limited range of footwear and uses.
Right: Strap-on crampons work with a variety of footwear but can be more finicky to adjust and put on. Hybrid crampons combine a toe strap with a heel lever.
Shawn Forry

Crampons come in a range of methods in how they attach to your footwear. Some will be better suited to specific applications.

Strap-on: Strap-on crampons fit the widest range of footwear, but their universal attachment system comes at a compromise in precision and rigidity. The webbing straps that attach the crampon to the shoe can be finicky and prone to freezing.

Step-in: Sometimes referred to as "automatic crampons," step-in crampons rely on a toe and heel bail that interlocks into integrated slots built into the footwear. Some ski-mountaineering crampons have dedicated tech binding inserts for the heel piece to further reduce weight. The Camp Race 290 crampons are likely the lightest full ten-point crampon in this category. Step-in crampons are an overall lighter design and are much easier to put on and take off. The downside is that they will only fit dedicated footwear. They are often the most rigid and precise in use.

Further blurring the line, Camp USA makes a super lightweight aluminum 10-point crampon that integrates into the heel of Dynafit tech bindings while having a standard bail toe.
Shawn Forry

Hybrid: These crampons, also known as semiautomatic, will have a toe strap and heel lever. These crampons are a middle-of-the road solution to the pros and cons of strap-on versus automatic crampons and are a solid all-around choice.

MATERIALS

For crampon construction, you essentially have two choices: steel or aluminum. Steel is infinitely sharper and more durable at the expense of weight. Aluminum crampons are suitable for all-around use when their limitations of durability and sharpness are considered. For penetrating bulletproof ice day in and day out, steel is the only logical and safe choice. Some models offer a good compromise of weight and penetration by having steel front points and aluminum heel spikes.

POINTS

While in appearance, crampons with a differing number and arrangement of points may seem like a manufacturer's cosmetic choice, each design is tailored to its intended use. For general mountaineering, glacier-walking, and ski mountaineering, ten-point crampons have become the norm. They offer adequate purchase and are lighter than full-on twelve-point crampons. For technical ice and mixed climbing on steep ascents, twelve-point crampons offer slightly more confidence and security.

How the front points are oriented will further dictate the intended use. Horizontal front points are best suited for general walking and moderate alpine climbing. Vertical front points

Anti-balling plates, while adding 1 to 2 ounces per foot, go a long way in function and safety, helping prevent snow from packing into the cleats, rendering the crampon useless.
Shawn Forry

provide better purchase into steep vertical ice and can be slotted into tiny cracks during technical mixed climbing. Twelve-point vertical front point crampons will be overkill and excessively heavy for most applications. Although front points can be replaced as they wear down, in general, keep your points in tiptop shape and routinely sharpen them. As with the knives in your kitchen, a dull crampon is far more dangerous than a sharp one.

Consider adding anti-balling plates to the base of your crampons to prevent snow from sticking to the bottoms. Conditions where snow will have the greatest tendency to stick are those that are favorable for making snowballs. Warm, wet snow will be the greatest offender. The negligible amount of weight added by the anti-balling plates is offset by the increased margin of safety.

Further blurring the lines are the toe-only five-point crampons by TechCrampon. At only 250 grams for the pair, these crampons only attach to the toe of Dynafit-compatible ski boots. While limited in application, these types of crampons are perfect for front pointing up steep couloirs. They will be severely limited in traversing or side-stepping and useless during descents.

SKI CRAMPONS

An often underutilized tool in the backcountry, ski crampons work in tandem with skins to achieve greater purchase during uphill efforts. Equally effective in traversing as they are in uphill skin tracks, ski crampons are also appropriate for rolling terrain. They add

Ski crampons can be an invaluable tool on steep icy slopes. Fixed ski crampons like these from Voile provide consistent traction throughout the stride of the ski. Note that a dedicated hinged Dynafit ski crampon will integrate into these bindings. Hinged bindings do not restrict the glide forward but rely on constant body weight to engage the crampon into the snow.
Shawn Forry

consistent purchase to the grip of skins, further minimizing energy output and the frustration of sliding backward. For anyone who has experienced the tenuous "pucker factor" while skinning uphill or especially traversing, ski crampons nearly eliminate this problem.

Ski crampons can either be fixed or pivot, and select models integrate into telemark, tech, or frame bindings. Crampons that pivot provide uninterrupted cadence as the ski is slid forward and engaged as pressure is applied to the foot. Fixed crampons are just that. While they increase drag while skinning forward, their "ever-ready" approach helps instill confidence that purchase will be there when needed, regardless if the ski is fully weighted. The other consideration is that fixed crampons are not adversely affected if heel risers are being utilized with the bindings.

The challenge with ski crampons can be when to carry them, since there is a limited range of conditions in which they work. When you want them, you need them; when you don't, they are unnecessary weight. They are great in firm ice, slushy spring corn, or "dust on crust" conditions, where skins generally struggle. At around 3 to 6 ounces, they add little weight but are generally bulky and awkward to pack. Keep them accessible by clipping them to the outside of your pack with a carabiner, and put them on before you will need them!

ICE AXES

Ice axes are to hands what crampons are to feet. The key distinction is that crampons, in collaboration with proper foot work and technique, are a proactive management tool. In the application of self-arresting, ice axes are deemed a reactionary tool to be used when things go awry. That being said, ice axes can serve many other functions, including chopping steps for more secure footing, adding balance and stability while climbing, and can be integrated into a climbing anchor or be used for vertical ascents in technical ice and mixed climbing. Mastery of the technique and proper use of an ice ax is of utmost importance; otherwise you're just traveling with a glorified human skewer.

While it's tempting to purchase the absolute lightest ice ax on the market, similar to crampons, ice ax design and materials clearly dictate their intended use and highlight their shortcomings. Aluminum is much lighter than steel but might not gain sufficient purchase in bullet-hard ice if you need to self-arrest. Axes without spikes are lighter still, but the handles are prone to fill with snow, increasing the weight and annoyance. Shorter axes, in the 50-centimeter range, are compact and stow more easily on the outside of a pack, but they will cause you to bend over more than a properly sized 65- to 75-centimeter ax.

As a whole, axes in the sub-8-ounce category should be considered only for mellow glacier routes, early season hiking, and ski mountaineering. A more substantial ax should be used when security in firm snow conditions is paramount.

POLES

Regardless of your mode of travel, pairing it with a set of poles will have the complementary effects of efficiency, safety, and utility. With the unpredictable stability of snow travel, poles are invaluable in maintaining balance, which can help prevent injury. Additionally, poles

TIP

If using poles for shelter construction, lash two together to double the strength. They will hold up better and be more stable under extreme wind and snow loads. This is no excuse not to shovel out your tent from snow at night! If your poles are too short to reach from the ground to the peak of the pyramid, pile up snow, rocks, or even your cooking pot at night to add height.

give you that extra reach to knock off tree bombs or probe rotten or suspect snow without putting yourself in harm's way. The versatility poles afford in camp with shelter setup makes them indispensable.

Poles can take quite the abuse during winter travel. If you're skiing, they will see increased strain when planting turns. You will inevitably use them to shed burdensome snow from snowshoes and skis, but be mindful of hitting carbon fiber poles against metal—you'll be chipping and weakening your poles. In camp, nighttime snow loads can quickly overpower their ability as a center pole for your shelter without proper reinforcement.

This all suffices to say that when considering a trekking pole for winter use, it will be better to err toward the slightly more durable end of the spectrum. Select poles that are at least 14 to 16 millimeters in diameter to stand up to the added abuse of winter travel. Carbon fiber poles are a logical choice, but dedicated winter carbon poles must be selected, as they will be reinforced and much more

Proper snow baskets will prevent poles from postholing into deep snow, increasing the risk of them snapping. Most popular trekking poles will accept snow baskets by simply pressing off the smaller summer basket and pushing on the wider snow basket.
Shawn Forry

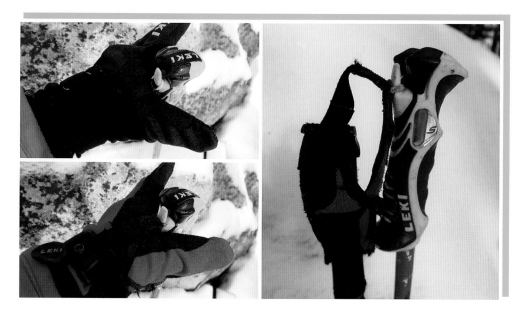

Leki's Vario S Trigger handles provide a quick and efficient means for securing trekking poles with gloved hands. The strap secures to the hand and is easily removed by pressing down on the handle's locking mechanism. Some dedicated Leki gloves have an integrated strap sewn in, eliminating the need for the strap altogether. Strap systems like this are secure while still releasing when needed; i.e., during falls or in an avalanche.
Shawn Forry

resistant to breaking than comparable summer trekking poles. An aluminum upper pole and carbon lower is a good way to save weight and lower costs.

Adjustable poles are much more versatile for shelter use and can compact when needing to stow on a pack. Opt for a two-piece pole over a three-piece pole to minimize moving parts that can break. Flick-lock poles are by far the most superior locking mechanism and will give you much less hassle in winter, when twist-lock poles are prone to icing up.

Make sure to install a proper snow basket on winter trekking poles. These wider baskets do a much better job of staying afloat on the snow. Opting to shave a few grams by using smaller summer-size baskets or removing them all together will result in a snapped pole in no time.

When it comes to how the pole connects to the hand, the Trigger S pole strap system that Leki incorporates is by far

the best on the market for backcountry use. When gloved hands will be the norm, the ability to quickly remove hands from the poles without having to take off gloves, undo buckles, and fidget with frozen straps saves heaps of frustration. The hand will also separate from the pole under extreme pressure, as when falling or, worse, when pinned in an avalanche. This

TIP

To keep your hands warmer, choose foam handles. If not included, wrap the bottom 8 inches below the handle with either hockey tape or foam to increase insulation on exposed aluminum.

little extra safety measure can go a long way toward preventing the pole from breaking and, even more important, preventing injury.

OTHER GEAR

PULKS

A seldom seen or considered adaptation for winter travel is use of a pulk. In simplest terms, this is nothing more than dragging a glorified kid's sled packed with your gear behind you. The ability to stay "afloat" in deep snow conditions is inherently limited by a few factors: the consistency of the snow, the surface area of impact, and the weight or force being applied to the snow. The combination of these three factors will determine our "wallow" factor.

In looking at the variables, the ones we have any control over are surface area and force. Our footprint in the snow can only get so large before things become awkward, clumsy, or excessively heavy. Regarding force, we can go on a crash diet prior to the start of the trip, but this will have limited results. One overlooked option is to remove pack weight from our

Here Larry Mishkar checks out the Apostle Islands by exploring frozen Lake Superior. Terrain like this is where pulk travel excels. Keeping weight off the back not only provides more "float" for skis but also keeps the back from saturating in sweat.
Larry Mishkar

Homemade pulks are fun and easy to make from a simple kid's sled, some length of fiberglass poles, and an old pack harness. Extensive testing by famed polar explorers Tyler Fish and John Huston revealed that the plastic used in a cheap kid's sled performed better than many high-end commercial plastics.
Larry Mishkar

bodies altogether. This can easily remove 20 to 50 pounds off our backs, which will directly translate to less overall force being applied to the snow.

Pulks are ideal in conditions that favor large heavy loads over flat, even terrain. Folks recreating on snow machine tracks or frozen lakes are primed to haul hunting and fishing gear to backcountry cabins with considerable ease. Even mountaineers with long approaches up glaciated valleys can benefit by using pulks to establish their base camps. Pulks can serve a dual purpose in camp by helping move firewood and snow around for establishing snow walls.

The idea is that efficiency is gained when measured against the increase in resistance versus the burden of shouldering excessively heavy loads. An added advantage of transferring packs to a pulk is that your back will be much less sweaty, further favoring more-uniform moisture management across the body. Nearly every successful unsupported ski expedition to the North Pole has utilized a pulk of some sort to carry the massive loads of supplies that could not physically be hauled on one's back. John Huston and Tyler Fish collectively hauled more than 300 pounds of gear and supplies during their historic unsupported ski expedition to the North Pole in 2009.

Where pulks become challenging and potentially frustrating is when terrain dictates traversing long stretches of steep terrain, areas with excessive blow-downs or other obstacles, and/or when snow cover is deep or not uniform. In deep snow a pulk will be more plow-like, and when dragging through uneven snowshoe or ski tracks, you'll spend more time righting the pulk due to its tendency to tip over in those conditions. It can take some time to get accustomed to the coordination required to navigate a pulk while wearing skis or snowshoes. Bear in mind that if using skis, your grip through skins, wax, or fishscales will be considerably less, since you'll have less force over your skis and more resistance with the pulk.

Commercially available pulks are available, and homemade variations are easy to make in a weekend afternoon. Basic equipment needed for construction will be a sled, two rigging poles (traces), and an attachment system. A toy sled can be easily modified by drilling some holes around the perimeter to accept cordelette for lashing equipment down. Fiberglass poles and mounting hardware can be sourced at a local hardware store or purchased online, and a pack with a removable hip belt can be donated as an impromptu harness.

The connection between the pulk and the hiker is important in balancing control and movement. Six-foot lengths of fiberglass pole provide enough distance to enable a natural stride, and the rigidity of the fiberglass prevents the pulk from slamming into your heels on steep descents. Fiberglass stays flexible at extreme temperatures and provides enough flex to help facilitate moving the pulk up, over, and around obstacles. Carbon fiber, which is lighter, would likely be more prone to snapping, as it becomes more brittle as the mercury drops. Be sure to handle the poles with gloved hands to prevent glass shards from getting into your skin. To minimize the plowing effects, keep the majority of weight low and toward the rear of the pulk. Make sure your connection and angle of the rigging pole to the sled provide a slight upward pull to help keep the pulk's nose from diving in to the snow.

The size of the sled is worth consideration as well. Longer sleds stay afloat better by more evenly distributing the weight and can haul more gear; shorter sleds are lighter and much easier to maneuver. Wider sleds resist tipping but are more prone to plowing; narrow sleds track better through snowshoe tracks. Most people prefer sleds with widths of 14 to 22 inches and lengths of 3 to 5 feet.

KITES

Generally, blustery conditions during winter are a surefire way to turn up a nose in disapproval. There is no better way to turn these unfavorable conditions into an opportunity than by incorporating a kite into your travel. Best paired with skis, kites offer an amazingly efficient means of crossing vast open landscapes that have consistent wind conditions. Fast becoming the new medium for travel in polar regions, through the adaptation of kiteboarding, kite-skiing is seeing huge advances in technology, safety, and technique while opening up new possibilities for extremely light and fast expeditions. The current record for top speed and distance covered in a 24-hour period stands at 73 miles per hour and more than 370 miles!

The coordination required to master basic kiting technique can be challenging due to the variation in snow and wind. Don't assume that by using a kite you're just along for the ride; kiting is a physically intense activity. Improper technique can be downright dangerous, as it's not uncommon to become airborne in certain conditions. Practicing on a smaller two-line, 3-meter oil trainer kite is preferred before stepping up to larger 10-plus-meter kites. Learning the basics of launching, landing, and maneuvering the kite will be essential before adding skis or snowboards. Kite size is dictated by surface conditions and wind speed. Obviously, the larger the kite, the more speed and force can be translated into movement.

Kiting is a great example of how the adaptation of sport and technology continues to push the envelope for ultralight long-distance travel. As this sport continues to grow and evolve, without a doubt, we will see more and more impressive undertakings.

Applying the right technique is a matter of gaining experience. In doing so, your comfort, efficiency, and enjoyment will be maximized.
Justin Lichter

CHAPTER 4

WINTER CAMPING AND TRAVEL: TECHNIQUES AND TIPS

TO PUT IT KINDLY, NO ONE WANTS TO BE THE TRAVEL COMPANION WHO'S A COMPLETE JUNK SHOW—frozen boots in the morning, a burnt meal, hours spent breaking down camp only to realize you left the tent poles in camp an hour into the day's travel. The unconscious efficiencies of a true expert further highlight the inexperience of the novice. Nothing defines mastery more than time and experience.

This chapter will highlight a few key considerations to help streamline your routine while in the backcountry. Bear in mind that the words on these pages will then need to be applied in practice. The established muscle memory of our brains and bodies is achieved by moving from unconscious incompetence to conscious incompetence. Knowing what you don't know lays the groundwork for getting out there to practice and refine your techniques. They say it takes 10,000 hours to achieve true mastery of any skill. While I think we all can strive to dedicate that much time in the backcountry, pooling our resources and collective knowledge can help expedite our heightened enjoyment of winter travel.

CAMPSITE SELECTION

A proper campsite is the foundation of setting ourselves up for success. It is a place to find reprieve from the day's travel, a place to wait out storms, and a place to kick back and enjoy our surroundings. Likely close to half our time during winter will be spent "in camp." If we get to design our house each night, why not put the best roof over our heads that we can? Selecting the proper real estate is the first step in creating a pro-grade base camp. A great campsite does not find us; we find it. As simple a statement as that is, a lot of factors go into choosing our campsite for the night. These considerations can be broken down into fore-sight, near-sight, and hindsight.

Take the time to survey whether your campsite location is adequate. It is important to consider questions like "Am I protected from wind and snow?" "Am I in a safe location?" "Am I minimizing my impact?" and "Is this campsite Instagram worthy?"
Shawn Forry

FORESIGHT

Jumping ahead to the "Leave No Trace" section, much can be anticipated before even stepping foot on the trail. A cursory review of the terrain we are going to encounter can provide a glimpse into the environment and surrounding we can expect to be traveling through. A concentration of tight contour lines on our maps indicates that finding flat ground may be a challenge, which might further dictate how far we can travel each day to find a suitable campsite. Endless expanses of flat terrain are great for finding a flat parcel upon which to park for the night but, depending on the tree cover, can also indicate more exposure to wind. Similarly, alpine campsites are visually stunning, but unless conditions are favorable, they will be somewhere on the spectrum of miserable to downright dangerous. Access to water may be a moot point if sources are frozen over. In addition, these lakeside sites are prone to cold, moist air settling in for the night. Our ideal site is going to provide us ample protection from the elements, be in close proximity to water, and be elevated high enough to avoid low-lying cold air sinks.

Our secondary layer of foresight is while on-trail, prior to departing camp, when we can do a similar route plan and map review. How stable is the weather today? Has there been an emerging weather pattern we should take note of, such as building storms or changing wind directions? Have the travel conditions been as we anticipated, slower or faster? What is our energy level and ambition for the day? All these questions can help to inform a broader sense of realistic travel expectations for the day. We should have a ballpark idea of how far we could reasonably travel for the day and then overlay these variables on our topo map. These factors should narrow down a finite area in which we can make an informed decision on possible campsite locations for the night. When we overlay these variables and foresee that they land us in an unfavorable location, we already know that adjustments may need to be made to our itinerary and travel. This basic process should help take much of the guesswork out of campsite selection. With a little forethought, there should be few surprises.

An old miner's cabin serves as refuge from the storm. Each night study the map to make a plan for the next day's travel. Maps not only allude to probable campsites but also inform of possible locations to get out of the weather.
Shawn Forry

NEAR-SIGHT

Despite our best intentions and guesswork, the ground-truthing process is the reality we must live in. Sometimes things went as planned for the day; sometimes things out of our control came up. An equipment failure, an epic blister saga, or a glorious tailwind on primo hard-packed snow can all throw a wrench in our best-laid plans. At some point in the day, as the sun is beginning to get lower in the sky, we should start to think about our true campsite for the night.

Usually around an hour before our preferred stopping time, we should start shifting gear from travel to camping. In this process we want to establish a critical eye for a proper campsite for the evening. It's OK to be vigilant in this process, maybe even erring toward princess-like preferences. That is why we have

Making a plan of action while high on an exposed ridge with weather coming in. Looking ahead to find a protected campsite will make for a more comfortable night's sleep.
Shawn Forry

allocated an entire hour for this process. Finding flat ground should be the most obvious first step. Looking at your current surroundings and the terrain ahead, consult your map for realistic locations. By this point you should have a good pulse on your travel pace based on the day's conditions. Where is the first possible location, based on the map and your foreground, where we could find a site for the night?

Once we are on suitable flat ground, it's time to transition to the second tier of refined campsite selection. Take note of wind direction during this time to help pinpoint sites that will be oriented toward the leeward side of the wind. Note that in blustery storm conditions, the leeward side will be where snow deposits, while the windward side will be snow scoured but exposed to the onslaught of tent-shuddering winds all night. The lower in elevation you can camp from the dividing ridge, the more you will be protected from this snow loading.

Paying attention to ambient temperature during the final selection process can sometimes mean a difference of 10 to 15 degrees of warmth, simply by avoiding the geographical cold air sinks. Discomfort from these cold air pockets will only increase as night descends. Locations near large bodies of water, creeks, and low-lying areas in steep terrain should be avoided. Cold, moist air will tend to settle in these areas, since it is heavier than warmer, rising air. While true that a 3.5-degree increase in temperature can be expected for every thousand feet we descend, elevating our campsite by even 100 feet from low-lying land can make a stark difference in our comfort level.

Seeking shelter among a cluster of trees provides protection from wind and drifting snow.
Shawn Forry

Locations in meadows or similar open terrain can experience heavy dew and surface hoar throughout the night. This moisture will deposit and freeze to everything exposed to the ambient air, creating another variable to manage in the ensuing days, as discussed in the "Shelters: Tricks and Tips" section of this chapter.

Lastly, and most importantly, we want to ensure that our campsite is in a safe location. Knowing what is above us is paramount to avoid camping in a potential avalanche slide path. These locations are easy to identify by the lack of tree coverage coming off steeper terrain, usually but not always consolidated to gullies and ravines. Knowing how far potential slide paths can radiate out is another key consideration. Broken branches and scarring on the upward side of trees are good indicators that they have fallen victim to previous avalanche activity. We need to be extra vigilant on low-visibility travel days. This short line of sight can lead to a false sense of security in our surroundings. Consulting the map to inform your surroundings and erring on the über-conservative side are necessary steps when visual confirmation is limited.

Here is the recipe for an ideal campsite location:

- Safe location away from avalanche slide paths
- Flat ground to prevent sliding around all night
- Protected from the wind to minimize convective heat loss
- Slightly elevated from the valley floor and away from open water sources to avoid cold air sinks
- Away from meadows and other large open expanses to avoid condensation

Setting up your shelter under the canopy of a large pine can help minimize the accumulation of snow on your shelter, since the tree will naturally shed snow away from its base. This equates to less shoveling in the middle of the night! The tree will also provide some additional wind protection and act as a source of heat. (Yes, trees and other living organisms emit heat and prevent radiational cooling at night. We're not talking about bonfire thermals here, but every little bit helps.) An added bonus: If a fire is required or preferred, you'll already in close proximity to dead and fallen branches as a fuel source.

TIP

HINDSIGHT

Every process deserves a proper feedback loop in order to prevent having to learn the same lesson again and again. Learning is the process of DOING and then REFLECTING, and this concept should be applied to our entire catalog of winter skills. For the sake of campsite selection, it is important to review what we learned from our ground-truthing process in the day's travel. The variable microclimates we are traveling through trump all textbook analysis and prediction. Depending on aspect, variations in the snowpack can limit or expedite travel. Learning the local weather patterns and rhythms can better inform future conditions with respect to winds and storm cycles. At the end of the day, take the time to reflect back on what worked and what didn't. This gained knowledge can (and should) be applied to the next day's travel.

SHELTERS: TRICKS AND TIPS

It should go without saying, but learning how to set up your shelter should take place in the confines and comfort of home. Regardless of whether you are purchasing a brand-new shelter or utilizing a proven one, familiarity in setup will help ensure that you can expedite the process when conditions are at their worst. For brand-new shelters, each one has its slight nuances to get a perfect pitch; and if you're using a familiar shelter, some small modifications will likely need to be made to adapt it for winter conditions.

Simple adjustments to make to each shelter while at home are to increase the length and diameter of guylines over summer preferences. Even lengthening the pull cords on zippers to shelter entrances is a creature comfort when you think about having to do everything with gloved hands. Longer guylines are essential in order to have the flexibility to adjust to varying stakeout points depending on conditions. Some nights, deadman will need to be used; other nights you may be on bare ground. The flexibility to elevate your mid or tarp higher off the ground for increased ventilation or shelter space is additional evidence to warrant longer guylines.

With regard to setup, site prep will be one of the first steps to ensure a restful night. Your camp scene will be much more stable and comfortable if time is taken to pack down and

After selecting a protected, level campsite for the night, first pack out a perimeter for your shelter, oversizing by 2 to 3 feet the entire way around.
Valerie DiPonio

Begin consolidating the sleeping platform, working your way step by step, edge to edge. Skis and snowshoes are best; hiking boots will take the longest.
Valerie DiPonio

Work your way perpendicular to your first line of tracks, ensuring first stomps with each step. Allow the base to settle. The more sugary the snow, the longer it will take to consolidate.
Valerie DiPonio

Create a cold air sink by digging an 8- to 10-inch trough around the perimeter of the sleeping platform.
Valerie DiPonio

Working from the outside, shovel snow 1 to 2 feet above the sleeping platform. This will protect your shelter from strong gusts of wind. The windier it is, the higher you should build your walls. Prioritize the windward sides of your shelter if time is limited.
Valerie DiPonio

Pack the snow walls with the base of your shovel to prevent them from eroding away in the wind.
Valerie DiPonio

Smooth out the base of your sleeping platform before laying out your shelter. Minimize walking directly on where you will sleep to prevent lumps. Make final tweaks to the sleeping platform once you get your sleeping pad laid out. Start to finish, this process will only add about 5 minutes to your camp setup while greatly increasing your comfort.
Valerie DiPonio

consolidate the snow. Failure to do this can result in undo amounts of loose snow entering the tent and a lumpy, uneven sleeping surface. Utilize skis or snowshoes (if available) to help with initial compaction. Further refinement and leveling can be done with a shovel.

Once the site is prepped, set up your tent by orienting the door to the leeward side to prevent snow from blowing in upon entry and exit. If you are on a slight incline, face the door to the downward side so that cold air doesn't settle into the tent. In extremely windy conditions, snow can be utilized to create walls around the windward sides of the shelter. Build them far enough away from the shelter so that snow can still shed from the roof but not so far away as to diminish the effects of the windbreak. Typically a foot away is ample.

Place your groundsheet, if you are using one, and sleeping pad inside the shelter and lie on it to ensure there are no uncomfortable lumps and bumps. Do this before the snow has a chance to ice up and harden. You can shovel out a 1-foot "porch" at the entrance of your shelter to facilitate easier entry and egress and further prevent snow from entering the shelter.

CONSIDERATIONS

Condensation

In no environment except winter is it apparent how much moisture is around us at any given point. The physical evidence of frost and frozen condensation serves as a visible reminder to how the elements are stacking the odds against us. Condensation within shelter systems is that annoyingly humid, junglelike feeling we experience in summertime. As temperatures drop, our once-damp shelter fabric becomes a frosty icicle.

While we are sleeping, numerous sources of moisture are accumulating within our shelter system. Whether you are under a floorless pyramid tarp or a fully enclosed four-season tent, there will always be sources of moisture brought in from the outside world. The direct exposure of a floorless tarp capped by a non-breathable fabric creates a steady stream of evaporative moisture buildup, only marginally reconciled by the added ventilation that tarps and pyramids provide.

We breathe a lot at night—about a cup of moisture will be expelled by our breath in an eight-hour period. Imagine pouring a cup of water directly onto your sleeping bag at night! Ever notice that frosty ring around the hood of your sleeping bag? There's your cup of water.

We're likely also drying out various articles of clothing at night within our sleeping bags. The perfect storm of contributing factors is if the overall relative humidity is high outside, most commonly observed during sleet, slush, and fog events. Never mind if you opt to cook inside the shelter and how much additional moisture will enter the atmosphere as you reach a boil. All this moisture has to go somewhere. The scenario we are trying to avoid is all this moisture ending up in our sleeping bags. All this is to say that our choice in shelter systems will directly affect how much moisture buildup we can anticipate having to manage.

Seemingly counterintuitive, ventilation will be our greatest asset in combating excess moisture. The thought of a drafty shelter when temps are well below freezing is enough to give any sane person pause, but the benefits of a modest amount of air movement at night to minimize moisture buildup in our sleep system will far outweigh the negatives. We are not

Cooking from the comfort of your shelter is wonderful. If weather permits, open a door while cooking to prevent the buildup of condensation under the tarp.
Justin Lichter

suggesting that you not batten down the hatches when gale-force winds are driving horizontal snow into your shelter, but simply saying that a steady stream of light air movement can be beneficial, especially at key times, like while cooking.

Another measure that can be taken to further minimize condensation buildup under the shelter is incorporating moisture-barrier curtains. These are simple sheets of any fabric draped like curtains from the roof of the shelter to compartmentalize the moisture expelled by our breath away from the rest of the tarp. This measure is best actualized through the addition of vapor-barrier clothing. In theory, all moisture buildup would be relegated to a small quadrant of the shelter, where the sleeper's head is. This is most commonly reserved for extremely harsh conditions with subzero temperatures and minimal opportunities for drying on multi-week expeditions. This small preventive measure can make a big difference when you're pushing the limits of comfort and equipment.

Packing and Maintenance

What do you do when you wake up to a frosted-over shelter? Ironically, the colder it is, the easier it will be to remove this frost layer before packing up for the day's travel. A simple shake of the shelter while erect will usually eradicate 70 percent of the frost. Try to resist doing any shaking until you are fully out of the shelter and all your gear is packed up; otherwise you'll end up with a light morning snow squall under your tarp.

The last thing to discuss with shelters is the wintertime reality no one likes to discuss. When the snow begins to pile up, no matter which shelter you've chosen, the reality is that you will need to leave the cozy confines of your sleeping bag to clean the accumulating mass of snow from the shelter and surroundings. The frequency of these maintenance intervals obviously correlates to the rate of snowfall and hierarchy of shelter choice; the more burly a shelter, the more weight in snow it can withstand. At best, the diminishing square footage under the shelter will become a minor nuisance. At worst, damage to the shelter could contribute to a bent pole or complete fabric failure. The universal truth is that lack of diligence in this endeavor will result in your, quite literally, being buried alive.

An effective preventive measure is to dig out your shelter BEFORE retiring for the night. By digging a trough and sloping the surrounding ground away from the shelter, you can buy yourself some time by providing a place for the snow to shed to. The protection of a tree's canopy can further delay accumulating snow, as the tree will act as a natural snow shed. It's common to toss and turn at night. Use these opportunities to give the shelter's rain fly a periodic tap to help encourage the accumulating snow to shed. Eventually this built-up snow will accumulate up the walls of the shelter. Never be fooled by the sound of silence. It's easy to think the storm has stopped, but it's more likely that you've been misled by the insulative nature of the snow encapsulating your shelter.

Kitchen Design

The option of where to cook comes down to two locations: nestled in the comfort of your shelter and sleeping bag, where the dangers of spills and flammable materials are ever present, or a dedicated cooking area. Conditions, experience, and personal preference generally will dictate which is right for you.

Winter kitchen setups can be some of the most elaborate designs and layouts. The sky is the limit with access to malleable materials like snow. Kitchen counters and shelves can go a long way to add comfort and ergonomics, if not style points. By shoveling out a pit about 3 to 4 feet deep in an arch or rectangular shape, you can create a surface that is at countertop level and also provides a natural windbreak. Carve out a shelf about a foot below the counter to create a level, protected platform for cooking. This protected area will help minimize fuel use and expedite cooking times. If you want to get even more elaborate, you can dig deeper in order to string a tarp overhead and carve in benches for sitting. Glam it up if you have the time and energy, especially if you are planning on basing out of this camp for several days.

Alternatively, you may just want to crawl into your sleeping bag and cook beside your setup. If you have a stove with a very controlled flame, like the Trail Designs Ti Tri, you can even cook in some shelters or just outside the door. It's very nice to be able to cook while in your sleeping bag; just make sure you don't burn or spill anything! If you're in a tarp, it can help to curl under your groundsheet to create a little cooking area in the shelter, slightly away from the wall. It should give you just enough room, with a buffer from your sleeping bag, pad, and tarp wall. If need be, unzip the door a little or reach below the tarp and cook just outside where it's still reachable from your cozy sleeping bag.

SLEEPING WARM

Your day's travel was challenging, scenic, and surreal. What better way to end the day than a perfect night's sleep? Much trepidation around winter camping is rooted in the fear of sleeping cold. Not just cold, but FREEZING cold. The pessimistic approach is to view sleeping in a cold environment as a burden to bear, surviving the night with a few winks and even more teeth-chattering shivers. For the more enlightened, a proper winter night's sleep means sinking into a cocoon of warmth, draped in lofty down and the body-molding comfort of thick sleeping pads.

As discussed in the Sleep Systems section, now that we have the proper equipment in tow, it's time to optimize its effectiveness. With a well-protected campsite in our favor we can now switch to more micro-level adjustments of creature comforts to ensure a restful night. Follow these fundamental simple steps to success:

Stay on your sleeping pad! Nothing loses heat from the body quicker than the convective chill of sleeping directly on snow. Prep your sleeping spot by leveling the area to prevent the perpetual slips, slides, and drifts that will send you into a tailspin of constant adjustments throughout the night. You can take this site prep one step further by creating a slight depression or trough for your body to nest into. Snow is easy to mold when soft, so do this prep work before the snow turns into ice from your body heat and weight. Items like boots and food bags can create bumpers down the side of your sleeping pad and even elevate the edges, further preventing you from slipping off your pad. Fight the urge to skip this simple preventive remedy.

Don't breathe in your bag! As tempting as it is to fully submerge yourself within the sleeping bag, by doing so you are introducing copious amounts of moisture inside your bag via perspiration from your breath. A wet bag is a sad bag. Use the draw cords on your sleeping bag to seal in the heat of your sleeping bag, and close the bag snugly around your face if using a mummy bag. Keep your face warm by using balaclavas and neck gaiters. Pulling a neck gaiter up to your mouth and then pulling a beanie down over the tip of your nose works well. With this method, you can breathe uninhibited and maintain the warmth on your face. For the coldest of nights, pull the neck gaiter over your mouth and breathe through your nose during the night. This may take some getting used to. It's also fine to breathe through the neck gaiter fabric, which will effectively pre-warm the air coming in but leave a patch of soggy fabric in the morning.

Minimize movement! For sleepers who are prone to tossing and turning, this will be the hardest practice to train yourself in. Every time you move during the night, your body's movements act as an air pump, pushing valuable heat out of the top of your sleeping bag. Furthermore, when you roll from your back to your stomach, or vice versa, it will take a few moments for the compressed insulation to loaf back up.

The beauty of using sleep systems like quilts and head insulation that moves with you is that, unlike with traditional mummy sleeping bags, you can get in the habit of moving within the sleeping bag without disturbing the orientation of the bag itself. The downside of this strategy with traditional sleeping bags is that you end up turning away from the head opening and breathing into the side of the sleeping bag hood.

Don't sweat it! Let's fully debunk the myth that sleeping naked is the warmest method for sleeping warm. The reason this effect is felt is that when sleeping in the nude, heat from your core is more easily able to circulate down to your extremities. What this model of thermal regulation depends on is that the insulation with the sleeping bag is the sole means of retaining warmth, thus not utilizing the ultralight ethos of multiuse—in this case, incorporating our insulating layers into our sleep system.

The opposite end of the spectrum is fully wrapping oneself in insulating clothing. This model relies on a microclimate of warmth keeping each extremity warm independently— the trifecta of down parkas, down booties, and down pants! Without some heat circulating throughout the bag, this model can feel downright cold.

The trick is finding the sweet spot, which will necessitate experimentation, since everyone is metabolically different. The bottom line is that we are ultimately trying to prevent being so frantic with fear about being cold that we overdo our insulation systems and begin to sweat. You will be the warmest when you first enter your sleeping bag. You are metabolically awake and have likely just eaten a calorically dense meal to keep your internal fires stoked. It is tempting to enter the sleeping bag wearing everything, but then you will overheat and begin to sweat, usually without noticing. As we nod off, our metabolic rate dips at about the same rate as our sweat begins to cool and condense, and our bags inevitably seep thermal efficiency. You'll be left with the dreaded damp chills and no means to add warmth back into your bag.

A better solution is to bring a few insulation layers into the sleeping bag with you. This will pre-warm them and provide quick, convenient access if you wake up chilled. Feet and core tend to be the areas that feel the coldest the quickest, while legs rarely need much attention. The opposite is true if you begin to overheat or wake up damp. Remove any unnecessary insulation layers, or open the sleeping bag briefly to let excess heat escape—all to prevent further sweating. If you anticipate getting cold, use the layers that you are pre-warming to add warmth to your feet by sliding your feet in the sleeves or partially in the pants.

Fill the void! Any dead airspace within your sleeping bag will need to be warmed by your body's heat. Unused clothing can be brought inside the sleeping bag to help fill these voids. Draping clothing over your core and extremities can promote additional warmth without sacrificing the circulation of warm air. Using a rolled-up jacket to bolster the draft collar is an easy and effective way to prevent loss of heat out of the top of the bag. If you're shorter than your bag's stated height limit, stuff any additional clothing or soft items down into the footbox of the bag to fill this unused space. Alternatively, you can tie off or fold under this unused section of the footbox to achieve the same effect.

Keep things cookin'! If you wake up chilled, do some light exercises in your bag to get your heart rate up and burn some heat-producing calories. Crunches or planking are easy and effective ways to get the internal furnace burning again. For an extra challenge, try swapping your socks from one foot to another. The frustration in doing so will surely get your pulse elevated!

Since it is common to be dormant for more hours during winter than in summer, remember that there will be a longer time period between dinner and breakfast. This dip in caloric intake can be felt by the effects of waking up cold. Keep the furnace burning all night by eating fatty "slow-burning" foods (like peanut butter) right before bed, and keep some snacks nearby for a midnight nosh. Keep some water nearby as well to stay above the hydration curve. Remember, it takes thin blood to get down to your extremities!

Cheat the system! If maintaining thermal regulation is challenging on your own, there is no shame in adding external heat sources to your sleep system. Hot water bottles are a great way to provide a temporary heat source during the night. Remember to factor the added fuel to boil this water into your fuel needs. Add boiling water to a water bottle that firmly seals, and place a sock or cozy over the bottle to prevent it from burning you. This will also extend the time the heat is released. Your water will still be warm by morning for a nice way to start the hydration cycle. Place the bottle in high heat-transfer areas like armpits, stomach, and the groin for maximum warmth.

Heed nature's call! There is an adage that you will sleep cold if you hold it all night—the theory being that it takes precious energy to keep the urine at body temperature. While not fully subscribing to this logic, one thing is for certain: All the tossing and turning you endure by NOT going to bathroom will surely keep you awake. It may seem a daunting task to leave the comforts of the nest and venture into the dark and snow to use the bathroom. Fight the laziness, and just get up! You'll have the added benefit of getting your pulse back up which, in addition to the relief of using the bathroom, will help you fall back asleep feeling warm again.

For the truly skilled, use of a dedicated pee bottle can be a wintertime game changer in the bathroom front. If sleeping in a floorless tarp, simply rolling over to one side and have at it—the true minimalist's method! No added fuss, gear or cultural standards. It's best to consult with your tent/tarp mate if this is an acceptable practice!

GETTING MOVING

The beauty of the morning routine during winter is that you have five-star hotel accommodations under the guise of sheer laziness, result being to stay in the warmth of bed as long as possible. This means (self-served) breakfast in bed, pre-warmed socks and clothing, and sipping hot drinks while reviewing maps and enjoying general morning musings. This can provide a helpful perspective if predawn starts under a glaze of ice and frost aren't your thing.

While the sequence of routine will shift slightly, the end goal will be to achieve the same results in an equally efficient manner in winter as in summer. This may trickle down to the order in which you pack up and even how you pack the contents of your backpack. By making minor tweaks to your overall process, you'll end up with a faster and warmer routine that gets you on the move and on the trail sooner. File these simple tips under the banner of "Wake up and GO!"

Stay in bed! Nearly every morning routine can be done from the warmth of your sleeping bag. Indulge in this fact, and use it to your advantage. Everything from eating breakfast, melting additional water if necessary, brushing your teeth, prepping and packing items, to reviewing maps should all be done while you're still in your sleeping bag. Don't get too complacent in this model though; precious daylight is burning. Plan on at least 45 minutes to an hour for an efficient wake-up routine in winter.

Pre-warm everything! Take the time to place any articles of clothing that you're going to be wearing in the morning inside your sleeping bag to pre-warm them. This is especially true if you're changing back into damp base layers, gloves, boot liners, and socks from the prior day's travel. Even pre-warming your insoles can go a long way toward getting those toes warm in the morning.

Sleeping with your boots inside your sleeping bag is a personal preference. This practice is hugely uncomfortable but helps set your feet up for success. Slipping your feet into frozen boots in the morning is not only nightmarishly frustrating but also a sure-fire way to increase your odds of getting cold-related injuries to your feet. Extremities are the hardest regions to keep warm, so setting off with the right foot forward in the morning is worth the discomfort of sleeping with your boots inside your sleeping bag.

The entire morning routine can happen from the warmth of your sleeping bag. Here you can eat breakfast, get dressed for the day, review your route plan and get 90 percent packed for the day.
Shawn Forry

Biting into a frozen energy bar is never a great way to start your morning. Pre-warm them by placing them in your sleeping bag at night or next to your skin prior to a break.
Justin Lichter

One key thing to highlight is that we don't want all that moisture in our boots to filter into our sleeping bags. Our efforts are geared toward keeping the boots warm and unfrozen, not drying them out. Placing them inside a pack liner or similar waterproof bag will help that moisture from permeating the sleeping bag.

Even food staples and hygiene items are more pleasant when warmed up. Biting into a nearly frozen protein bar is a good way to break a tooth in the morning. Trying to put in contacts with frozen solution never works either. If traveling by ski, place your skins in your insulating jacket when you first wake up to get a jump on warming up the adhesive backing for better adhesion in the morning. Use water bottles that seal well so you can sleep with your water so it doesn't freeze solid and turn your bottles into dead weight. Basically, if it CAN freeze, it WILL freeze; anticipate what these things might be before you go to bed.

Plan ahead and prepare! Reviewing the day's travel now or the night before is the best way to prevent future unpleasantness. Knowing what hazards lie ahead, where flowing water or future camping could be found, are much easier questions to answer under the protection and warmth of camp, especially if weather conditions are looking unfavorable. A food plan can be set aside and packed in an accessible place for the day. These extra measures will minimize how many times you have to get inside your pack during the day, preventing unwanted moisture from entering the contents or getting on the maps, and helping streamline meal breaks for the day. Having two separate food stuff sacks can help organize this system. One food bag holds dinners and breakfast, while the other contains all snack and lunch items and can be packed in a more accessible location.

Pack accordingly! The sequence in which items are packed can streamline both your morning and evening camp scenes. Once you're fully dressed, the sleep system should be packed first. Unneeded clothing and food items can now go in and be sealed off in some sort of waterproof system like a trash compactor bag. The shelter can now come down and be placed near the top for easy access when arriving at your next campsite. This leaves only snacks for the day and the insulating layer you're wearing to be packed last. Any additional water storage can be wrapped in the insulating jacket to prevent freezing during the day. This model creates a highly efficient system in the event of extreme weather.

The action is GO! Ten steps to get you on the trail quicker:

1. Wake up! Put on gloves and insulation top layer to maintain warmth while completing morning chores.

Keeping frequently needed items toward the top of your pack is extremely important for efficiency, especially during inclement weather.
Justin Lichter

2. Eat breakfast and sip water. Look over maps quickly while eating.

3. Pre-warm clothes and dress for the day. Sequence clothing so that only the insulation layer must come off prior to departure.

4. Deflate sleeping pad while brushing teeth, and pack any ditties in their stuff sack.

5. Put on footwear and transition into packing.

6. Pack sleep system, extra food, and cook gear.

7. Use the bathroom.

8. Take down tarp.

9. Pack shelter, snacks, and insulation layer.

10. GO!

MOVING DURING THE DAY

The day's travel should stand at the forefront of our motivation for winter travel. If the camp scene is our respite and recovery, the travel is the reward of our efforts. Here we

Pristine beauty through challenging conditions is a natural motivator.
Shawn Forry

experience the blanketing of white through tranquil forest and mountainous environments, an opportunity to see familiar terrain in a different light. As conditions erode the edges of our comfort, a balance must be struck to maintain presence in the passing surroundings while moving efficiently to maintain thermal equilibrium. With a few tweaks to common summertime travel systems, we can maintain our "cake and eat it" duality. We'll dive into a few key concepts to help keep us ambling down the trail at an enjoyable pace and presence.

STAYING DRY

A mantra to incorporate into your vocabulary is "If it's not dry, it's drying." The foundation of this concept is that with wintertime's smaller margin of error in consequence versus risk, we must take every precaution to maximize our abilities to maintain warmth at all costs. Our layering system is the heart of this equation. Being constantly surrounded by moisture and minimum sunlight is a recipe for accumulating sogginess in our clothing and equipment when measured over a multitude of days.

The first step in this overarching concept is to reduce the chances of getting wet in the first place. As obvious as that sounds, the conditions are forever against us. Every time we kneel in the snow, sit for a break, brush snow with our gloved hand, or have the unfortunate

"If it's not dry, it's drying." Never leave your gloves or any other article of clothing lying around in the snow where it will get wet or, worse, lost. Store gloves inside a jacket pocket to keep them dry and warm during quick tasks or to dry out during the day's travel.
Shawn Forry

timing to have a "tree bomb" of snow drop down our backs, we are being exposed to moisture. Over the course of a day this can escalate to enough moisture build up to necessitate wringing water droplets from our gloves and socks, in addition to a general feeling of dampness. Simple mindfulness of this limitation goes a long way toward prevention. Keep a small section of foam pad handy for sitting on at breaks or sit on your pack (something we would never condone in the summer), immediately brush snow from clothing if contact is made before any melting can occurs, and get in the habit of "de-bombing" laded branches of snow with a trekking pole before ducking under them. Additionally, keep zippers closed when ventilation is not required, and minimize the amount of time you're opening up your pack to the elements throughout the day. Completely brushing snow from yourself and footwear prior to entering your shelter further helps keep moisture in check. A frequent self-audit while traveling will keep you in-check and mindful of when and why dampness is occurring.

When things inevitably do get damp, your body is a key source of consistent heat. Jackets with internal pockets

To prevent the icy surprise of a tree bomb dropping down the back of your neck, take the time to clean overhanging branches of snow before passing under them.
Justin Lichter

Multitask whenever possible. Taking every opportunity to dry items is essential for long-term moisture management. Minimize contact with the snow by sitting on a foam pad or pack.
Justin Lichter

are perfect for tossing in damp socks and spare gloves while on the go. Tucking items down your waistband is another convenient way to utilize the heat coming off your thighs without being overly chilled by having these damp articles along your skin. Items can always be on the "dry rack," either throughout the day's travel or inside your sleeping bag at night. Think of every source of heat, including your body, as a finite heat source from which you are trying to extract every last BTU.

Seemingly counterintuitive is the notion that things will sun-dry in subfreezing conditions. We have science to thank for the concept of sublimation, which is the act of solids skipping the liquid phase and going straight into the gaseous state. On a sunny cold day, laying out your sleeping bag will actually help remove some of the moisture buried deep in the insulation and atop the shell. The colder it is, the more effective this process will be due to the temperature gradient of the item and the ambient atmosphere. (The same is true for why hydration is so important when we are traveling in subzero conditions!) While not nearly the thermal efficiency of summertime drying, every little bit helps ensure our clothing and equipment continue operating at maximum potential. These small things are all a nod to the idea that "if it's not dry, it's drying."

STAYING WARM

Overdressing is likely one of the most common mistakes of winter travel. Consumed by the fear of being reduced to a frigid state of misery, we fail to listen to the feedback loop between our body and our brain. This is the intersection between staying dry and staying warm. For perspective, during extreme physical output, it's not out of the question to be stripped down to a short-sleeve base layer in subzero temperatures. The lack of awareness or acceptance in these times to reduce layers directly leads to a breach of rule #1, and we find ourselves damp from our own efforts.

If we think of the analogy of layers as an onion, a similar correlation is defined with how, what, and when we wear various articles of clothing. In the matrix of base, wind, water, and insulation layers, there is a dizzying array of combinations in clothing, effort, and weather conditions to maintain an appropriate comfort level of heat. On the flipside, with properly selected clothing, this spectrum of flexibility can easily cater to any condition we might face. The underlying intent is to reach an acceptable thermal balance of being *slightly* chilled but comfortable when travelling. Obviously, the far ends of the spectrum are rapid shivers and being drenched in perspiration; any tolerance we have for being on the *slightly* chilled side of equilibrium will go a long way in minimizing the effects of sweat buildup in our underlying clothing layers.

Despite the fact that it's below freezing, windy, and snowing, stripping down to just a base layer and wind shell is often required to prevent overheating.
Justin Lichter

The inconvenience of stopping to "de-layer" is one of the highest contributors to complacency in this rule. The frustration of micro-adjustments to refine clothing choices is nestled in the reality of stopping to pack, repack, unclip, re-clip, re-layer, and de-layer while ultimately trying to reach the end of day's destination by dark. The other contributing factor is that heat is not distributed evenly across regions of your body. For example, a hat will cover your forehead, ears, and the nape of your neck, but each of these areas has varying coverage needs.

A common routine for maintaining the proper heat output is to know that we are going to warm up as we begin to travel. During summer it is a common practice to fully strip out of isolative camp layers and down to hiking attire prior to departing camp. For winter we refine this practice slightly to depart camp "as is" and only de-layer once we begin to heat up. To overcome the initial hurdle of chilly extremities, it is ideal to hold on to a bit of excessive core warmth until this warm blood begins to fully circulate. The discipline to stop and de-layer in a timely manner is paramount to ensure that we preserve the thermal integrity of our isolative camp layers. We may even forgo the use of poles/trekking poles until we achieve warmth in our hands. Upon initially departing camp, we may find it preferable to stow hands inside jacket pockets. Swinging blood down into our hands and feet through leg kicks and arm windmills is a common technique to "cheat" warm blood into these extremities and give the temporary perception of warmth. Even the sternest of hikers can be caught in a series of jumping jacks and other heart-elevating cardiovascular acts prior to camp departure to help accelerate the warmth of travel.

Pete Townsend's famous "windmills" in the band The Who actually stem from his extensive polar expeditions. Moves like this force warm blood down into the tiny capillaries in the fingers for temporary warmth. The sensation is only temporary, so keep the inner furnace stoked to keep pushing that warm blood around the system. No time for lounging now!
Justin Lichter

The latest dance craze? Possibly. Shoulder shrugs with hands at a 90-degree angle pump a surprising amount of blood into the hands. Best tried without anyone around, or with music playing.
Justin Lichter

While not as effective as arm windmills, a similar technique can be used to force warm blood down into the feet. Better yet is to increase the heart rate through jumping jacks, deep squats, and constant movement.
Justin Lichter

Preventing overheating and being saturation from sweat is key to staying warm and dry no matter the season. Many folks are scared of underdressing in winter. Be proactive. Stripping excess layers prior to a climb and opening ventilation zippers help prevent the dreaded clammy cold chills.
Justin Lichter

Once moving and warm, it takes a surprisingly minimal amount of clothing to maintain our equilibrium of output and environment. Knowing which areas of the body to vent and which to cover is the product of experience and experimentation. Ultra-thin wind shells over a long-sleeve base layer are a perfect combination for keeping the chill at bay over the core. Side vents work well for minimizing the overheating of legs, an area that routinely requires very little in the way of warmth and protection. Hands and feet commonly need more warmth while also being some of the sweatiest areas of the body. It can seem a Sisyphean task to properly regulate the heat in hands and feet during winter, as there are fewer options for adjustment.

Feet especially are largely affected by our mode of transportation and the overarching need to seal moisture out. The application of vapor barriers is a worthwhile tool to consider if subzero conditions are present in order to fully realize the benefits of VBLs in maintaining foot and hand insulation.

To maintain warmth during any routine break, it is essential to capture the heat coming off our bodies, especially our core and head. Finding a safeguarded location, away from wind and precipitation, goes a long way in extending the comfort of a break. Tarps and mids are quick to set up for a midday break if packed appropriately in our packs. Once our physical output is reduced during a break, it doesn't take long to cool and chill past the point of comfort. Counterintuitive to nature, it is essential to throw on an isolative layer immediately after stopping, regardless of how overheated you may feel. The objective is to trap all the excess heat coming off our bodies to carry us through the duration of the break. It is much easier and more

Throw on a puffy jacket immediately after stopping for a break to trap the heat coming off your body. Note Trauma sitting on a folded-up Tyvek groundsheet to insulate himself from the cold.
Shawn Forry

efficient for your body to stay warm than to warm it back up once chilled. Throwing a waterproof jacket over the isolative layer can further prevent heat loss through convective wind. Don't be timid about using all those hoods on each of the various layers you are wearing! They help seal in the heat dissipating out of the top of jackets and trap the heat coming off your head. Don't forget to sit on the foam pad or your pack during breaks as well to prevent the chilling effects of losing precious heat through your bottom.

STAYING SAFE

Linking these strategies can go a long way toward feeling success and competence during the day's travel. Some days can feel overwhelmingly blustery, but this should not detract from the fundamentals of staying warm, dry, fed, and hydrated. If any of these foundational blocks is

TIP

To prevent the damaging effects of chilblains and windburn, slather Vaseline over exposed skin. Inuits have been doing something similar for centuries by using animal fats. You'll also have the added benefit of a sense of additional warmth on the areas covered, since Vaseline acts as a minor insulating layer as it prevents convective heat loss.

Between a rock and a hard place—finding reprieve from the weather during a break. "Do I need to go back out there?" "Should I set up camp here?" are questions to ask yourself to inform proper decision making.
Justin Lichter

diminished or eliminated, the stage is set for consequences to set in. The humiliation of having to cease a day's travel should never trump safety. A series of questions to ask yourself is "Do I need to be right here, right now, in these conditions?" The answer should unanimously be YES! Otherwise, set up the shelter and call it a day.

Taking survey of the broader picture can add objectivity. Factoring in alternative routes, food rations, weather patterns, and the goals of the trip can help reprioritize and illuminate smart decision making. It is important to highlight that major incidents in the mountains are rarely the result of a singular poor decision. The creeping accumulation of seemingly benign "red flags" set up the domino effect of dire consequences. Ignoring degrading weather conditions, getting too destination driven, and/or failing to operate from a place of competence are only a few reasons negative consequence occur. Being honest with one's abilities and erring on the side of caution are both ingredients for smart decision making in the mountains.

STAYING EFFICIENT

Winter travel, no matter your method, is always going to take considerably more effort and time than summertime treks. Expectations regarding mileage per day and travel times should follow suit. The effort required to saunter down the trail during summertime pales in comparison to breaking trail in fresh-powder conditions. Mobility will be reduced with

Plan on at least a 30 percent reduction to your pace in the wintertime. Keep an "all day pace" mentally, and trade off breaking trail as frequently as needed.
Justin Lichter

By thinking two steps ahead, efficiency opens up possibilities to enjoy your sense of place.
Shawn Forry

the additional layers being worn, and the additional weight underfoot and on your back will diminish stamina. Heading into each day's travel with an "all day pace" is the cure-all for adding efficiency to your travel. There is no sense in trying to fight the conditions, so work with them. As frustration seeps in, our movements become forced and overexerted. Slowing down, setting realistic expectations, and being present to changing conditions will help optimize efficiency during the day. As a rule of thumb, plan on at least a 30 percent reduction in your pace and daily mileage from summer, even more as the beginner's learning curve takes shape.

Simple steps to incorporate forward thinking in the day's routine can prevent delays in transitions, which can surprisingly add up to a gross amount of lost time during the day. Before stopping for a break, think about the type of break location you are looking for, which layers you are going to put on, and where they are in your pack. What are you going to eat, and what is required in the preparation? What other tasks are required during this stop? Bathroom? Equipment adjustment/repair? Map review? Think of the sequence of these actions to maximize efficiency. Reviewing maps while eating and adjusting layers for the next section of travel go a long way in carving a few more minutes out of the day. The more you can consolidate breaks and adjustments, the less you will have to stop and waste time. Stubbornness in old habits will forever be the limiting factor in developing this skill set.

STAYING HYDRATED

The irony of being surrounded by water without the ability to drink is only accentuated when afloat upon a rescue raft in the middle of sea. In winter, access to water is greatly hindered when it's constantly in the frozen state. Furthermore, one of the biggest misconceptions of outdoor winter pursuits is that your level of hydration is markedly less. While true that you will likely sweat less during a typical day in winter than a 105°F tromp across the desert, winter hydration is prioritized by the body's ability to circulate warmth. Winter air is also notably drier, and your lungs work harder to humidify and warm this air. This is even more vital when at altitude. Have cold hands? It may help to drink more.

Think of the body and its circulation system as a giant engine. In winter we are told to let our car engines warm up before we begin our commute to work in the morning. The reason is that, due to the colder conditions, your engine's motor oil will be thicker, hence not adequately lubricating the smaller recesses of the engine. The heat of the engine must warm up the oil, increasing its viscosity to ensure the lubrication needs are meet on all rotary surfaces. The same is true for the human body.

As we become dehydrated, our blood literally becomes thicker. The capillaries in the far extremities of our body need warm, thin blood to appropriately flow and warm the surrounding cells. The primitive instinct of the body to shunt warm blood to our core to preserve primary bodily functions further exploits the challenges of not only staying hydrated but also staying warm in winter.

We get it. It's hard to drink when it's so dang cold out! Further frustration commonly stems from ill-fated attempts to remain hydrated from frozen water bottles and hydration bladders. Key strategies to combat dehydration in winter are to become opportunistic in your approach and to add indulgence. Much the same approach to hiking through arid desert environments, any open source of water becomes an oasis of opportunity.

Due to the excessive amount of time it takes to melt snow or ice for water, every opportunity you can find to source flowing water adds valuable minutes to your day, especially important when daylight is already extremely limited. It can become impractical to pause midday to melt more snow for consumption. Not to say you shouldn't if needed, but expect about 30 minutes of downtime to process about 1 liter of water. It can be equally as discouraging to be out of water as it is to find an open source of water that is inaccessible or challenging to reach. Caution should be applied when trying to access open water sources. Creekside snowbanks can collapse; openings in frozen-over creeks can present as deep troughs, with challenging consequences if you happen to fall in. Retrieving water using a thin cord tied to a water bottle can be an effective solution with enough patience. Keep your skis or snowshoes on to get water, as they will spread out your weight and help minimize impacts. Inch toward the water, and kick steps and flat platforms along the way. Getting soaked and hypothermic should never be the outcome of trying to stay hydrated. Only utilize water sources

Left: Beyond helping you stay hydrated, every open water source, no matter how small, becomes an opportunity to shave the hours it takes to melt water off your daily routine.
Right: When water is scarce, searching for a safe place to access it should not be ignored. While this creek bed is only about 3 feet deep, sometimes you'll come across 20-foot-plus wells.
Justin Lichter

where hazards can be mitigated. Keep in mind that larger creeks or rivers are less likely to be completely frozen over. If the ice on lakes isn't too thick, you may be able to punch through with a trekking pole point or handle, or you can carry an ice screw. Also keep in mind that puncturing the ice can often weaken the surrounding area.

The real question becomes: If access to water becomes scarce during the day, how do you manage sourcing and carrying enough water to stay fully hydrated throughout the day? Anyone who has attempted to use summertime strategies in water management has likely quickly been confronted with a frozen water bottle or hydration hose. A key shift will be in the morning and evening camp routines. Under the warmth and protection of your shelter and sleep system lies the convenience to dedicate time in the day to not only enjoy a hot beverage but also prepare enough water for the day's travel.

So how do we ensure that our nightly efforts to adequately prepare ourselves to stay hydrated pay off? We need this freshly melted water to stay in liquid form, not only through the night but also throughout the next day's travel. As previously discussed, we can use this freshly boiled water as a heat source inside our sleeping bags through the night, effectively serving double duty. Storing your water bottle inside your pack wrapped in an insulating layer that you are already carrying will also prevent premature freezing. Yes, these methods will take more time in the morning and render your water inaccessible during the day, but these minor inconveniencies can go a long way to maintain hydration, as well as sanity. An in-between compromise is to store your immediate water needs in an external bottle, wrapped in a cozy, and placed upside down in a side pocket of your pack. Make sure to place the bottle upside down, or else the lid might freeze shut. During each snack break, you can refill the external water bottle to ensure hydration stays accessible. Alternatively, but not the most comfortable, you can store your water in an inside pocket in your jacket, making a sling to hold your water bottle or water carrying system underneath your exterior layers. Use an Aquatherm-type insulator product, or simply carry your bottle upside down so the lid doesn't freeze on and an ice lens doesn't form, preventing water from pouring out.

When you melt snow for water, try to densely pack the snow into the pot. Colder, drier snow has less moisture content than ice or other types of snow, so it can take longer to get quantities of water from it. When it first starts melting, you will often get a burning smell. This is completely normal and, if you have some water available, can be alleviated by adding a small amount to the pot before you put it on the flame. As the snow melts it will shrink and occupy less and less volume in the pot. As this happens, keep adding snow to keep the pot full. You will need multiple fillings of snow to get one pot load of water. If you can find corn snow or ice, it will be much more efficient (in time and fuel) than melting cold, dry snow. This may entail digging down into the snowpack or choosing a specific campsite based on the snow conditions.

With a few minor adjustments to our daily routine, achieving basic requirements like nutrition and hydration will become commonplace. These two vital functions are the very foundation of safe and effective travel. Taking the time to find a diet and routine that works for you will set you up for future success.

STAYING ENERGIZED: FOOD, COOKING, AND OTHER CONSIDERATIONS

Most conversations in the backcountry eventually evolve into a food-porn dialogue of greasy food, sweet treats, and a general disdain for dehydrated nonsense. The priorities and considerations for winter travel can be both enlightening and discouraging. Traveling in a literal freezer can open food options that are a non-reality during summer's heat. The comfort to consume elaborate meals in these same temps can marginalize extravagance in favor of efficiency. The bottom line is that there is a high need to consume ample calories to stay warm and satiated. For perspective, it is said that the body burns the same number of calories in 5 minutes of shivering as it does in 1 hour of sitting still. Not that we should ever be in a state of shivering during a winter trip, this is stated merely to highlight that in general the body is going to burn 500 to 1,000 calories more per day in winter to cover the same metabolic output. Travel is more challenging, our bodies are working harder to maintain thermal regulation, and breaks will be minimal due to the cold. This all adds up to more time on the go at a higher output, despite the shorter travel days. Your food plan should match this accordingly.

Hiker hunger is real! Thanks to famed hiker Scott Williamson for helping us recoup precious calories during a town stop along our winter PCT trek.
Justin Lichter

The biggest factor we want to consider is getting the most bang for our buck in terms of calories and those that take the least amount of time and effort to consume. Calories-per-ounce is a common metric for comparing food staples. By following this formula we can minimize outright food weight while maximizing the nutrition and caloric efficiency of the foods we are selecting. It is no wonder that dehydrated foods are the hallmark of backcountry meals—it makes no sense to carry water weight.

A common misconception is that sugary treats are going to have the highest calorie efficiency. While tasty, these empty calories do very little to fuel us down the trail and minimize our pack weight. Fats are the densest in terms of calories (9 calories per gram), while both proteins and sugars weigh in at 4 calories per gram. What this means in practice is that fatty foods like nuts, nut butters, and fried foods have more than twice as many calories than any other food staple for the same weight. This is why good old trail mix has become the mascot for backcountry travel. While shopping the grocery store aisles, get in the habit of looking at the calories per serving or, more precisely, doing some basic math to factor the calories per ounce. A general rule of thumb is that foods with 100 calories per ounce or less are less efficient and are either very sugary or filled with water weight. Aim for foods that average about 140 to 150 calories per ounce. Nuts and nut butters have upwards of 200 calories per ounce, while straight fat has nearly 240 calories per ounce! What this equates to in practice is that with careful regard to calories per ounce, we should be able to anticipate 2 to 2.5 pounds of

Picking the right foods will have a huge effect on your energy, pack weight, and overall backcountry enjoyment. The progression from grocery store to stuff sack can seem overwhelming. The food highlighted here fueled Pepper's unsupported FKT of the Colorado Trail. More than 76,000 calories and 34 pounds of food were carried from the start. Nutritional and calorically dense foods were a priority.
Shawn Forry

food per day, or about 4,000 to 5,500 calories daily. That's plenty to keep you motoring down the trail.

Math obviously has its merits, but palatability should also be considered, if not prioritized. Very few people can stomach straight butter or olive oil for days on end. If your food options are not appealing, there is a high probability that you won't eat them. There are plenty of food options that are both tasty and high in calories: almond butter, chocolate, trail mixes, granolas, dried meats and cheeses like Parmesan, chips, and pretzels, to name a few. Olive oil or butter is a great additive to any dinner to bulk up calories and add taste. Trail hunger only goes so far toward making unpalatable foods palatable. If it doesn't sound appealing in the confines of your kitchen, it's probably not going to cut the mustard in the backcountry.

Food	Calories per Ounce
Canola or Olive Oil	240
Mayonnaise	200
Brazil Nuts	185
Fried Pork Rinds	175
Mixed Nuts	170
Pringles	170
Peanut Butter	166

Food	Calories per Ounce
Fritos Corn Chips	160
Ruffles Potato Chips	160
Ritz Crackers	158
Hershey's Milk Chocolate	152
Chips Ahoy! Cookies	150
Peanut M&M's	147
Coconut (dried, sweetened, shredded)	143
KIND Energy Bar	140
Pork Bacon	140
Cheese and Peanut Butter Crackers	140
Doritos & Chips	140
Wheat Thins /Triscuit Crackers	140
Plain M&M's	140
Powdered Nondairy Creamer	140
Snickers Candy Bar	136
Popcorn	135
Chocolate-covered Doughnut	135
Pepperoni	130
Chex Mix (prepared per package instructions)	130
Chow Mein Noodles	130
Granola	129
Ramen Noodles	124
Saltine Crackers	120
Cracker Jack	120
Pop-Tarts	117
Lipton Noodles and Sauce	116
Hot Cocoa Mix	115
Cheese	110
Sugar-sweetened Drink Mix	107
Nutri-Grain Bars	106
Pasta (100 percent semolina)	105
Stove Top Stuffing Mix	103
Instant Rice (e.g., Minute Rice)	102
Lipton Dinner	102

Food	Calories per Ounce
Bulgur (uncooked)	100
Fig Newtons	100
Quick-cooking Oats	100
Grape-Nuts Cereal	100
Jell-O Instant Chocolate Pudding	100
Fruit Roll-Ups (store-bought)	100
Protein Powder	100
Coconut (raw)	100
Cream Cheese	100
Nonfat Dry Milk	98
Instant Potato Flakes	98
Instant Miso Soup	98
Summer Sausage	95
Dried Fruit	92
Flour Tortillas	89
Spam	85
Pitted Dates	84
Cheese Whiz	83
Beef Jerky (store-bought)	80
Honey and Jelly	80
Bagels, Pita, Bread	78
Turkey Bacon	70
English Muffins	61
Fresh Avocado	60
Tuna (in oil)	52
Hummus (prepared)	47
Canned Chicken (in water)	40
Beef or Chicken Bullion	40
Tuna (in springwater)	30
Canadian Bacon	30
Bananas	26
Tofu	18
Fresh Fruit and Vegetables	5–15
Coffee or Tea (no milk or sugar)	0

One of the great advantages of winter travel is that food spoilage will be nonexistent, so we can leverage that in our favor. Butter can easily be carried as a calorically dense additive without the worry of liquefying. Cheeses will last days longer, and even items from the freezer aisle at the grocery store are not out of the question.

We also want to consider food prep time. Meals like breakfast and dinner can be eaten within the confines of a warm sleeping bag. Meals throughout the day should have careful consideration toward minimal prep time. When temps are consistently below freezing during the day, snacking and/or grazing is a better approach than meals that require a lot of prep time. In summertime we might have the luxury of carefully crafting the perfect tortilla wrap with multiple ingredients delicately sliced and diced. For wintertime breaks during the day, factor about 15 to 20 minutes before a chill begins to settle in—far less if conditions are not favorable. Take the approach of single-serve food items that can easily be unpackaged. Energy bars, trail mixes, and string cheese are easy to eat on the go and require zero prep time. These types of foods can even be left in an easily accessible side pocket for quick access as energy reserves begin to deplete. If single-serve items are handy, you can even start snacking before the designated break time to help to make sure you are consuming enough calories despite the short window to stop. Keep your gourmet meals for the evening, and prioritize the "stuff your face and go" approach to your daytime meal selection.

STAYING RESPECTFUL: LEAVE NO TRACE

As outdoor recreationalists, protecting the natural spaces we travel through is one of the highest priorities toward being environmental stewards and ambassadors of preservation. Winter is one of the most tranquil times of year to be in the backcountry. Yet despite a lower user count, it is of upmost importance that we preserve the untarnished aspect of winter travel for the next passerby. In winter, every step we take and camp we make will be a temporary reminder of passage through a corridor. With the topography of winter acting as an optical blank canvas, it doesn't take much to negatively alter the visual aspect of our camp and travel scene, and create lasting disturbances.

Similar to summer travel, the fundamental ethos of Leave No Trace (LNT) still applies, with a few special considerations and alterations. As with any ethos, the underlying principle is that we do the best we can. In doing so, we not only increase the safety of our travel but also heighten the personal satisfaction that we are minimizing our impact. This foundation is akin to the overarching ethos of ultralight travel: minimal weight, minimal effort, minimal impact. The tie that binds these concepts is our overall awareness and skill set. As we encourage the next generation to explore these wild places, education and mentorship are two of our highest priorities.

Plan Ahead and Prepare

Proper preparation prevents piss poor performance. The emphasis to adequately prepare for your trip will minimize the "suffer-fest" potential and, in the worst-case scenario, the strain of emergency resources. Type II fun is laughable to recall in hindsight, yet it should not be the result of the irresponsible winter trekker. During your planning process, take the time to familiarize yourself with the local regulations, weather conditions, and anticipated hazards.

Winter conditions can change frequently, especially in regard to avalanche conditions. Understanding the underlying snowpack will greatly inform your travel plans and route. Make sure your skill set matches the skills required to have a safe and successful experience. If a particular skill is deficient, travel with a knowledgeable partner to gain experience, attend a local winter skills course, and/or plan your trips in a logical progression so as to not bite off more than you can chew. Day trips are great ways to practice with low consequences in order to solidify systems and concepts.

Best practices to consider:

- Plan for the worst with regard to extreme weather, hazards, and emergencies.

- Monitor snow conditions in the days leading up to your trip, and confirm and update your findings while in the backcountry. Carry an avalanche beacon, probe, and shovel—and know how to use them. Make sure your partners do too. Remember, you won't be able to save yourself!

- Educate yourself by taking a winter backcountry travel course.

- Travel with competent partners to increase your skills; never travel alone your first time in unfamiliar conditions. Leave your itinerary with family or friends.

- To minimize the chance of waste being left behind, repackage food into reusable containers/baggies.

Travel and Camp on Durable Surfaces

Traveling in snow conditions is one of the least impactful ways to experience the backcountry. As winter transitions to spring, all evidence of travel will literally melt away, leaving the underlying ground untrammeled. The effects of wind and continued precipitation will also contribute to eliminating any visual presence. As winter transitions to spring, it can also be one of the most fragile times of year with respect to the underlying vegetation and emerging mud season. Frozen lakes can be one of the least impactful campsites to consider. With eerie overnight groans coming from the expanding ice, it can be both a terrifying and memorable camping experience. Be sure all your wash water and bathroom visits still remain at least 200 feet from the water to minimize pollutants entering the watershed come spring thaw.

Best practices to consider:

- When possible, camp on compacted snow or rock surfaces void of fragile underlying vegetation.

- Be mindful of your overall camp location with regard to avalanche slides paths, cornices, and exposure to wind.

- Establish your camp out of view of prominent travel routes.

- Expedite the effect of wind and snow by taking the time to break down any snow benches, wind barriers, and snow structures you constructed. Disguise sites by shoveling a uniform amount of powdery snow over any impacted areas. Naturalizing the area by filling in any snow pits will also increase the safety of other travelers. No one will enjoy skiing into your unseen fire pit or snow bench during low-light conditions!

Dispose of Waste Properly

"Pack it in, pack it out" is one of the more recognizable tenants of LNT practices. We should extrapolate this one step further by stating, "Pack it in, pack more out," striving to truly leave each place better than we found it. The term "waste" can comprise many subjective measures. A balance will need to be struck in practicality and due diligence, as only the most dedicated trekker can truly pack out all waste.

Accounting for human waste is one of the more challenging aspects during winter; the reality is that the ground will most likely be buried under snow and/or completely frozen. In cold conditions, you will also want to be highly efficient in your bathroom visits to maintain basic comfort. Find areas protected from wind to increase comfort. Stomp down a stable platform to prevent off-balance mishaps and to allow ample room for the "drop zone." Kick snow over the area after urinating to cover unsightly stains in the snow. Urine becomes increasingly more yellow over time as the water separates from the mineral waste.

Hiker Michael ""Nacho" Vaz does the right thing and packs out multiple empty plastic jugs found at a water cache along the Continental Divide Trail.
Michael Vaz

Best practices to consider:

- Pack it in, pack it out. Pack out everything you bring with you. Burying trash and litter in the snow or ground is unacceptable.

- Be mindful of where you prep food to minimize crumbs and small food scraps landing in the snow. It is nearly impossible to pick food residue out of snow, so proper preparation is important.

- In fragile alpine environments, pack out solid human waste using a WAG BAG. In lieu of packing it out, cover and disguise human waste deep in snow away from travel routes and at least 200 feet (70 adult steps) from water sources. When possible, kick down to ground level before defecating to allow for adequate coverage.

- Use natural toilet paper when possible. Snowballs are winter's bidet. Burn or pack out toilet paper or wipes.

- Water is nature's best solvent. A handful of icy snow is a great exfoliator for cleaning hands.

- Use biodegradable soaps sparingly for dishes, if necessary at all. Remove all particulate from pots before cleaning by using a pot scraper, your finger, or licking clean. Strain dishwater into a sump hole.

- Do a camp sweep prior to departure. This will ensure not only that you don't leave any precious (and expensive) gear behind but that all crumbs have been accounted for.

Leave What You Find

Few things change during winter with regard to leaving what you find. One additional consideration would be to preserve any natural snow or ice formations you come across for the next visitor to enjoy. The wind and sun do magical things to the snowpack, and formations morph daily.

Minimize Campfire Impacts

Fires conjure up the most primitive requirements of backcountry travel. We all enjoy the warmth of a campfire, especially during wintertime. Improper fire technique can leave visual scars on the land, unnecessarily reduce resources, and leave a scavenged appearance to the forest. Fires should be viewed as a luxury, not a necessity. They take considerable time to prep and dismantle and should be a refined tool during extreme conditions and/or situations.

Stumbling across the tracks of famed Wolf OR-7, the first recorded wolf to enter California since the 1920s. Something as rare and precious as this should be preserved for the next hiker to enjoy.
Shawn Forry

A small twiggy fire is all that is required to cook a meal on. Resources are limited in the alpine.
Justin Lichter

Best practices to consider:

- Fires should not replace a proper camp stove. If cooking by fire, use more fuel-efficient wood stoves rather than open fires.

- Use dead and downed wood if you can find it. Minimize taking dead branches from standing live trees, as the point where the branch meets the trunk can act as an entry point for insects.

- Put out all fires completely. Even in winter and buried in snow, fires can smolder and flare up after your departure. Collect and scatter ashes, and disguise the fire pit.

- Avoid burning large logs to ensure that all branches burn completely and fire-scorched logs are not left behind.

Respect Wildlife

Winter is an especially vulnerable time for animals. They are at their most depleted in terms of energy reserves and are trying to survive the harsh conditions. While wildlife sightings can be rarer during wintertime, we should continue to observe wildlife from a distance. Tracks are easy to discern, and we should resist the temptation to follow them.

Best practices to consider:

- Never feed wildlife or leave food behind to be eaten. Buried food will easily be discovered by wildlife.

- Make sure wildlife has adequate access to water sources with regard to your campsite, especially during winter, when most sources can be frozen over.

- Protect wildlife and your food by storing rations and trash securely. Follow all food storage regulations per a given area.

Even the elusive hiker trash raccoon should be respected.
Shawn Forry

Be Considerate of Other Visitors

Coming across another backcountry user in winter can be a surprise for all. Being mindful of our visual and auditory impacts will enhance the experience for everyone. Respect for all forms of travel will prevent prejudices from negatively altering our perceptions and biases.

Best practices to consider:

- Be respectful of other users. Travel only in approved areas with regard to motorized versus nonmotorized travel. Share the trail, and be courteous. We all want to have a good time.

- Yield to downhill and faster traffic. It is far easier to step off the trail while going uphill.

- When stopped, move off the trail. Do not take breaks on blind corners, and be extra alert to oncoming downhill traffic.

- Separate ski and snowshoe tracks where possible, and avoid hiking on them when possible.

- Follow all local regulations regarding pets. Not everyone loves your dog like you do. Pack out or bury all dog feces.

- Keep noise to a minimum. Sound travels farther in cold conditions due to less foliage and ambient noise.

The backcountry is a winter playground for all users regardless of mode of travel. Be considerate of dedicated use trails to not only keep noise levels down but also to be mindful of safety.
Shawn Forry

Be considerate of other backcountry users . . . and ALWAYS allow them to break trail through slushy swamps first!
Justin Lichter

I'M SURE YOU'VE HEARD IT BEFORE, BUT IT'S MORE IMPORTANT TODAY THAN EVER: SAFETY IS THE FIRST PRIORITY. Things can quickly take a turn for the worst in winter, and before you know it a common situation can spiral into a potentially lethal one. Typically it takes two or three poor decisions for the dominos to start to fall and lead to a very dangerous situation.

It is important to know how to break the chain of poor decisions. Winter travel is all about decision making. It can be tricky and take some experience to know how to step in and take control. Rely on your experience. Take a minute to decide and think through all the possible outcomes. Sometimes it's as simple as stepping back and realizing that you need to take preventive measures immediately. This could be as minor as adding another layer or immediately warming up your hands or as major as setting up your shelter and calling it a day or even deciding to reevaluate the trip.

Quick Decisions

One day on the winter PCT hike in Oregon, we trudged through 2 to 3 feet of snow during a pouring rain. It continued to pour throughout the night and the next morning. I remember dreading leaving the tarp in the morning. We were also headed higher as we climbed toward one of the high points in Oregon, near Mount Thielsen. About an hour into the morning, the rain changed over to snow. For the umpteenth time I wrung out my soaked gloves to try to warm my hands. I thought my hands would warm, as they usually did once the blood started pumping from hiking in the morning. But instead of gaining sensation in my hands, I was losing feeling. I tried putting my head down and hiking harder and faster, but when breaking trail on snowshoes you are physically capped at about 2 to 3 miles per hour. After wringing out my gloves again, I couldn't feel my fingers and desperately tried to get them back into the gloves' finger slots. With each passing second I could feel my hands getting colder and colder and more useless.

Knowing I would quickly cool down even more, I made the difficult decision to stop hiking. It was tough and tedious, but I took the time to unbuckle and open my pack. I grabbed another layer for my upper body, stripped off my rain poncho and rain jacket, and added another insulation layer. I threw everything back on and grabbed my overmitts out of my rain jacket. I then stashed my poles on my pack so I wouldn't have to hold them and could keep my gloved hands inside my poncho and less exposed. Lastly, I threw the overmitts on and continued. I balled my hands up in my gloves and kept them in the sleeves of my rain jacket. It took nearly an hour of hiking to fully regain feeling.

In 2 minutes I had made a decision that could have exacerbated the issue. In the 2 minutes I stopped moving, numbness was spreading and coming on even more quickly. But I knew what needed to be done and had to get more uncomfortable before things could get better. Relying on experience, I quickly broke the spiraling chain of events that could have led to a serious problem. If I had waited much longer, I would no longer have been able to use my hands to open my backpack to get the items I needed.

Almost all aspects of winter travel can lead back to decision making. It can be dangerous to zone out and let your mind wander like you can during a summer trail hike. You need to be on your "A game" at all times and evaluating any number of factors—conditions, route selection, navigation, your personal health, hydration, and sensation in your extremities and exposed skin, to name a few. Safety is maintained by awareness and risk calculation. Each route selection will involve some decision making and evaluation of calculated risk. Do you want to add elevation gain or try to contour? What's the chance that the slope will slide? How much longer will it take? What are the potential outcomes? It's nearly the same as choosing a financial investment. There are some unknowns in the process, but you do what you can to minimize the

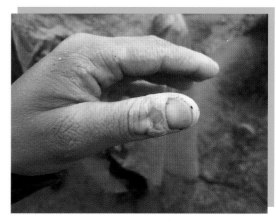

Wet, shriveled hands can be the start of loss of dexterity.
Justin Lichter

unknowns and make decisions based on the calculated risk. Some people are more risk tolerant; others are more risk averse. This all needs to be factored in and acknowledged when discussing options as a group. It is important to remember that everybody's personal bias and comfort level are different.

It is also important to acknowledge that ignorance is rarely bliss. Ignorance can get you into trouble, but so can knowledge and expertise. Clearly, if you don't know the dangers of avalanches, for example, you can get yourself in a dangerous situation. But it is also common for experts and frequent backcountry skiers to get themselves in trouble. The classic line we hear repeatedly is, "I've skied this slope (or slopes like it) a million times and have never had a problem. It'll be fine." Don't take a more experienced person's word as a given. In the backcountry, it is very important to question authority, question each decision, and not take anything for granted.

DECISION MAKING

Decision making is a crucial skill that helps keep you safe. When traveling in winter you must be on top of your game, whether it's searching for clues of the trail, keeping on route, navigating obstacles, overall route selection, or choosing safe and efficient travel paths. All these will require constant processing and evaluation of the surroundings, coupled with your experience and knowledge to lead to a decision. Some of the decisions will be effortless and subconscious, like in summer; others will require more conscious thought. Since decision making will be continuous, it is also an easy way to lose time and efficiency. Keep things streamlined and discuss as you go so that the person in the lead who is breaking trail can also keep moving as much as possible. If you stop often to discuss options and check out a map, you'll be surprised how much time you can lose by the end of the day.

Still, don't rush into a decision. Weigh all pros and cons and the potential outcomes. On a more psychological level, I also think it is important to look internally if you are struggling

Developing Sound Risk Management: The Four Stages of Competence

> Good judgment comes from experience, and a lot of that comes from bad judgment.
>
> —*Will Rogers*

Regardless of where you are on the spectrum of your development and competency, we all go through an experiential learning process composed of both success and failure. To achieve a state of mastery, it is important to understand what doesn't work in order to highlight severity of consequence and our process in decision making. "Mastery" is defined here as the state in which we can not only perform a task by second-hand intuition but also articulate, mentor, and teach our process to others (*Reflective Competence*). We can all think back to our first outdoor trip and recall all the "rookie" mistakes we made. We laugh at them now, and they are invaluable learning experiences that should not be shadowed by shame or judgment. The key to this learning curve is understanding when and, more importantly, why we are getting in over our head.

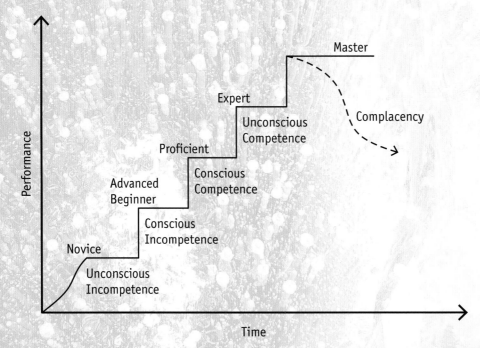

Justin Lichter

This process of awareness is called *Conscious Competence* and is essential to proper risk management. No matter where we are on the spectrum of skill development, at any given moment during an outdoor pursuit, we are balancing our competencies and our awareness thereof.

Let's use a classic example of a first winter camping experience. In our eagerness to get out and experience the serene beauty of winter, we may be unaware that our canister stove might not perform as anticipated or of the ever-lurking avalanche danger. On a risk scale, one will have very minor consequences, while the other can have dire outcomes. We are in a state of *Unconscious Incompetence*; we don't know what we don't know. In these moments our greatest Type II stories are born, with tales of "So there I was" and other near misses. These are often the times when we are at greatest risk. If we survive these introductory experiences, we'll likely move from *Unconscious* to *Conscious Incompetence*. We now know what we don't know.

For many of us this is a great place to get to. We now realize we might not have all the skills required to make safe decisions, but we are acknowledging the dangers inherent to the activity. Our decision making generally becomes more conservative, and we have a foundation of where we need to invest time to fill gaps in our skill set. Reading this book is a great first step in moving from *Unconscious Incompetence* to *Conscious Incompetence*. With this newfound awareness, the art now is to get out there and get hands-on experience to grow these skills.

As we continue to invest time and energy into developing our skill sets, we will eventually arrive at a platform of *Conscious Competence*. We know what we know. For the average backcountry user, this is a great place to be, and where some of our most informed and appropriately challenging outings will take place. We know how to plan and mitigate for risk and, with the absence of unforeseen challenges, likely have some of our most enjoyable moments in the backcountry. This cycle innately breeds confidence.

Where this cycle can become dangerous again is when this confidence dips into *Unconscious Competence*. We know something so well that we fail to even think about it anymore. Here you can see the lines blur between overconfidence and lack of competence. Our "Hero Halo" is born and reveals itself in comments like "I've been here a thousand times," "I've skied this line without incidents," and "I am the expert here." Following a group-think mentality, putting our trust in this person can have compounding negative consequences—the blind leading the blind.

The challenges are to always be our highest critic with the choices we are making. Pausing to simply confirm and articulate why you are proceeding with a certain risk-management plan is a great way to address our unconscious confirmation bias. As leaders in the backcountry, this is a great process to role-model to others in order to mentor safe backcountry practices.

to decide. Why are you leaning toward one thing over the other? What are your personal strengths and weaknesses and comfort level, and how do they affect your thought process and ultimately your decision? This way you know the root of your choices and realize the "why" of each choice, allowing you to acknowledge weaknesses and use this knowledge to improve your skill base.

Group dynamics can also lead to unsafe decision-making situations. Make your comfort level and your preferences known to the group so you can discuss the options openly and intelligently. Each person should also be able to accommodate changes on the fly and adapt personal preferences without leading to tension or strain in the group dynamics. Remember one decision does not necessarily affect the next decision, so it is often not a great solution to say "I got the benefit this time; you'll get it next time." Some people are more risk averse; others are more risk tolerant. Typically, that will have more impact on each individual decision and it's the reason each collaboration should be weighed as an individual event.

In winter it's important to err on the side of caution. Things can quickly spiral downward, and one small mistake can lead to a serious problem. So be safe and be cautious. If there are any doubts, choose the safer option.

WEATHER FORECASTING

Many small details can help you predict the weather and help you plan ahead. In winter it is imperative to have an idea of what conditions you might hit. This may be as simple as checking the weather forecast compulsively before you leave each resupply location. You may also be able to use your satellite messenger or cell phone to get updates. Knowing the weather forecast will lead to preparedness in planning and route selection. You may want to push more miles one day when it is nice out so that you can hunker down early the next day when it's stormy. Or you may have route options to avoid potentially dangerous areas based on new snowfall or wind-loading potential.

A barometer on watch or a GPS unit can also help tell you when the weather is changing. And it can change fast, especially in the mountains. If you watch the Weather Channel, you know it's impossible to know exactly what will happen. But if you're educated about weather indicators and prepared for weather conditions you're likely to encounter, you'll be a lot better off. It pays to pay attention to the wind's direction as well as the shape and movements of the clouds.

CLOUDS

When high-level cirrus clouds—those high, wispy clouds or streaks—are building, it means a storm can be heading your way within 48 to 72 hours. Lenticular cirrus clouds echoing a peak as they rise into the sky—like the profile of a lens—also can mean a storm is headed in within about 48 to 72 hours. A blanket of cloud cover and spindrift can mean high wind on the peaks.

The march of the storm usually goes like this: First the cirrus clouds come in. They're followed by cirrocumulus clouds—small, puffy clouds that can be rows or ripples. Next are the

Spindrift off the North Sister shows strong winds up high and wind loading.
Justin Lichter

cirrostratus clouds that cover large areas. Those are followed by altostratus—smoky midlevel clouds—and nimbostratus clouds bring the steady precipitation.

Keep an eye on cumulus clouds, which might be nice, puffy, cottony clouds like at the beginning of *The Simpsons*. But these cumulus clouds can quickly turn into nasty cumulonimbus clouds, the breeding grounds of fierce thunderstorms and other violent bursts of weather. In high mountains like the Rockies or Sierras, tall cloud tops, like cumulonimbus clouds, can build from friendly cumulus clouds in minutes, and quickly drop the temperature 30 degrees. It can snow any month of the year, and that snow can accumulate at rates of 3-plus inches per hour.

TIP

Look for spindrift coming off peaks to show you how windy it is going to be above tree line and help determine route selection. This will also help tell you what aspects are getting wind loaded.

WIND

Wind direction also plays a major role in predicting the weather. If you understand weather patterns, you know that in the Northern Hemisphere, winds around a low-pressure system circle counterclockwise. So if you're hiking in the Sierra Nevada and winds start coming from the south or southwest, a storm might be coming in. Typically in the Sierras, the winds pick up from the south or southwest around 24 hours before a storm and continue as it approaches. If you're hiking in New England and the winds start coming from the north or northwest, temperatures are probably going to get colder.

TIP

Some personal locator beacons (PLBs) that offer two-way messaging, like the Garmin inReach, can text out a message to a number and get an automated message returned of the weather forecast at the location of the GPS unit—your location. You can even set this up as one of your main contacts so that it doesn't count as a message when you are billed. Check this website for more information: http://wx2inreach.weebly.com.

ORIENTEERING, NAVIGATION, AND SIGNALING

FINDING YOUR WAY

There's lost . . . and then there's really lost. The first lost is more of a temporary misplacement and can easily take care of itself. The second lost is the "I really don't know where I am and may not be able to get back to where I need to be" and is more serious. This is the type of lost you will need help to solve, the type you may or may not be prepared for. It's also possible that your maps no longer cover the area you have wandered into or, worse, you don't have any maps at all.

WHAT TO DO

Step 1: Don't Panic!

Stay calm; stop and look at the map or topography, using your last known point as a reference. People often consider just one possibility and attempt to make the terrain fit their assumption. Unfortunately, they're often in a different spot than they think they are.

Consider all the possible places you could be on the map. Narrow it down to what fits, using landmarks to triangulate your location on the topo map. You can always retrace your steps to get back on track. If you can determine your location without a doubt, you may be able to figure out a different route to intersect your planned route.

If you're totally lost, STOP. Remain calm and evaluate the situation. Remember, "Undue haste makes waste." Try to remember any landmarks you passed or how long ago you made a turn that changed your course. Can you identify any obvious features (trails, roads, bodies of water, cliffs, changes in vegetation, etc.) that you recently passed? Think about how long you have until dark. If it's going to get dark before you can return to any known points, stay put and set up camp. It's better to set up at a place when you know you're lost than to push on in the dark and get even more lost.

If you're hiking with a group, talk things over and figure out a reasonable plan of action for determining your location and getting back on track. Don't act rashly! If you head out in one direction on a whim and have to backtrack, you end up wasting a lot of extra energy and time, and probably increase your worries.

Step 2: "X" Marks Your Spot.

If you need rescuing when you're lost, it can take hours or even days to be found. Help rescuers find you by making a small smoke fire, or, if it's not too much effort, find an open area and lay out rocks in an "X" or a triangle formation. Also lay out some brightly colored clothes or your pack. Use something that will reflect sunlight onto planes flying overhead or anything else that might help rescuers pinpoint your location. If you're lost at night, don't camp near running water. The water sounds will make it harder for you to hear voices of people nearby.

If you've called for a helicopter rescue or used a PLB (personal locator beacon), be ready to give details about your, or an injured patient's, condition. Details should include urgency, name, age, sex, and location. Also provide your best estimate of location, whether you intend to move, and, if so, where you intend to go. When a helicopter or plane flies over, stand toward it with your arms held in a V shape if you need help. If your arms are in a straight line at a diagonal, like a slash, it means "All OK."

If you've managed to find your way before a rescue team arrives, change your PLB signal or call them back to call off the rescue effort. It costs a lot of money to organize and deploy rescue services—and you can be held liable for those costs. If you do call a rescue service, try to make their job as easy as possible by using the signaling tactics mentioned. This will increase your chance of survival and speed up the rescue process.

Note: Three blows on a whistle is a universal signal for help.

ALWAYS leave an itinerary and trip details with people you trust. Ideally, make sure they're in touch with one another as well. When heading out on a long hike, I always give people my planned itinerary and resupply spots. I call or e-mail from each stop to let them know where I am and roughly when they should next hear from me. If they don't hear from me and it's more than a day late, they can initiate the search-and-rescue system, providing an idea of where I should be.

TIP

We can't emphasize this enough: If you have a map, regularly check your position on it; note where you think you are, and make a mental note of the time you are checking. You'll get to know your pace and where you should be at these intervals. Also check the time at known points, such as bridges, peaks, and other obvious landmarks, as well as road, river, and trail crossings. That way, if you get lost you will have an idea of how far from those features you've traveled and will have a better idea of where you are on the map.

EMERGENCY NAVIGATION

Without a compass or an altimeter watch, there are a few easy tricks to get your bearings.

Timekeeping and Navigation

One of the most important tenets of good navigation is checking your location on the map at random intervals and matching your location with the time. This gives you an idea of both your pace and location. If you get off course, you can refer to the last time you were still on course and have a better idea of where you are because you know where and when you were last on course. You can then make plans to either double back or adjust your route to get back on track as necessary. You can also count how many steps you take in a certain amount of time and then estimate about how far you have traveled by knowing how long your stride is and if you maintain roughly the same steps per time period.

Wear a watch, and know when sunset will occur. If your watch fails, knowing when sunset will occur can still help you figure out what time it is and how much daylight you have left. Cover the sun with your thumb, palm facing you. Each finger above the horizon represents 10 to 15 minutes before sunset.

You can use the sun to tell direction using two methods. The hour hand of an analog watch can help you determine direction, as can a stick in the ground. In the Northern Hemisphere, the sun

Route finding above 17,000 feet in the Dolpa region of Nepal
Justin Lichter

is due south at noon (it's easier to tell before and after summer, when the sun travels lower in the sky). In the Southern Hemisphere, the sun is due north at noon (again, it's easier to tell when the sun is lower in the sky).

When using an analog watch in the Northern Hemisphere to determine direction, point the hour hand in the direction of the sun, keeping the watch face flat. Halfway between the hour hand and the 12 is south. So if it is 5 p.m. in the Northern Hemisphere, south will be between the 2 and the 3. North is opposite that; west and east are perpendicular. In the Southern Hemisphere, point the 12 on the watch face toward the sun. Halfway between the 12 and the hour hand is north.

Alternatively, you can place a 3-foot-tall stick, your trekking pole, or something else upright in the ground. Mark the location at the end of the shadow. Wait about 15 to 20 minutes, and mark the tip of the shadow again. Draw a line connecting the two marks. This shows you an approximate east-to-west direction; you can calculate north and south by drawing a perpendicular line.

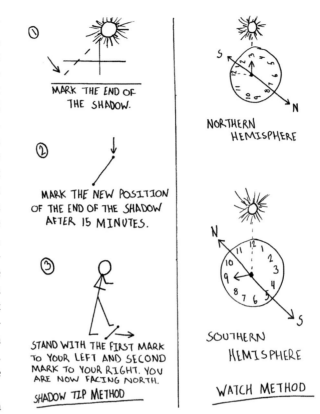

Justin Lichter

Nighttime Navigation

We don't recommend traveling at night when you are lost unless it is truly an emergency. The likelihood of getting increasingly lost or experiencing an injury increases while traveling in the dark. If you do travel at night, make sure to take all the precautions that you would during the day—and more. Try to avoid potential avalanche slopes, but if you must cross them, go one at a time. Take extra care when crossing creeks or rivers in the dark.

Here are some nighttime navigation tricks to help you stay on track.

If the moon rises before the sun has set, the illuminated side will be the west side. If the moon rises after midnight, the illuminated side will be the east. This can provide you with a rough east–west orientation at night.

If it is a crescent moon, you can draw an imaginary line from the top tip of the crescent to the bottom tip and continue the imaginary line to the horizon to find due south.

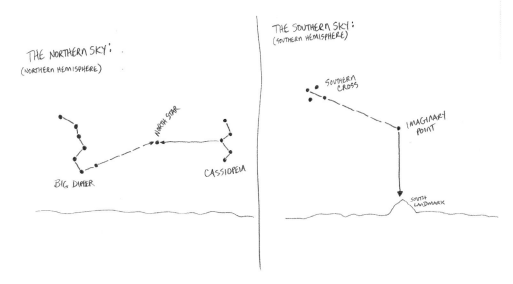

Justin Lichter

In the Northern Hemisphere you can tell north by finding the Big Dipper and Cassiopeia and locating Polaris (the North Star). These constellations and Polaris never set. The Big Dipper and Cassiopeia are always directly opposite each other and rotate counterclockwise around Polaris. The Big Dipper is composed of seven stars, with the two stars forming the outer lip of the Dipper known as the "pointer stars" because they point to Polaris. Imagine a line from the outer bottom star to the outer top star of the bucket, then extend the line about five times the distance between the pointer stars. The North Star will be along this line. Cassiopeia has five stars that form a "W" on its side. The North Star is straight out from

TIP Try this trick if you can't find a map with distances between trail junctions or the key distances you want to know. Hold a string to the map's scale, and mark the string to match miles, half miles, and more if you need to. You can then use the string to measure distances on the trail or map, which will give you a fairly accurate measure of distances. Since the trail or path you took or will take is not a straight line, it is hard to accurately measure the distance of a convoluted path without using a string. Bend the string to follow the curves of the route, then mark the end of the section that you desire to measure on the string, or hold your finger in place. Measure the distance on the string using the map's scale in the legend. This method will give you a more accurate distance.

TIP

It is a common misconception that if you are lost, you should try to follow a creek or river downstream to civilization. This is often not the best approach. In some areas rivers flow directly into the ocean and there is no civilization along the route. In other places the river has carved a canyon with dangerous drop-offs and no possible exit. In the Intermountain West of the United States, many water sources eventually flow to inland basins, only to evaporate in the summer heat. A map will dictate what you should do. If you don't have a map, it is best to get a view from a high point and make your plans and travel path accordingly. Your knowledge of settlements and the specific area you are in will also guide your egress route.

Cassiopeia's center star. After locating the North Star, you can locate true north (the direction to the North Pole) by drawing an imaginary line straight down to the horizon.

In the Southern Hemisphere look for the Southern Cross. It has five stars, and its four brightest stars form a cross that tilts to one side. The two stars that make up the long access are the pointer stars. To locate south, imagine a distance five times the distance between the pointer stars, and extend this distance from the lower pointer star. The point where the imaginary line ends is in the general direction of south. Look to the horizon, and locate a landmark below this point to act as a bearing.

WINTER FIRST AID AND ULTRALIGHT WINTER FIRST-AID KIT

Winter conditions can pose additional challenges to your standard summer first-aid considerations. This includes the typical summertime concerns of blisters, rubbing, chafing, and general muscle and joint aches and pains; however, in winter you also need to be extra cautious about frostnip, frostbite, and hypothermia. Ironically, a warm storm in winter can lead to more dangerous hypothermia conditions. When snow levels rise and temperatures hover around freezing, with a cold rain or wet snow, it can be very hard to maintain your core temperature.

Our typical winter first-aid kit varies by location, nature, and duration of the trip. A few items always remain the same, but quantities change and other items get inserted or deleted based on the various factors.

PROACTIVE VS. REACTIVE

One important factor that helps pare down a first-aid kit is being proactive rather than reactive with any issues that arise. We typically plan trips to know how long between resupplies, potential exit points, conditions present, temperatures, and many other issues that factor into preparedness for potential emergencies you might face.

Furthermore, by stopping at the first instances of pain to assess the situation, you can often prevent an injury from becoming worse, even debilitating. Popping a couple ibuprofen, applying Vaseline to chafed of windburned area, or taping a rubbing on your foot before it becomes a full-blown blister can go a long way toward keeping you moving forward—as can stopping and adding layers, or loosening boot buckles or shoelaces to aid in circulation.

Training

We have some medical certifications ranging from EMT (emergency medical technician) to WFR (wilderness first responder). We have been involved with treating medical conditions in the backcountry that have required transportation afterward. In the backcountry, or wherever you may be, the main thing to realize is that there's only so much you can do no matter how much equipment you have. You learn to make do with what you have. Put simply, the ultimate goals are (1) do no further harm, (2) make the patient comfortable, and (3) transport your patient to higher care as quickly and safely as possible.

Location and Duration

Location plays a large role in the contents of the first-aid kit. Is the hike in the United States? Is it in Africa, Nepal, or South America? What are we going to be able to find in those countries, and what are the risks that are present? In parts of Africa anti-malaria medicine is crucial, no matter the time of year. In other places we carry preventative meds for waterborne illnesses. In the United States, how much time will it take to get to the closest resupply town with a supermarket, pharmacy, or doctor to restock your kit or seek medical attention?

This all leads to considering the duration of the hike and the duration between resupplies. Basically, how much of each item will be required to get you to the safety of society and a place where you can stock up on more meds or more supplies. Carry enough of what you think you will need if something happens, enough to get you to the next opportunity to restock.

The Kit

- **Duct tape:** Used mainly for foot care. Rip a larger piece that is bigger than the blister and then a smaller piece that is slightly bigger than the blister. Turn the smaller piece and attach the two pieces together, with the sticky sides facing each other. Adhere the tape to the blistered area or hot spot, with the larger piece facing out. The smaller piece prevents the tape from sticking to the injured area and makes it easier and less painful to remove, while also preventing the injured area from additional injury from prying the tape off.

- **Ibuprofen:** Pain and swelling relief.

- **Aquamira or denatured alcohol:** Used occasionally as hand sanitizer.

- **Bandanna or cloths:** To make slings and compression wraps; wrap a ziplock bag filled with snow for icing injuries/swelling.

- **Needle and thread:** To pop blisters; also to make clothing or pack adjustments or alterations in the field. Can also be used to make slings or other items if needed.

- **Small multi-tool knife with nail clipper as main tool:** To cut fabric or other things; foot care to prevent issues.

- **Trekking poles:** Crutches or splints.

- **Leukotape:** Can be good for foot care, hot spots, blisters, and other things since it is super sticky.

- **Sunscreen:** Just because it's winter doesn't mean you don't need sun protection. The sun and reflection off the snow can still create skin damage and sunburn.

- **Dermatone/Vaseline-type product:** To help protect against cold and windburn.

- **Neosporin:** Topical antibiotic ointment for cuts and abrasions.

- **Superglue:** To repair small tears in packs, tarps, and tents. Also used for closing wounds.

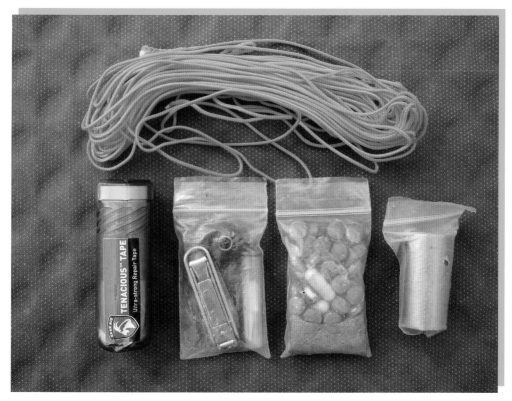

Cord, Tenacious Tape, duct tape, thread, needle in small plastic tube, small Gerber multitool with nail clipper, ibuprofen, and multivitamin
Justin Lichter

TIP

Willow bark has an active ingredient similar to aspirin. In fact, that's what aspirin is derived from. If you are not allergic to aspirin and have an injury, muscle pain, or fever in the backcountry, break off a piece of willow and chew the bark to release the salicin. Or you can make a tea by steeping the bark in hot water.

Note: All items listed above are usually downsized—torn from the main roll of tape into smaller rolls and other items repackaged into small baggies or smaller containers to save weight and space.

When traveling to second- or third-world countries, we usually fill prescriptions before leaving and bring Imodium and broad-spectrum antibiotics like Cipro and Tinidazole to combat the effects of waterborne illnesses.

Other Considerations

The following conditions should be considered, depending on location and/or climate.

Snow Blindness

Bright sunlight in a snow-covered area can cause snow blindness, which happens when ultraviolet light damages the cornea. Initial symptoms include a feeling of grit in the eyes, pain in and around the eyes that often increases with movement of the eyeball, teary and red eyes, and a headache that usually increases with continued light exposure. Additional exposure can cause permanent eye damage.

Blisters

Catch them early and you will be much better off. However, this isn't always an option, especially in winter, since it can be hard to stop and take off your shoes or boots in cold weather or during a storm. If you need to, set up your shelter quickly for some extra warmth and protection from the weather. If you can catch a blister or another injury early, you won't regret taking the extra time to set up your shelter. It will prevent a lot of pain and potential downtime in the future.

When you find a blister, cover it with moleskin or duct tape. We usually like to wait for a more "permanent" treatment until the end of the day, when we have a more sterile environment and don't need to put on our shoes or socks again for a while. In the evening, clean the area and sterilize your needle by holding it in a lighter's flame. Come into the blister from the unaffected skin along the side. Bring the needle into the blister and then gently drain the fluid out. Don't tape it up for the night. Instead let it get airflow and dry out. The next morning, tape it up as discussed above to protect the fragile skin so that another blister does not form in the same spot.

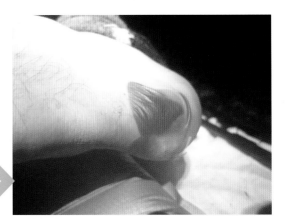

It is hard to stop in the winter. This is an example of not being proactive. Earlier I had said, "I think I feel a little rubbing." When I took off my boot at the end of the day, it looked like this.
Justin Lichter

Chafe

Chafe is usually less of a problem in winter than the summer. Generally, if chafe is happening it means you are hot and sweaty. If this is the case, flush the area gently with water to remove the salt buildup that can further irritate the skin. Try removing a layer of clothing and washing your clothing. If that doesn't work, consider Vaseline or another skin lubricant to protect the area.

Frostnip

Frostnip can lead to frostbite if not treated or conditions taken care of quickly. Frostnip is usually on the face, ears, or extremities and can be painful. If you have frostnip, warm up the area immediately. Usually covering the area and/or getting out if the windchill be enough to take the edge off and get thing back on track.

Frostbite

Frostbite is deeper tissue damage than frostnip and is the result of longer exposure to cold conditions. Frostbite is the result of frozen tissue. Frostnip is the first step as the skin gets cold and loses circulation. You may feel numbness or tingling before you lose feeling in the area. The longer it is exposed to the cold, the deeper the injured tissue and the more serious the injury will be. Be aware of the sensation in your face, toes, feet, ears, and hands, as these are the most susceptible areas. Skin will look dull, whitish, and pale.

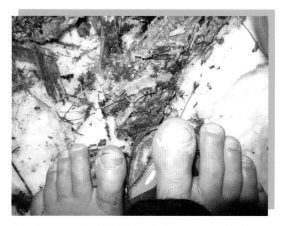

The white, waxy look of frostbite before it is rewarmed
Justin Lichter

If you are traveling with someone, he or she can monitor your face for the signs. If you are alone, you need to be aware of the loss of sensation to any of these areas. You can also periodically cover your nose and cheeks with a gloved hand to provide some warmth to the skin. If your hands are cold, place them in your armpits or groin to keep them warmer. Also make sure to scrunch and make faces and move your fingers and toes from time to time to increase the blood flow. If you lose feeling in your hands or feet, stop to assess the damage. If it doesn't seem deep, rewarm the affected areas by using body heat or placing the injuries next to a hot water bottle. Do not insert the frostbit area into hot or warm water. You want to rewarm the injured areas slowly.

Most importantly, if you don't have the proper equipment to keep the area from refreezing, refrain from thawing the injured tissue. It will do more damage to thaw the

> **TIP**
> Ziplock, bread, or other plastic bags can be put over your socks or hands to create a vapor barrier liner and increase the warmth of your extremities by not permitting air exchange to help you get out of the backcountry or through a dangerous situation.

area and have it refreeze and will raise the chance of infection. Do NOT massage areas with frostbite to rewarm them.

Hypothermia

Hypothermia occurs when your core body temperature drops below normal. There are varying stages of hypothermia, and if you do not warm the afflicted person up, he or she will continue to deteriorate into worsening stages.

Snow will quickly melt into your clothing and zap your body heat without the proper layers. Dehydration and lack of food will also increase your chances of hypothermia.

To treat hypothermia, it is imperative to warm the body. The first step is typically to add layers or strip off wet layers of clothing. Replace lost fluids and eat to gain calories that will help warm the body.

Hypothermia can result in sluggish thinking, poor decision making, loss of dexterity, and an unexplained feeling of warmth. Ultimately it will lead to an inability to take care of one's self, unconsciousness, even death.

It is crucial to rewarm a hypothermia patient as soon as you see the early stages. This can be done by body-to-body contact inside a sleeping bag or near a fire. Make sure to remove any wet clothing. In a serious case of hypothermia, take care not to rewarm the body too rapidly. Also, once rewarmed, make sure not to let the body get cold again once removed from the heat source.

Not to be a Debbie Downer, remember that cold does strange things to your body. Never write off someone whose body is cold as being dead. In extreme cold bodily functions can slow down to preserve tissue and vital organs. Ironically, it is very difficult to tell if someone is dead in the field until he or she has been warmed up.

EMERGENCY COMMUNICATIONS

An important part of a first aid kit, especially in winter, is being able to communicate in case something happens. In some locations this can be accomplished with your cell phone, but that is not a viable option in most backcountry locations. Here are a few ideas, along with their pros and cons.

- **DeLorme InReach:** This reliable two-way messenger allows you to communicate with people at home while you're in the backcountry. Communication can pair with your cell phone but is mainly through text messages or Facebook. You cannot place voice calls. This product doubles as a GPS and can also receive weather forecasts (http://wx2inreach.weebly.com/details.html). You will need to pay an activation fee and have some sort of monthly plan to activate the device.

- **SPOT communicators:** You can send messages and SOS messages but cannot receive messages, nor does the device serve any other function while on trail. Requires a monthly plan.

- **Cell phone GPS:** Your cell phone can act as a GPS device, but the battery doesn't last very long when this function is in use. You will need to carry extra batteries or a battery pack and will still likely not be able to communicate with anyone at home in case of an emergency because the phone cannot send messages through satellites.

- **Satellite phone:** A satellite phone can send texts and voice from remote locations. Service can be interrupted under tree cover, cloud cover, or without a clear view of the sky. Service is also very costly. If you are serious about getting a sat phone, keep in mind Iridium versus Globalstar service. Iridium is the only truly global coverage satellite provider. Globalstar's network does not cover some areas on the Earth (including the poles, portions of Africa, extreme southern South America, areas over the oceans, and some areas over India, Nepal, and Tibet).

AVALANCHE CONSIDERATIONS

Avalanches are one of the many dangers present in winter. This section is by no means a comprehensive treatise on avalanches. There are many books on the market that delve specifically into the nature of avalanches and travel through dangerous terrain. Instead our goal is to provide a quick overview of what to watch out for, how to deal with some of the dangers and challenges, what equipment is mandatory in your kit, and some details on rescue techniques—basically, the important takeaways from what could be a weeklong avalanche course.

Sometimes it feels as though the more you know about avalanches, the more you don't know. It is not an exact science. The best you can do is be cautious and observant and make smart decisions. Avalanche forecasts are prepared by experienced professionals but are by no means a given. Once in the field, there are a million different variables that can affect each individual slope. If you have any concerns or doubts, play it safe. It's always better to be safe than sorry.

AVALANCHE BASICS

Avalanches typically happen on slopes between 30 and 50 degrees. Anything at a lower angle than 30 degrees typically doesn't start "rolling"; anything over 50 degrees usually cannot hold enough snow to slide. (This can be different in maritime snowpack areas, where wet snow can stick on very steep faces and cliff areas.) It helps to think of avalanches as a dynamic event that turns the snow into a fluid motion that can almost seem like a liquid before it settles and cements into its final resting place. Keep in mind that an avalanche doesn't necessarily need to be triggered from the top. Also, it is important to remember that just because an avalanche has already happened in an area doesn't mean it is safe to be there. There can be remaining hang fire above or instability along the sides. If a slide has happened, it is a warning of inherent instability, whether it was natural or human triggered.

A natural slide is one that has occurred in the backcountry without any human trigger, and is an obvious sign of danger. Other key indications of potential danger include overhanging cornices, rapidly warming temperatures, strong direct sun, rapidly changing weather conditions, rainfall on top of the snowpack, a storm or heavy snowfall, intense bursts of snowfall

Pepper crossing an avalanche slope. Note the "flagging" on trees, with the uphill branches missing on the lower areas, and sporadically spaced small trees, indicating frequent avalanche activity.
Justin Lichter

at more than 1 inch per hour, unstable layers within the snowpack (specifically surface hoar, crusts, facets, or graupel), convex terrain features, *whoomfing* or settling snow, cracking, hollow drumlike sounds, temperatures below freezing for days on end that create faceting, and wind events that are transporting snow. Wind can transport and load slopes even faster than a snowstorm. Keep an eye on this, as wind-loaded slopes are typically significantly more dangerous than wind-scoured areas.

Conditions that show a potential avalanche path, such as flagging on a tree (uphill side of the lower part of the tree without lower branches, or with broken branches), an obvious gully or pathway that's been scarred and has no trees or has younger trees toward the bottom, or a recent debris field at the run-out, should be noted as you travel. Be cautious when entering any of these areas or crossing any of these slopes. Be very wary of the compression zone since this often seems like a safe and efficient area to travel but actually can be one of the most dangerous. Keep in mind that a slide can run 2.5 times its vertical fall.

By the nature of an avalanche, you can trigger a slide seemingly anywhere on the face of the slope, below the slope, and even remotely. This is very unpredictable, and you need only hit a weakness in the snowpack, whether it's a shallow area on top of a rock or a layer of facets, to trigger something. The top of the slide path is called the head, and the bottom of the debris pile is called the toe. You want to be particularly aware of the compression zone.

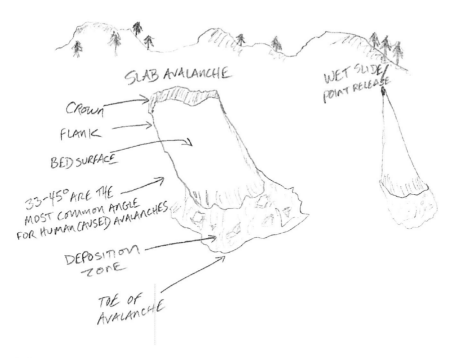

SLAB AVALANCHE

WET SLIDE/POINT RELEASE

CROWN

FLANK

BED SURFACE

33-45° ARE THE MOST COMMON ANGLE FOR HUMAN CAUSED AVALANCHES

DEPOSITION ZONE

TOE OF AVALANCHE

Justin Lichter

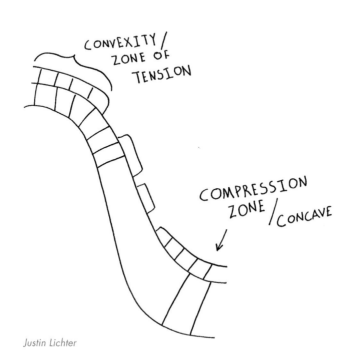

CONVEXITY / ZONE OF TENSION

COMPRESSION ZONE / CONCAVE

Justin Lichter

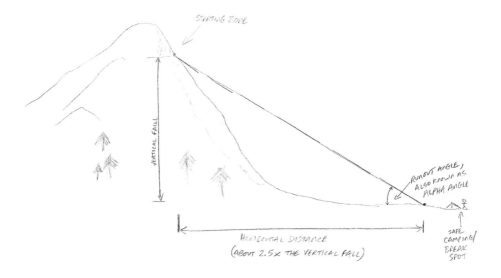

When choosing a safe travel route, campsite, or break spot, remember that the run-out can go more than 2.5 times the vertical fall of the avalanche. Under some circumstances it can be up to 2.9 times the vertical fall. Use your topo maps to measure the potential vertical fall and an inclinometer or eyeball to gauge the angle to give you a good idea of a safe spot. Clues in your surroundings will also help you determine safe areas.
Justin Lichter

Although many areas in this zone are relatively easy paths, it's potentially a very lethal location—in the event of an avalanche, you'd be buried at the bottom of the debris pile. Also, take note that with enough momentum, some large avalanche paths can travel uphill; for example, on the opposite side of a valley bottom.

Mountains are often affected by wind before, during, and after storms, which plays a large role in the snowpack and the snow conditions. Wind events can add slab layers and instability to the snowpack, along with transporting snow. The skies can be clear and cloudless, but wind-loading can add weight to a snowpack just as a new storm does. It is important to always be aware of what might be happening around you. Look for signs like spindrift off the peaks that show snow transport. Wind can move lots of snow and add cornices to saddles and ridgelines. Winds can start in one direction before a storm, switch directions altogether as the storm moves in, and then move the snow to a completely different aspect after the storm passes. For example, in the Sierras the winds often start from the southwest before a storm and end up coming from the north or east after the storm. Be aware of wind-loading, cross-loading, and wind-stripping to help determine safe travel areas and danger zones.

You also want to be aware of terrain traps. These are areas where the terrain will prevent you from a possible escape in the event of an avalanche; the avalanche will be funneled through this terrain, or funnel you into an area of extreme danger. Some examples of terrain traps are a couloir, gully, cliff band, abrupt transition at the bottom of a slope, trees at the bottom of an avalanche track or run-out, or an hourglass-shaped chute. These areas can produce bad consequences. Sparse trees are not very effective anchors, while very thick trees can help hold a slab in place. Likewise, rocks showing through the snowpack can anchor a slope, while rocks hidden beneath the snow can create weaknesses and depth hoar. Always have a contingency plan in case something happens, and know the potential "safe spots" to try to get to and to view your partner from. When at a safe spot near a tree, remember that fractures tend to break from anchor to anchor, meaning it can be safer to stand on the uphill side of a tree or group of trees.

In springtime when the daytime temperatures warm, the days grow longer, and the sun angle increases in the sky, the snow conditions often change. Corn snow begins to become the dominant type of snow on the ground, and the snowpack can become more uniform and stable. Springtime slides tend toward wet, point release–type slides rather than dry slides (unless new snow or rain events occur, the snowpack has not re-bonded well with freezing temperatures overnight, or some general instability remains in the snowpack). Overall, springtime slides are a lot less dangerous and destructive. They typically start slowly and gain momentum, sliding like a game of dominoes rather than the instantaneous, unpredictable, and potentially devastating release of a dry slide. Wet slides generally start around a point source like an exposed rock or cliff band and are tied to the warming of the snow. Roller balls are another sign to look for as a precursor to wet slide danger.

Rollerballs
Justin Lichter

Wet slides usually don't occur early in the morning, waiting until the sun has started to bake the slope. Wet slide instability can be dangerous but not in the sense of dry slides. You know a spring snowpack is losing its stability and overall bonding when your feet begin to posthole above your boot top. At this point, be careful to avoid rock outcroppings or other potential starting points. If you are postholing to that effect, you'll also want to be careful when crossing snow bridges, frozen lakes, or other areas where it is critical that the snowpack is cohesive.

It is worth specifically noting that in spring, the snowpack can be dangerous on the days following the first couple of nights where the nighttime low temperatures did not rebound below freezing. This can prevent the snowpack from refreezing and re-bonding, thereby creating a weaker snowpack when daytime heating begins. It can also allow melting snow to lubricate crusts or the ground, providing a slippery bed surface for the avalanche to slide on.

SAFE TRAVEL TECHNIQUES

With the background and nature of avalanche danger in mind, there are many ways to try to mitigate and take precautions to avoid and minimize the risks associated with traveling in avalanche terrain. We always recommend traveling with an avalanche beacon, probe, and shovel and, most important, knowing how to use them.

Instructors for many avalanche courses will teach you how to dig pits, assess the snow layers, and assess the potential weak layers. These courses are very helpful and highly recommended. We are not going to go into the details of how to dig a pit and assess the snowpack. We do stress that you should assume the dangers are present and adjust your behavior accordingly. Be observant; learn from what you are seeing, and how the snowpack is reacting to you, while keeping in mind that the snowpack changes throughout the day and by elevation, aspect, and location.

Since this book is focusing on travel, we are assuming you are headed from point A to point B, and are in a similar mind-set as we were during our winter PCT trip. You want to move and make progress. With that perspective in mind, we did not dig one pit to analyze the snowpack on the trip. In fact, I rarely dig a full-blown avalanche pit on any backcountry trip. Typically I will quickly dig some hand pits to determine the types of snow crystals, and any crusts or potentially weak layers in the top 3 feet of the snowpack. I do this since, while on skis or snowshoes, your body weight only affects the top 1 meter of the snowpack. From this information, along with hands-on knowledge of previous conditions in the area, research before heading out, and reading the avalanche forecast for the area in detail, I have

A loaded, dangerous slope shows clear signs of avalanche history. Plan your route accordingly if the snow conditions are unstable. Either stay on the ridgeline or plan to go down and around.
Justin Lichter

built a bank of knowledge to determine what layers to worry about, and on what specific aspects and elevations. This analysis helps guide my travel choices and areas to avoid.

When you are traveling through avalanche terrain, the most important thing is to make smart decisions. Problems can arise quickly and often spiral downward rapidly with multiple poor choices. Break the chain of bad decisions and you've stopped the snowball effect, pardon the expression. It is important to practice safe traveling techniques. Make sure all parties know how to use their rescue equipment efficiently. Don't travel alone, unless you are willing to take the risk and/or going to travel completely out of avalanche terrain. Travel one at a time across potentially dangerous areas (slopes, compression zones, etc.). This at least gives you the opportunity to have a rescuer if something happens. When you travel one at a time, make sure the party that is spotting is watching closely and is in a safe spot. It is important that this person watch closely, because often people caught in slides are located much more quickly when there is a last-seen point. This can reduce the search area dramatically. When choosing a safe spot, be careful—avalanches often can rip out larger than you'd expect. Brace yourself or hold onto a tree if possible. Be ready for the worst, even if you think you look stupid. If something happens, it will happen so quickly that it will be hard to prepare yourself. Safe spots are locations that are protected from the slide path. If dropping in from the top, be wary of cornices above or that could break. You may want to test slopes from the top by placing ski cuts in them and then travel from safe spot to safe spot. Remember, not every descent has to be straight down the hill; sometimes a diagonal or zigzag descent is safer.

If conditions are very dangerous, travel exactly in one another's tracks. Travel one at a time, moving from safe spot to safe spot and keeping eyes on the other person or persons in the group. Be careful not to isolate slabs by your ski or travel tracks with the group. Isolating a slab could reduce its tensile strength and allow it to separate from the areas that were keeping it in place. There are case studies where the tenth skier on a slope triggered the avalanche. Just because the first nine skiers went down safely, doesn't mean the danger is gone.

It is also critical to understand overall group dynamics and how this affects decision making. It is important to take everyone's perspective into the decision-making process; don't shy away from expressing your own thoughts and opinions, even if you are less experienced than others you are

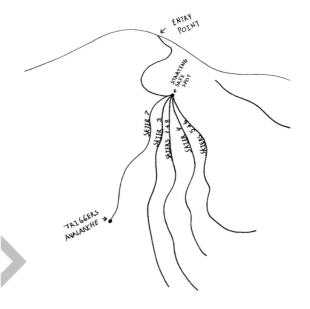

Always be aware. It's not always the first skier, or the second, that triggers an avalanche. Anybody can end up isolating the slab. In this example from Tunnel Creek, Washington, the seventh skier triggered the avalanche, possibly by finally isolating the slab or hitting a trigger point. Decision making and group dynamics also came in to play. To read more, the *New York Times* did a great case study (www.nytimes.com/projects/2012/snow-fall/#/?part=tunnel-creek).
Justin Lichter

traveling with. Take advantage of everyone's experience, knowledge, comfort levels, and observations to make your decisions and guide your activities and route selection. When traveling with a group, remember to check that everyone's beacon is on and transmitting each day, and make sure your battery charge never drops below 60 percent. Some beacon manufacturers say you can use the batteries down to 40 percent, but this isn't standard industry practice, since this would give you only 1 hour of search time and 20 hours of transmit at 14°F, which isn't that cold. Hence most ski patrols recommend changing batteries when they reach 60 percent. And remember, always use alkaline batteries in your beacon. Rechargeable batteries are unacceptable, and lithium batteries hold a constant charge and then quickly drop to 0 percent—not a good characteristic in an avalanche beacon.

EQUIPMENT

There are three pieces of essential equipment when traveling in avalanche terrain: beacon, probe, and shovel. Other products are available and can be helpful, but they are not essential. We are focusing on ultralight travel and will quickly detail some viable options with good concept but probably not worth the weight on long-distance trips. Avalung products, made by Black Diamond, are a clever concept. By creating a reservoir of oxygen, they give a victim more time to be found. However, they are generally heavy packs and better suited to day trips into the backcountry. Plus, if you are in an avalanche, your pack might get ripped off or you might not even have time to put the tube in your mouth. The "floatation" packs with inflatable "airbags" are another great invention. These literally are lifesavers in avalanche situations, partly due to their ability to keep the victim afloat while "surfing" the avalanche—potentially even more so because of the protection they provide around the neck and head to prevent trauma. These airbags work by the Brazil Nut Effect. Basically, think about a jar of mixed nuts being shaken, whereby the larger Brazil nuts end up at the top. In an avalanche situation, you'll need to have sufficient time to "shake out" to the top, so if you are toward the bottom of the slide path, the airbag likely won't work. The other problem from our perspective is that these systems are heavy; the inflatables take up space and can't be put into other packs not made by the manufacturer. Thus, you are tied to a heavy backpack that isn't made for the style and duration of the trips we are discussing.

Helmets have become increasingly common on downhill skiers and are sometimes seen in the backcountry. These can be worthwhile to carry on day, overnighter, or backcountry ski trips where the clear intention is to get some turns. On distance-oriented trips, helmets are burdensome, unpackable, not practical for temperature control, and extraneous.

Beacons are your lifeline, but they are only as good as the operator. It is important to practice, practice, practice and become competent and efficient at using your beacon. Practice every season to keep your skills fresh. You don't want to be rusty in the event of an emergency. Many mountain towns have beacon parks with six or eight beacons buried. You can turn avalanche signals on and off and practice single and multi-burial scenarios. Another option if you want to practice beacon scenarios is to borrow beacons from friends. Place a beacon in a Tupperware-style container, on and in the transmitting mode. Have a friend bury it, and then find it. If you want to go one step further, mount a Tupperware-style container onto a roughly 2 x 2-foot piece of plywood or carpet. Carpet or duffel bags give a more realistic probe strike feeling, but remember that if you probe someone's head or shoulder, it will feel different than striking his or her abdomen. Now you'll have something that will help you go from beacon search to probe strike.

Beacons have made huge strides over the past ten years and are getting much more user-friendly. Most backcountry beacons weigh upward of 10 ounces or more. Although probably technologically doable, there hasn't yet been much innovation into making lighter-weight beacons. While not the most technologically advanced for searching, the Pieps Micro is functional and currently the most streamlined beacon on the market, weighing in at just over 5 ounces. There are smaller beacons made for dogs, but these will not suffice. They transmit only and don't have a search mode.

Probes are important to help locate buried victims. A probe is basically a collapsible pole to use to stick down into the snow. It saves time in pinpointing the location of the victim so that you only have to shovel where it counts. Probes come in various lengths and materials. Length is a balance. You want to be able to probe deeply into the snowpack to find the victim, but in reality, if the victim is buried more than 2 meters (6 feet) below the surface, it is unlikely that you'll be able to save them. Choose a carbon fiber probe if you are OK with spending a little extra. They are strong and the lightest poles available. There are different "cinching" (for lack of a better word) mechanisms. Try them out, and find the one you think is the easiest and quickest to use. All probes should have distances ticked off on them.

Shovels are also a necessity in avalanche terrain and will generally be very helpful on a winter trip anyway. You can shovel out or pack down your campsite, use it as a base for the pole of your tent or tarp (so it diffuses the pressure and doesn't sink into the snow), or cook on it if it has a metal blade. Although it's a bit heavier, it's critical to get a metal-bladed shovel. Although lighter in weight, plastic blades tend to break in avalanche debris. Other super-lightweight shovels I've tried, like the Arva Ultra Shovel, which seems to be the lightest on the market, also bent while performing routine shoveling. You don't want that to happen while counting down the minutes in a rescue situation.

TIP

Cell phones—for that matter, anything with an electronic voltage regulator (cameras, black diamond heated gloves, etc.)—interfere with beacon function. Do not keep your cell phone (on or off) anywhere on your person; and if you must, keep it as far away from your beacon as possible. I highly recommend shutting off your phone and putting it in your backpack. In the event of an avalanche, also remember to keep your phone away from your beacon while searching.

RESCUE TECHNIQUES

In the event of an avalanche, remain calm and logical—and remember, move fast but don't rush. Do it once, and do it right. Make sure the scene is safe to rescue the victim (no hang fire or other avalanche potential). Assess the situation. Did you see the victim caught in the slide? Was there a last-seen point you could use to narrow down the search area? Are there any terrain traps that would have caught or funneled the victim? Are there any clues on the snow, like a glove, hat, or ski? If there are clues, these need to be explored immediately. There are multiple case studies where a glove or ski was sticking up through the avalanche debris but the rescuers immediately started a beacon search instead of checking the clues. They assumed the ski or glove had come off the victim's body. However, when they finally lifted up the glove, the victim's hand was right there. By the time the beacon search led them to the glove, it was too late.

Suffocation is the main cause of death for avalanche victims, with trauma being the next factor. Suffocation occurs because the victim is buried under the snow and exhaling warm, carbon dioxide–filled air into a small air pocket in front of their face. When the avalanche debris slows, it settles like cement. The buried person's breath melts the snow in front of his or her face and then refreezes, creating an ice lens, which blocks off all air flow. The carbon dioxide then builds up in the pocket of air that is being re-inhaled.

You want to try to reach the victim within 2 to 3 minutes. Eighty percent of victims survive if they are out within 10 minutes. Success drops precipitously after that, with survival dropping to 40 percent at 15 minutes and less than 10 percent at 35 minutes.

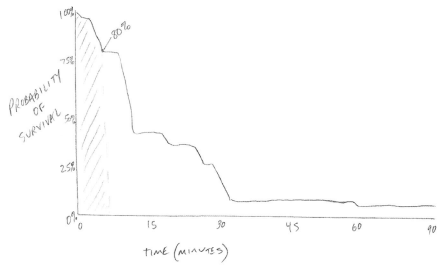

Justin Lichter

It can be difficult to travel through avalanche debris. If you don't have visible clues, make your beacon search through the debris. Be smart about it—your first pass is your best chance, especially if you are uphill of the slide, since it will take a lot longer to search uphill than downhill.

If you have multiple people involved in the beacon search, make sure you don't interfere with one another's search. You all need to have your beacons in search mode.

Use what you see—a last-seen point, glove, ski, terrain trap—to help guide your search area.
Justin Lichter

Beacon range is 40 to 50 meters (about 120 to 150 feet), so use this to your advantage when thinking about how far to the flank of the slide path you would need to go to pick up a reading and how far apart your zigzags could be through the debris while still making sure to cover it all. Be efficient and smart about using the beacon's range to your advantage. But remember, a beacon is simply a computer with a processor. It cannot process as fast as your brain. Move deliberately and not too fast, or else you will move faster than the beacon can process and end up below the signal. Move in a zigzag from the last-seen point using the coverage distances to your advantage. As soon as your beacon picks up a reading, ditch the zigzag and follow your beacon.

After you have picked up the signal, remember that the numbers on all newer beacons are in meters. (Older beacons don't have numerical readings.) Use these readings as a relative reference—you're getting closer or farther away, not as a specific distance number. Often the closest reading you will get is in the 1- to 3-meter range before you'll need to start probing.

Multiple Person Rapid Beacon Search

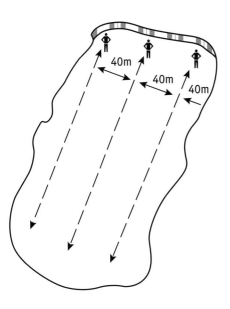

Single Searcher Search Path

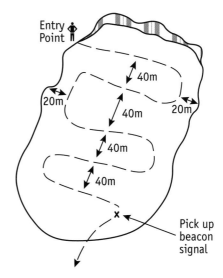

Justin Lichter

When you get to your closest number, pinpoint the search by getting on your knees and holding your beacon directly above the snow's surface. Make a "box" of one arm's reach, using your lowest readings.

When you have your narrowed-down "box" from your beacon search and have the location with the lowest reading, mark it. Then begin to probe the area. Start at the location of the lowest reading. If you don't have a strike, begin to spiral out from that reading location. Keep in mind as you continue your spiral out that if the victim is buried vertically (standing), there may be only 4 to 6 inches to get a probe strike because of the narrow profile. Always probe directly vertical and 10 inches or less apart. Don't overcomplicate this—you do not want to probe perpendicular to the slope. Your probe at every insertion should be straight up and down. If it is angled at all and you are probing 6 feet down, you'll end up with a wide area that has not been probed 6 feet under the snow. Think about the letter "X." If you extend the legs down another 6 feet, how far apart are the lines? Too far.

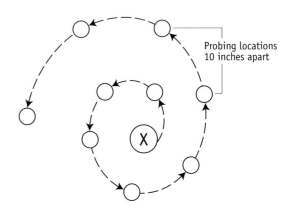

Probing locations 10 inches apart

A probe strike will usually feel a little squishy, but still firm. It'll feel a lot different than a rock, but can be a little difficult to discern from a tree limb. Don't move the probe once you think you have a strike. Instead, leave

Justin Lichter

the probe exactly in place, look at the measurements on the probe to determine the depth to the strike, and step back one to one and a half times the distance on the probe. Step down the hill, and start shoveling.

Shoveling is the slowest part of the rescue, so you want to make sure your beacon search is quick and efficient. Instead of shoveling a hole, shovel into the slope to meet the probe.

Remember when you were a kid on the beach, trying to dig to China? That's the example of what NOT to do. You don't want to get down to the victim with a tiny hole the size of a silver dollar, only to realize that you've hit the victim's midsection. The victim needs air, and needs it ASAP, but it will take a long time to expand that type of hole to find his or her airway. Plus, you'll likely be stepping on top of the victim and have nowhere to place the snow. You don't want to have to move the same snow twice when it cascades back into the hole. Use the terrain to your advantage.

Take the depth of the probe strike and move back one and a half times that distance. If you have enough people, set up an assembly line of shovelers, moving the snow away from the burial area, and rotate to keep them fresh and to keep the snow away from the digging area. Shoveling into the slope this way will also help create a platform to move the victim out onto once he or she has been rescued so that you can begin performing first aid, and will help you get to the patient's airway quickest.

Remember, the deeper the victim is buried, the less likely the rescue will be successful. Someone at the bottom of the slide path when the avalanche occurs will usually be buried deeper as the snow comes down the slope on top of him or her. On the other hand, someone near the top of the slide path when it starts will have a better chance of being near the surface. If trapped in a slide, kick off your skis so that they don't drag you down and get your legs twisted. The easiest way to be found is to have a body part showing when the movement stops; that's why experts say swim and try to stay afloat. Then, as the snow slows down, make sure to raise a hand. Whatever additional distance or visibility you create, the better your chances of being found. If your hand comes above the surface, you have a great chance of being rescued quickly. Once the snow settles, you won't be able to move, so make sure to get one arm straight up and the other hand over your face. As the snow slows, use the hand over your face to expand the air pocket in front of your face as much as possible. You may have been cartwheeled going down with the slide, so once things settle, you may want to drop some saliva out of your mouth to determine which way is up.

ACCESSING AND ASSESSING SNOW BRIDGES AND ICE

Getting water can be an extremely dangerous activity on a winter hike. Obviously, you don't want to get wet when the temperatures are cold, because this can quickly lead to hypothermia. However, you often need to get in a very precarious position in order to access the water and are resting precipitously on snow or ice that could easily break free, landing you in the drink.

Be extra careful when making any moves over water. Pack down the snow with each step to help stabilize it. Test ice by hitting it hard with your poles. Usually if the tip doesn't break all the way through, creating water that bubbles to the surface, it should be fairly strong—but no guarantees.

Ice comes in many forms and layers and can look stunning. It can be efficient and easy to travel over frozen lakes, but test the ice carefully first. Generally, "black ice" 1 inch thick is safe and supportive for a person, where upwards of 3 inches creates an acceptable margin of error to account for variable ice conditions. So-called black ice is actually perfectly clear, but when over water it appears black. This ice is the strongest, since it is uniformly frozen and void of air pockets. Gray ice, on the other hand, is typically frozen slush and riddled with air pockets. It can take upward of 6 to 8 inches of gray ice to equal the strength of 1 inch of perfectly clear black ice.

This snow bridge looked dangerous, but with temperatures below freezing, it was pretty solid. The same probably wouldn't be true had it been warmer out.
Justin Lichter

Seeing an open water source, we stopped to get water in Bubbs Creek on the way up Forrester Pass. This shot was taken right after we got Pepper out of the creek, hence the hole in the ice the same shape as Pepper's skis. *Justin Lichter*

To test the ice, try chipping away at it with your trekking pole. If you are unsuccessful, it is probably good to go. If you are going to be consistently crossing ice fields, a small hatchet is an ideal tool to verify the thickness of ice. Also be careful if you can see multiple layers of ice; try to chip away through the layers to see what's going on. Sometimes the ice can be rotten, with water layers trapped between the ice layers. If you want to add a few extra ounces to your pack weight, you can also carry an ice screw so that you can ascertain the thickness of the ice, and possibly bore through to get water.

Being on a frozen lake the first time can be very unnerving because the ice often groans, creaks, cracks, and makes other strange noises. The closest comparison would be that it sounds like a whale. Even though it may not seem unsafe, the ice is shifting, forming, melting, or doing other things that lead to these noises. Be wary!

As you plan your route across a frozen water source, scan the horizon for inconsistencies in the ice. It can sometimes be hard to distinguish open water from wind-scoured black ice. If you see mist or steam rising, it is assuredly open water. If you see what look to be frozen flowers on the surface of the ice, this is an indicator of an opening that just recently refroze and is likely thinner than surrounding areas. Keep in mind that water with current will freeze last or not at all. Water around the inlet or outlet of a lake can be most susceptible to

The unpredictable nature of ice requires constant assessment, especially along narrow creeks such as this. Having a small hatchet, while heavy, greatly expedites the checking process, increasing confidence and minimizing exposure to hypothermic consequences. Three inches of clear black ice is adequate for bearing human weight.
Larry Mishkar

thin ice, and sections of a river that pinch down will likely have rapids flowing underneath.

Shelf ice can be especially tricky to assess. This occurs when a layer of ice forms and then the water level underneath drops and freezes again, creating a hollow pocket in between. This ice will inherently sound thin and weak, but it might be perfectly fine to travel across. The only sure way to assess what is going on is to chop through both the shelf layer and the underlying ice layer. Again, we are looking for a minimum of 1 inch of black ice with 3 to 4 inches adding more peace of mind.

Bear in mind that on large frozen lakes, it will be common to find slush in the middle of the lake. This is especially likely after a large dump of snow covers the ice. The weight of the snow on the ice bows the ice layer down, causing the surface water to push up through any natural cracks in the ice layer. This slush layer is especially notorious for taking a long time to refreeze because of the insulating properties of the overlying layer of snow. Don't be alarmed if, when traveling across a frozen slush layer, you break through to icy water below, only to reveal thick black ice farther down. Besides soaking your feet and nearly having a heart attack, disaster may be averted.

Trekking or ski poles are extremely useful for testing snow bridges and snow near waterways, since often the snow can melt out from underneath in these areas. Stabbing the snow bridge or snow you are going to step on can reveal a lot about the area. Some of the things you can learn are: Is there an air pocket underneath that might collapse? What's the thickness of the snow? Is it too thin to be supportive? Is it all sugary and faceted and going to be very tough to deal with? Keep in mind that snow bridges will be strongest at night and first thing in the morning, when temps are the coldest.

Besides the obvious open water here, the presence of "frost flowers" can indicate recently frozen and thin ice. These areas are common around flowing water that froze over from a recent cold snap.
Calvin Croll

Pressure cracks in ice are actually a good sign that the ice is expanding; horizontal expansion means the ice is also growing in thickness. Don't be freaked out by eerie sounds the ice is making, much akin to that of whales.
Larry Mishkar

There are some high-stakes scenarios if you do fall into the creek or lake. Make sure you assess these when you choose to get water so that you can determine the safest location. You may not want to try to get water from a creek that gets covered by snow shortly after the opening, especially if the creek is moderately deep and there's any chance of getting swept downstream. Also, test lake ice carefully near the shallow shoreline before setting off or trying to get water near the deepest part.

If you do fall in and get wet, it's not the end of the world; but maintain your calm. It can be very difficult to get out, because the ice around the opening becomes weaker and the snow may shift as you try to clamor out; plus, you probably even have your skis or snowshoes on. We believe it helps to leave your skis or snowshoes on when trying to get water, because they will prevent you from postholing through the snow and help distribute your weight on the snow or ice. However, once you do break through, snowshoes or skis make it more challenging to get out.

When you are in the water, you'll want to scramble up to the edge of the ice or snow and lean onto it with your upper body, first checking that it will support your weight. If it won't, break off the weak areas until you get to a stronger spot. Lean onto the snow or ice with your upper body, and try to distribute your weight as much as possible over a wide area. As your upper body gets more stable and horizontal, begin to lift your legs out of the water and shimmy your entire body onto the ice or snow. Scoot horizontally, with your weight disbursed, until you are certain you are on a supportive area. You may have to release your skis or snowshoes to get back out; just make sure to hold onto them as you do so that you don't lose them.

Once you are safe from the immediate danger you have a few options to manage the situation and prevent hypothermia. You can quickly and efficiently stop, strip down, and wring out all your wet layers; put them back on; and continue traveling to stay warm. This will help to more quickly dry out your layers from the inside, since they'll have less water. Be careful with this strategy in winter—the ability to do this depends a lot on outside temperatures and overall terrain challenges, since you'll likely be unable to maintain body heat if there's a long impending downhill. As you are traveling, if you sense you are unable to regain your body heat through exertion, go immediately to Plan B.

The other option is to stop and set up camp. Strip down and wring out the layers; then get in your sleeping bag and warm up. Later, once you are warm, you can put the layers back on one by one in your sleeping bag; that will help dry them out. Alternatively, you can collect wood, start a fire, and hang your wet clothes near the fire to dry.

RESCUE AND SIGNALING

Rescue during winter and in mountainous terrain can be extremely complicated, if not impossible. It is imperative to think and plan ahead, and be proactive if you think you'll need outside help. During periods of bad weather in winter, you must be self-sufficient. You cannot rely on any search-and-rescue (SAR) agencies being able to help. You need to be ready to be self-sufficient for days on end. Helicopters often can't fly for multiple days because of winds and visibility. Decision making plays an even more important role in winter should things take a turn for the worst and you decide you need help. You'll need to assess engaging SAR, helping SAR responders find you, deciding whether you should continue traveling to try to get out of the backcountry or to a different location, determining your best escape, and be planning ahead more than ever because everything takes longer in winter and things can spiral downward faster. You can quickly go from fully functional to losing the ability to use your hands effectively—and not even be able to tie your shoelaces or put your gloves back on properly.

Timing is critical when deciding whether to activate SAR. If you have a PLB or get cell phone reception, this is a much quicker activation. However, SAR still may not be able to help for days, depending on the weather. You need to be self-sufficient and able to wait if need be. When you are deciding whether you need help, it is important to keep in mind how long it could take to get rescued. If you are on your own and only relying on an itinerary that someone at home is monitoring to make sure you check in at various intervals, you may be out even longer before SAR gets activated. Decide your best escape route for the situation, or your route to a safe place to wait it out for SAR or until the storm ends.

SIGNALING YOUR LOCATION

Neither of us is one to carry extra stuff for that just-in-case situation. We like to get creative and use what we have or what we can find to make things work. However, in winter it can be especially helpful to have a PLB. If you don't, here are some options and techniques to signal for help with what you may have with you:

- Three of anything is considered the universal sign for help. This includes three consecutive blows on a whistle (use two fingers if you aren't carrying a whistle) and three successive flashes from a headlamp or flash on your camera (it helps to be in an open area). Many headlamps now also have strobe features.

- Lay out bright clothes in a line or a triangle in an open area.

- Try using your cell phone to call or text; 911 calls will work on any network. If texting, text your location and condition to your entire contacts list. Save your battery by only turning on your cell phone for a few minutes each day.

- Make a fire in an open area to signal your location, or make three fires in the shape of a triangle. If it is daytime and a fire will be hard to see, add wet leaves, green wood, or green vegetation to create smoke and make your fires more visible.

- Use your cell phone or GPS screen to reflect the sunlight between two fingers. Point the sun reflection at your target, and move it back and forth between your fingers to signal.

- Pull a metallic-lined food wrapper tight and reflect the sun's light with it, signaling the same way as above.

- If the ground is snow-covered, pile dark-colored objects like rocks or branches in an X shape in an open area on top of the snow. If you can't get to the rocks, you can walk and pack down the snow so that it is clearly human-made. When doing this, keep in mind the orientation of the X, since ideally you want the shadow in the trough to be present in the snow most of the day.

- If you move to a different location, make sure to leave signs indicating your direction of travel and your planned route.

TIP When making a triangle or X as a locator for SAR responders, remember that you are signaling to someone in the air. Try to contrast the color of the rocks against the ground. If you are on snow, get dark-colored tree branches or rocks. If you are in a meadow, get light-colored objects. Also, make the triangle bigger than you might think you need. The sides should be at least 3 feet wide and 18 feet long.

BUILDING FIRES

Fires are a key tool for survival and comfort while winter camping. In normal circumstances I never build campfires. I can count on one hand all the times I have built a campfire in three-season camping. Most of those times the campfire was a miniscule twig smudge to create a little bit of smoke to help to keep the mosquitoes at bay. During winter, an occasional fire can be very comforting and help dry out gear that otherwise wouldn't dry.

Keep a lighter deep inside your pack in a ziplock baggie for worst-case scenarios. I usually keep one with my stove, and inside my pot, where it is unlikely to ever get wet. If I am cold and wet, I know I can set up my shelter and get warm and dry in my sleeping bag. This prevents me from having to struggle or expend extra energy to make a fire when it is raining and cold. However, it is also essential to know how to start a fire in any situation and with wet wood. Feeling comfortable making a fire can get you out of trouble and is one of your last lines of defense.

How to Build a Fire with Wet Wood in Winter

Step 1: You need to accumulate some small pieces of wood, twigs, or dry leaves to get things going. This may entail searching under trees, finding dead limbs and branches, digging into lower layers of the duff, or using the inner layer of tree bark. Depending on your location, the optimal fuel sources for starting a fire will vary. Also collect wet wood or large

Use larger, wet or semi-rotten pieces of wood as the platform for the fire, as you can see in this photo. This prevents the fire from melting into the snow, wetting out, and then extinguishing itself.
Justin Lichter

Note in the photo how the sticks are piled in a "tepee," beginning with smaller dry twigs on the bottom. This photo shows how you can use sticks as "drying lines."
Justin Lichter

Dead lower branches of tree conifers are often dry. Use these as fuel for your fire—they should be easy to gather and leave less impact on the forest than cutting down trees.
Justin Lichter

One method to start a fire is the lean-to method. Note the small dry twigs leaned against the bigger stick, and the tinder on the inside. In the Sierras and Cascades, wolf lichen can be used to help start the fire.
Justin Lichter

pieces of rotting bark. These virtually unburnable pieces will be the base for the fire to keep it from burning into the snow and snuffing itself out.

Step 2: Dig a hole into the snow with a flat bottom and about 1 foot deep, and lay down the unburnable base. On top of that, make a tepee with small sticks and put some twigs and dry

TIP If you are getting cold, you have a few options to stay warm: (1) Keep moving/hiking; (2) Do jumping jacks to get your blood moving; (3) Make a fire; (4) Make sure you eat something with a relatively high calorie content. Your body needs calories to stay warm. On cold, rainy days it is tempting to push through without stopping. Your body needs to refuel. Make sure to keep some snacks and a lunch handy so you can take quick breaks or eat while you are walking.

TIP

In an emergency situation, if you have some dry cotton like a bandanna, you can make a char cloth to help you start the fire. Use your stove and place 2-x-2-inch squares of cotton in your pot. Cover it. In a few minutes you should start to see a decent amount of smoke. When the smoke stops, shut off your stove and let it cool down. You should have squares of fabric that will catch a spark and burn slowly. When you blow on them, they should help catch your tinder on fire. You can also use any petroleum-based product, like Chapstick, DEET-based repellent, or Vaseline, and your toilet paper stash to help get your fire started. Voile Straps and Fritos make surprisingly great fire starters, further highlighting their versatility!

debris in the middle. Try to light the debris and small sticks using your lighter. If need be, pour a little bit of your stove fuel onto the debris and sticks. You can also soak a stick or dip it into your fuel bottle before adding it to the fire. Don't go too heavy with the stove fuel. You don't want to use it all in the first try; you might need to add more if the first attempt doesn't work.

Step 3: If the fire catches, let the sticks burn a bit and create some coals before you start to add more wood and slightly larger pieces. Slowly build up the size of the additional wood so that you don't drown your fire. If necessary, add a little more stove fuel to get things going. White gas is very volatile and flares up and quickly dies down. Alcohol burns for a longer time but at a lower temperature. Either can be beneficial. Fire travels upward, so it can help to try to put the fuel underneath things you are attempting to make catch.

Step 4: If your fire still isn't lighting, remember to start small. Use small pieces of dry tinder. It can also be helpful to use your knife and strip off the wet outsides of the pieces of wood that you are using. Try to get down to dry areas, and keep your fuel in a dry place. An abandoned bird's nest can make great tinder, as can dead lower limbs on evergreen trees.

Flash back to those days of making s'mores over the campfire, and use multipronged branches stuck into the snow around the fire as drying racks for socks, boot liners, gloves, and any other wet items.

Oh $#!* Moment: If the fire still isn't starting, no matter what you are doing and your sleeping bag is drenched, you need to set up your shelter and put on dry clothes or head for the car or for civilization, depending on the time of day. Know when to cut your trip short and head for the nearest trailhead. This often will not be the same trailhead you started from. Don't worry about that! You can get back to your car later. For now you must think about your immediate well-being. Keep moving and eat occasionally, even if you are not feeling hungry. Make sure to reference the map occasionally to keep on target. Head for civilization.

You do what you can to get you through until you have the opportunity to swap out incorrect gear for the conditions. Don't try this at home!
Justin Lichter

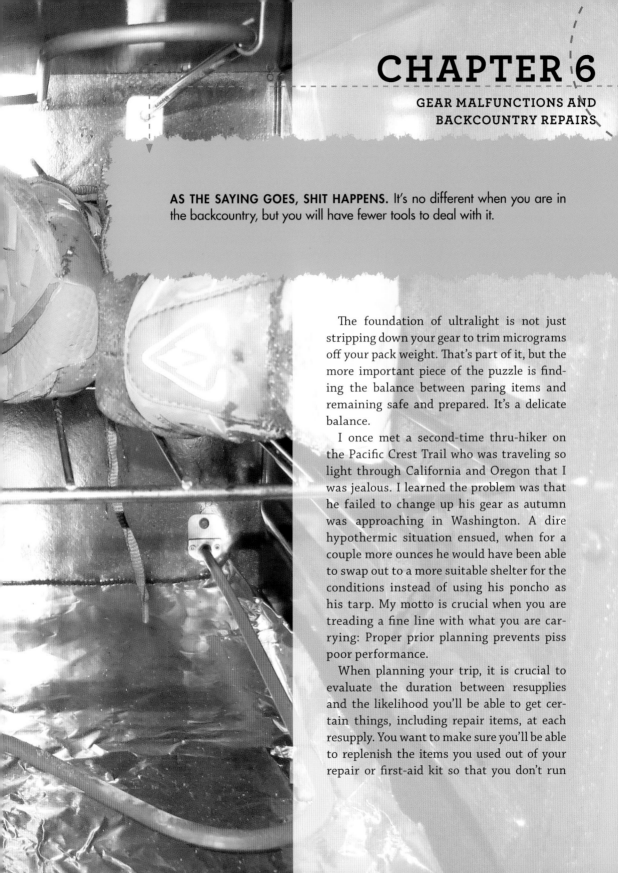

CHAPTER 6

GEAR MALFUNCTIONS AND BACKCOUNTRY REPAIRS

AS THE SAYING GOES, SHIT HAPPENS. It's no different when you are in the backcountry, but you will have fewer tools to deal with it.

The foundation of ultralight is not just stripping down your gear to trim micrograms off your pack weight. That's part of it, but the more important piece of the puzzle is finding the balance between paring items and remaining safe and prepared. It's a delicate balance.

I once met a second-time thru-hiker on the Pacific Crest Trail who was traveling so light through California and Oregon that I was jealous. I learned the problem was that he failed to change up his gear as autumn was approaching in Washington. A dire hypothermic situation ensued, when for a couple more ounces he would have been able to swap out to a more suitable shelter for the conditions instead of using his poncho as his tarp. My motto is crucial when you are treading a fine line with what you are carrying: Proper prior planning prevents piss poor performance.

When planning your trip, it is crucial to evaluate the duration between resupplies and the likelihood you'll be able to get certain things, including repair items, at each resupply. You want to make sure you'll be able to replenish the items you used out of your repair or first-aid kit so that you don't run

Our Simple First-Aid and Gear Repair Kit

Item	Use
Ibuprofen	To relieve pain and swelling
Bandanna or cloths	To make slings, compression wraps, and act as a buffer for icing injuries/ swelling
Ziplock bag	To ice injuries (with snow, ice, or cold water); can be used as an occlusive dressing and for food storage
Needle and thread (or dental floss)	To make slings, repairs, or alterations in the field; to pop blisters
Small knife/multi-tool	To cut fabric and other items; to tend to blisters
Trekking poles	To lean on like crutches to help take weight off an injured leg while walking; to splint a broken bone or damaged joint
Duct Tape	To care for foot or finger issues and repair gear (but not sleeping bags or things I don't want a sticky residue on after permanent repair)
Tenacious Tape*	Fabric rips, clothing rips, sleeping bag repair, temporary inflatable sleeping bag repairs
Zip-ties	Skin and binding repairs (do not work great in the cold)
Voile Straps x 2 (9- and 15-inch)	Attach skis to pack, repairs, shelter setup; attach frozen skins to skis; overall, extremely versatile
Torx Screwdriver	Dynafit binding repair
MaxiGlide Glide Wax	Wax for bad snow conditions and sticky snow
Foam Padding (1/8-inch thick, 3 x 5-inch piece)	Pad pressure points in ski boots
CAMP Skin Wax	Fend off sticky snow conditions
JB Weld Quick Set	Epoxy for binding repair

* When using Tenacious Tape for fabric, sleeping bag, and inflatable sleeping pad repairs, it can be useful to cut it with rounded corners. This will prevent the edges from catching on things and result in a longer lasting repair.

out. Know the quantities you might burn through based on the duration between restock locations, and tweak your kit based on the location of the trip, climate, season, and the equipment and travel mode you are using. There are a few items that always remain the same, but quantities change and other items get inserted or deleted based on these factors. You can pare down your kit as you go depending on what you are using, what gear swaps you are making, and what items are becoming dead weight. If you use an item during a stretch, pick up a replacement at your next resupply or make sure you have enough in case something else happens.

Get creative if need be. That's part of the fun of going ultralight. Create solutions with only what you have on your back. Everything you carry could be used for repair. For example, I have used the cord from my shelter guylines for a shoelace. There's no wrong way—as long as you've made it back safely and have enjoyed the experience.

REPAIRING EQUIPMENT

Sleeping Bag

Restoring durable water repellent (DWR): The DWR on a sleeping bag will wear off over time. This is pretty easy to restore with a standard DWR treatment like Revivex Air Dry Waterproofing Spray.

Leaking down: All bags will lose a few feathers here and there. Most manufacturers use a tightly woven material for the shell or a down-proof liner to help prevent this. But it is inevitable that a bag will lose a few feathers. Sometimes they're lost at the seams; other times the quills poke through the shell or liner. If this is happening, try to grab the feather through the opposite side of the sleeping bag and pull it back into the bag. The hole should be small and close up after the feather is pulled back through. If you can't do that, the feather is destined to come out. A few feathers won't affect the bag's performance. If you're losing feathers because of a rip in the shell material, or something bigger than a small hole with a protruding feather, you need to fix it.

Fabric tears: If you are out camping or hiking, use a patch of nylon repair tape or some Tenacious Tape. Carry both Tenacious Tape and duct tape. The Tenacious Tape works well for gear repairs, since it sticks amazingly and comes off without leaving any residue, unlike duct tape.

Broken zipper: It is pretty easy to replace a slider. If the coil is damaged, the repair becomes more complicated. Getting it professionally done by a gear repair service or tailor is recommended, because the entire zipper must be removed and replaced. If there is damage to only one or two teeth of the zipper, remove them with nail clippers. Pinch the damaged coil back as far as you can; the zipper should slide right across the missing teeth.

Most commonly the zipper will fail to engage both sets of teeth together. If this is occurring, the zipper might just need to be adjusted. As we use zippers, the clearance between the zipper and the teeth can slowly expand. Take a pair of pliers and *gently* squeeze both sides of the zipper to close the gap. Do a little at a time until the zipper engages the teeth as normal.

Keeping the zipper track clean and free of debris will also extend the life of your zippers. Abrasive, sandy environments are the harshest on zippers. Wash with soapy water and rinse. You can lubricate your zippers by rubbing a candle over them.

To replace the zipper slider, get a slider that matches the one you are removing. Letters printed on the slider tell you the size you need. If the stop and end are sewn into the bag, use a seam ripper to carefully remove stitching around the lower ends of the zipper tabs. When the zipper's end is visible, pry off the metal stop at bottom of the zipper. Take care to not tear the tape at the base of the zipper teeth; it can unravel. With the stop off, slide the old zipper slider off. Take the new zipper slider and guide it onto the track tape (the coils or teeth). Start on the side the stop was on, if applicable. If there was a stop, replace it, then feed the opposite track tape in and test the zipper. If the stop was just sewn in, insert both track tapes into the top grooves of the slider, pushing them through to the slider's bottom. Use a pin if necessary to work the track tapes through. Pull tapes gently to make sure the slider is sitting evenly on the tracks. With both tapes threaded through the slider, gently pull it up until the locked track teeth appear at the bottom; make sure they're even and track evenly. If the metal zipper ends were sewn into the bag itself, sew a new stop at the top of the tracks with needle and thread. Sew the zipper back into the sleeping bag, following the guidelines of needle holes left from where stitching was removed for repair.

Sleeping Pad

To find a hole or leak in an inflatable pad, submerge the inflated pad in soapy water. Remove the pad, and with the valve closed try to push out the air. The soapsuds should bubble in the area with the leak and show you where you need to place the patch. Place the patch as directed in the package instructions. Make sure to let the glue set before using the pad. If doing this in the field in the cold, make sure to warm up the pad and the patch before trying to adhere the patch. It will stick and stay on a lot better if both the pad and patch are warm.

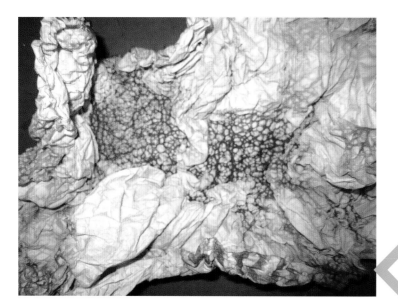

Be careful of some Laundromat dryers. Many have very high heat settings that can melt nylon or other materials into cauliflower.
Justin Lichter

Shelter

A few things can break on shelters, depending on the type you're using. Tarps are the simplest to repair because you're usually just dealing with fabric. Handle any fabric rips as mentioned above for fabric tears in sleeping bags.

To deal with a broken zipper, you may be able to replace the slider on the rain fly, but probably not on the inner tent because it is sewn in at the stopper. It can also be tricky to replace the coil on the inner body for the same reason, even if you are an experienced sewer. If the zipper breaks on the tent, get creative and do what you can to get through the trip safely. Guy out the rain fly to provide better coverage and hold the fly taught. Use your rain gear if you need to cover some holes in the system.

If your tent pole breaks, it's unlikely that you are carrying the sleeve that came with the pole for repairs. Use duct tape with a stick to help splint the pole around the break, just as you would do in a first-aid situation for a long bone injury. Another alternative is to see if you can tie off to a tree or use your trekking pole to create the necessary support for setting up the tent.

Clothing

Generally, treat the same as above for fabric tears if it is a nylon layer (wind shell or rain jacket) or zipper repair, with the exception of base layers, non-nylon, or "soft" layers. For those types of layers, you'll want to break out your needle and thread and sew up the rips.

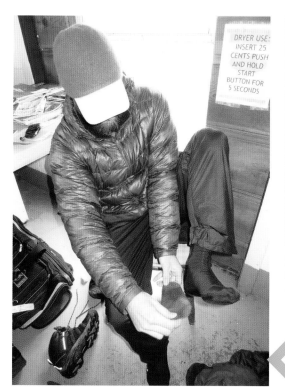

Nighttime chores include repairing gear to help keep it functioning at its best.
Justin Lichter

Using a powerful dryer led to miniature insoles and painful miles until replacements were found.
Justin Lichter

Trekking Poles

Poles usually snap. If a pole snaps, it is pretty much done. You may be able to jerry-rig the pole to a functioning state, though, by extending the remaining pole sections to a manageable height and doing the best you can.

Shoes

Get used to it. Shoes wear out and start to break down; laces break. As long as they are still comfortable, normal wear is manageable. For more significant wear, use duct tape to fill in heel rips, or wrap mesh rips in duct tape to close the rip to prevent snow from getting in. Tie broken laces together, or adjust the lacing technique to accommodate the length you have. Alternatively, you could cut a length of cord for a shoelace.

Do what you can to alleviate problems and make temporary fixes until you can get into town and can make a more permanent fix or get a replacement.
Justin Lichter

Ski Boots

The main things that are going to break on your ski boots are the buckles, tightening system, or liner. Duct tape should take care of most of these with a little finessing. Since some ski boots have buckles that are screwed on, make sure to carry a small multi-tool. These screws can loosen over time during long trips. Some buckling systems are riveted. Rivets sometimes break and can be a pain to fix in the field. The easiest way is to tie the buckle tightly back through the rivet hole using a piece of cord. Carrying a couple of small zip-ties can also be helpful in case of an emergency.

You can also get snow or ice built up on the metal areas where the tech binding cinches on the boot. This usually happens when your boots have hit water, enabling the snow to stick to the metal. This usually is pretty easy to solve by knocking or chipping the snow or ice out of the cavity. However, be careful using your trekking poles to bang your boots, especially carbon fiber poles. Try to chip with the tip. You can create small chips in the carbon fiber; this will create weaknesses and make it easier to snap your poles.

Skis

Skis can chip, delaminate, experience core shots or edges ripping out, or full-on break. Most of these issues are critical failures and won't be easily resolved in the field. Chipping of the top sheet or delaminating can be resolved fairly easily. For minor chips, you don't have to do anything. For more severe delaminating, you want to superglue the top sheet back in place and clamp it down to prevent further delamination. Similarly, when an edge rips out, you'll want to superglue it back into place and clamp it down to let it set in place. If you don't feel like you can do a good enough job in the field, wait until you are in town, since it will be harder to repair the repair once it is glued in place. If you are doing these fixes in

Repeated bashing into the ski in tour mode led to dents in the front of the boot that needed to be punched out numerous times to prevent losing valuable toe room. Also, the screw holding the carbon fiber in place came out. Note the cord used to fasten it instead.
Justin Lichter

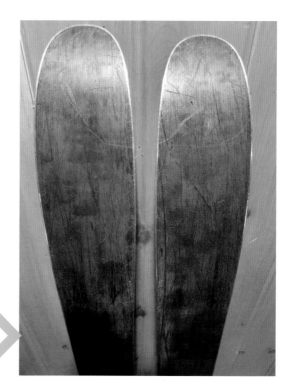

Beat-up skis are bound to happen in less-than-ideal conditions or on long trips. The superficial wounds in this picture can easily be taken care of with a good waxing and tune-up. Core shots require P-Tex for proper repairs, and edge problems should be repaired by an experienced tech for the best results.
Shawn Forry

The wrong conditions can add tons of weight to your ski setup and make any glide virtually impossible. A few ounces of weight in wax can be a lifesaver.
Shawn Forry

the field, make sure the ski and the glue are warm so that the glue sets faster.

Core shots are not the end of the world, but you'll probably wait to repair them until you can get to town, since you'll need an iron and some base repair material, like P-Tex. If your ski breaks or snaps, you are probably hung out to dry. Depending on where it breaks, you may be able to keep using the ski to help you make the quickest exit to a road without postholing. Ideally, the break will be near the tip or tail so it doesn't affect the performance that much. If the break is right underneath the binding, it will be a challenge to keep your foot locked into the binding. For an emergency fix, create a bridge on top of the ski with a flat piece of wood or metal, and then duct tape and superglue it.

Less of a repair, but just as important to the overall maintenance of your skis (and your overall mental health), is waxing them regularly. Hot wax them with the appropriate color wax when you are in town, and carry some easy-to-apply liquid/gel wax for the backcountry. Sometimes snow conditions are so heinous that the snow will clump and stick to the base of your skis, adding pounds and pounds to your skis—and friction that will make you feel like a fly trying to escape glue paper. It's frustrating as hell, but a quick wax application can help temporarily.

Ski Bindings

Bindings can be a little complicated, and there's a wide range. The toe piece on one of the original AT bindings, Fritschi, had a notorious tendency to break. This was a difficult field repair. The issue has been resolved for a while now, but generally we'd still steer clear of Fritschi, Marker, and other bindings that claim they're AT bindings. Not because of poor quality or breaking problems, but because they are darn heavy and built more for in-bounds and freeriding, and occasional backcountry or side-country use, where there's minimal touring. We're not going to go into field repairs for these types of bindings; instead we're going to focus on what people will likely use.

Tech Bindings

Tech bindings are generally pretty simple, with minimal moving parts. Screws could loosen or rip out. A simple small Allen wrench or screwdriver should help in the event the screws loosen. A small tube of superglue or epoxy can be useful if the screws rip out. One of the more common issues is ice buildup underneath in the footplate on the toe piece. This happens more frequently under certain conditions. One is when snow gets packed in underneath the boot and then gets wet, or melts and freezes. Another is when warming snow or corn snow gets underneath the boot and then freezes in the evening or in the shade when the temperature drops. This issue can make it difficult, if not impossible, to release the boot from the binding. It can be very frustrating. To resolve this issue, make sure to carry a thin knife, like the Vargo Wharn Clip knife or the Baladeo 22-gram backpacking knife. Use the openings in the side of the binding to chip away at the ice. It's debatable how long it works, but it can also be helpful to spray PAM on your bindings and on the top sheet of your skis to prevent snow buildup.

When you are camping and get out of your skis in the evening, make sure to get all the snow out of your bindings. Otherwise you could have a tough time getting your skis on in the morning. Most of these ultra lightweight bindings and boots are made for ski racing and not for constant overnight use. They are designed to be used hard for one day and then sit in a house drying out that night and the next day.

One of the downfalls of tech bindings is that in the right—or wrong—conditions, the binding can get iced up and not allow your boot to be released—making it very hard to switch from downhill to tour or get your ski off. The easiest and quickest way to solve this is to use your knife in the slits in the bindings to chip away at the ice buildup.
Justin Lichter

Telemark Bindings

Telemark bindings are generally pretty low maintenance. As with anything with screws, the screws could rip out. Another issue is that the heel plate or toe plate breaks, which usually isn't a critical failure. The spring could pop out, which is typically as simple a repair as screwing it back in. A more major problem is the rivets breaking and the toe bail over the duckbill popping free. This creates a major loss of control. There is no easy fix to regain as much control, especially on downhills.

Skins

Skins have three main parts that can go wrong: {1) the attachment points, (2) the glue, and (3) the skin itself. If the attachments go on the fritz in the field, it can be frustrating but isn't a deal breaker. You can use what you have in your repair kit to create a temporary fix. Zip-ties, duct tape, and superglue can all work, depending on the exact issue. A friend who is a polar explorer usually rivets his skins to his skis before he sets off on an expedition so he knows he won't have any problems with the skin attachments during the trek. Granted, this is for polar exploration, so it clearly isn't recommended for the type of rolling and mountainous terrain we are often traversing; we just wanted to mention this as an option. It's a good example of thinking outside the box and doing what works for you and for the terrain you'll be encountering.

The second issue with skins that are getting tired, when they have been used a lot and repeatedly taken on and off the skis, is that the glue can stop sticking. This can also occur when your skins get wet. These are two different issues. Well-worn skins can be re-glued. This is a resupply or town-time task. You won't want to do this in the field, nor will you want to carry extra skin glue. You'll see this issue coming for weeks if not months before you finally decide that you either have to retire the skins and get new ones or re-glue them.

Another issue of wet or frozen skins can happen in certain temperatures and snow conditions, or if you walk across running water in your skis with skins on. This can create a couple of issues: (1) Snow may now stick to your skins, and (2) the glue may not work as well. To handle issue number one, you may want to carry a small chunk of "skin wax." This wax can

Over time the plastic holes can stretch out or crack, making you susceptible to losing the clip. Keep an eye on the wear and tear, as these tail clips can take a beating and often flip off the tail of the skis.
Justin Lichter

be rubbed on without heating and creates just enough of a coating to prevent snow from sticking to the skin.

Always try to dry out your skins when you have the opportunity. This may be as simple as fastening them to the outside of your pack for the downhills or when you're not using them, or laying them out during a break. This will also help keep the glue working better. Also try not to get dirt, pine needles, or other debris in the skin glue. If the glue isn't sticking as well because of wet skins, this isn't a critical failure. The ski attachment should still be able to hold the skin on sufficiently; however, you may just see some separation between the ski and the skin if you pick up your ski; that separation will disappear as you weight your ski.

Snowshoes

With snowshoes you can break straps, frames, or the material inside the snowshoe, allowing you to float. These all can be major nuisances but should be repairable with the items in your repair kit. Remember, not everything has to be a permanent repair but, at the minimum, should make do until you can get out of the backcountry and either effect a repair better, since you'll have better tools and supplies, or replace the broken item.

Straps can be repaired using zip-ties, duct tape, or cord, just as we noted previously for ski boots and other items with straps. The material can be repaired by either using duct tape or sewing it, depending on the type of material the manufacturer used for the platform. If you are confident and want to really get creative, you can overlay another piece of plastic or something and sew it or even try melting it together. Be careful; the goal is to "create no further harm." The frames are generally made out of metal, so the fix is usually duct taping it back together, and maybe splinting it with another small piece of metal so the frame doesn't saw through the duct tape.

APPENDIX A:
WINTER GRAB AND GO GEAR CHECKLIST

Here's a generic checklist to use as a guide for an overnight adventure if you're scrambling to pack up and get out the door. This can of course be catered to the season, destination, and type of tour/trip, but you'll find it a useful reference tool for gathering your gear and making sure you don't forget anything.

Carrying System   Weight

❑ Backpack or pulk   _____

❑ Hip-belt pockets   _____

Mode of Travel

❑ Type of travel equipment—skis, snowshoes, etc.   _____

❑ Boots, overboots   _____

❑ Trekking or ski poles   _____

Sleep System

❑ Sleeping bag   _____

❑ Sleeping pad   _____

❑ Shelter and tent stakes   _____

❑ Groundsheet   _____

Clothing

❑ Waterproof pants   _____

❑ Base layers   _____

❑ Socks   _____

❑ Mid/Insulating layer   _____

❑ Rain pants   _____

❑ Rain jacket   _____

❑ Underwear   _____

❑ Wind jacket and pants   _____

- ❑ Leggings _____
- ❑ Accessories—shoes, cap, sunglasses _____
- ❑ Warm accessories—beanie, gloves, balaclava, mittens, overmitts, neoprene or VBL socks _____

Food and Water

- ❑ Stuff sack(s) (for food bag) _____
- ❑ Cookware (pot, stove, windscreen, spork, fuel, lighter) _____
- ❑ Water treatment _____
- ❑ Water bottle(s) _____
- ❑ Water bladder(s) _____
- ❑ Snacks, meals, drink mix, etc. _____

Necessities and Accessories

- ❑ Map, book, notebook, trail info, knife, pen, spare batteries, first-aid kit _____
- ❑ Toiletries—toothbrush, small toothpaste, floss, contact lens solution, glasses, toilet paper, trowel, etc. _____
- ❑ Personal items—credit card, ID, keys (if necessary), cash _____
- ❑ Electronics—phone, headlamp, camera (with extra memory card), GPS unit, satellite tracker, etc. _____
- ❑ Repair and first-aid kit—ibuprofen, Tenacious Tape, cord, Voile Straps, JB Weld, screwdriver, duct tape, etc. _____
- ❑ Avalanche safety items—beacon, probe, shovel _____

APPENDIX B:

GEAR LIST FROM OUR WINTER PACIFIC CREST TRAIL TRIP

Item	Backpack (WA)	Snowshoe	Ski	Backpack (SoCal)	Pre-Trip Notes	Post-Trip Notes
Packing						
Granite Gear Virga 2 (Pepper)	18.7 oz					Light and simple. Enough volume for bulky winter gear. Improvement over original Virga.
Granite Gear Crown V.C. 60 (Trauma)	34 oz	34 oz		34 oz		
Granite Gear Snow Leopard V.C. 46		44.2 oz			Custom Cuben Fiber with carbon framesheet	Beaver tail perfect for carrying snowshoes. Perfect blend of weight and performance.
Granite Gear Leopard AC 58			53.3 oz			Comfortable to 45-plus pounds. Easy to carry skies as needed. Side pockets do not hold items well during falls while skiing. Make sure things are strapped in/fastened.
Mountain Laurel Designs Exodus (Pepper)				16.2 oz		Go-to pack for three-season outings.
Mountain Laurel Designs Pack Pockets (2)	2.4 oz	2.4 oz	2.4 oz	2.4 oz	Storage for camera, sunscreens, snacks, etc.	Easy to access. Attachment to Mountain Laurel Designs packs could be improved.
Granite Gear Air Zippsack (medium) (2)	3.4 oz	3.4 oz	3.4 oz	3.4 oz	Food storage	Two-food bag system, perfect for separating morning/dinner foods from daytime snacks.

Note: Green boxes in the chart indicate Group Gear Shared.

Item	Backpack (WA)	Snowshoe	Ski	Backpack (SoCal)	Pre-Trip Notes	Post-Trip Notes
Pack liner	1.8 oz	1.8 oz	1.8 oz	1.8 oz	Trash compactor bag	Lasted about one month. Hard to find name-brand compactor bags; off-brand thinner.
Sleeping/Shelter						
Katabatic Sawtooth 15-degree quilt (Pepper)	24.8 oz	24.8 oz				Amazing warmth and coverage. Could push into single digits as needed.
Katabatic Palisades 30-degree quilt (Pepper)			18.2 oz	18.2 oz	Down inner, combined rating of 0°F	Amazing warmth and coverage. Perfect wet-weather system with Mountain Laurel Designs overbag. Good to single digits.
Montbell Down Hugger 900 #2 (Trauma)	24 oz	24 oz	24 oz	24 oz		Worked well the whole trip. In conjunction with Spirit quilt on cold nights.
Mountain Laurel Designs Spirit 38 Overquilt		18.3 oz	18.3 oz		Overbag for moisture management, wearable	Light plus compact for synthetic. Just large enough to act as overbag. Closure system could be improved.
Katabatic Bristlecone Bivy (Pepper)	6.0 oz	6.0 oz	6.0 oz	6.0 oz	Custom Cuben Fiber floor	Helped with spindrift under tarp and keeping quilt systems together. Used with XTherm inside for added warmth.
Granite Gear Uberlight Dry Sack	0.6 oz	0.6 oz	0.6 oz		Ensure dry sleep system	Extremely light. Prone to wearing out from Velcro abrasion from overbag.
Therm-a-Rest NeoAir XTherm	17.4 oz	17.4 oz	17.4 oz	17.4 oz	Used in conjunction with Goodnight pad, mummy 20- x 72-inch, R-Value 5.7	Unbelievable warmth. Used entire trip. Packs compact. Repaired one hole by valve after 2,400 miles.

Item	Backpack (WA)	Snowshoe	Ski	Backpack (SoCal)	Pre-Trip Notes	Post-Trip Notes
Therm-a-Rest ProLite XS (Trauma)	9.0 oz			9.0 oz		"The Kidney Bean."
Tyvek groundsheet	4.6 oz	4.6 oz	4.6 oz	4.6 oz	Longer lasting than polycro	Good durability. Retained moisture. Would likely use heavy-gauge plastic in future.
Mountain Laurel Designs Cuben Duomid (Pepper)	14.6 oz	14.6 oz	14.6 oz	14.6 oz		Amazing balance of strength/space/weight. Confining during storms. Wish door was on end not side.
Vargo Titanium Ascent Tent Stake (8) (Trauma)	2.4 oz	2.4 oz	2.4 oz	2.4 oz	Use skis as deadman for winter setup.	Great holding power in extreme wind. No pulled stakes. Needle stakes easier to place in frozen ground.
Cooking/ Water						
Trail Designs Ti-Tri Sidewinder	3.5 oz	3.5 oz	3.5 oz	3.5 oz	Burns wood, alcohol, Esbit	Great versatility. Simple and light. Slow to melt snow, but we knew that going in and had the time/darkness.
Vargo 1.3 L Titanium Pot (Pepper)	5.4 oz	5.4 oz	5.4 oz	5.4 oz	Big enough to melt water if needed; fill hot water bottle at night	Perfect winter size. Lip on pot not large enough for Caldera Cone.
Evernew 1.3 L Titanium Ultralight Pot (Trauma)	4.6 oz	4.6 oz	4.6 oz	4.6 oz	Big enough to melt water if needed; fill hot water bottle at night	Winter size. Normal size is 900 milliliters.
1 L Platypus Plus Bottle	1.3 oz	1.3 oz	1.3 oz	1.3 oz	Alcohol for backup	Enough fuel capacity for 10-plus days and melting snow.
Vargo ULV Titanium Spork	0.2 oz	0.2 oz	0.2 oz	0.2 oz		

Item	Backpack (WA)	Snowshoe	Ski	Backpack (SoCal)	Pre-Trip Notes	Post-Trip Notes
Lighter (2)	0.8 oz	0.8 oz	0.8 oz	0.8 oz	Mini-Bic, spare in ziplock bag	Spare crucial for winter trips. Common to drop lighter in snow with gloved hands.
Platypus 2 L Water Bottle (2)				2.6 oz		
Nalgene 1 L Canteen	2.1 oz	2.1 oz	2.1 oz			Easy access with wide mouth. Horrible quality. Broke four-plus bottles between us.
Vargo Titanium Water Bottle	3.9 oz	3.9 oz	3.9 oz		For hot water bottle, more durable with freezing bottles	Versatile for winter. Could put on stove or fire. Lid handle prone to breaking but not needed. Wish it came in 1 liter option.
1 L Gatorade bottle				1.0 oz		Cheap and simple. Go-to bottle for warmer temps.
Vargo Titanium Wharn-Clip Knife	1.0 oz	1.0 oz	1.0 oz	1.0 oz	Sharp and light	Simple and compact. Did not miss not being able to fold for closure. Extremely sharp.
Snowshoe System						
MSR Women's Lightning Ascent Snowshoes	58.6 oz	58.6 oz			Per pair; women's version lighter/narrower	Perfect snowshoe for variety of conditions. Extremely durable. LOTS of miles. We were not nice to these!
NEOS Adventurer Overboot		35.2 oz			Per pair. Size XL	Crucial for cold/wet conditions. Likely saved our trip after frostbite incident. Closure system needs improvement.
Oboz Sawtooth Low (Pepper)		33.6 oz				Good balance of weight and durability. Opted against waterproof version for quicker dry time.
Salomon Ultra Mid GTX (Trauma)		29 oz				Used GTX version inside NEOS to try to prevent getting wet from trapped condensation.

Item	Backpack (WA)	Snowshoe	Ski	Backpack (SoCal)	Pre-Trip Notes	Post-Trip Notes
NRS Hydroskin Neoprene Socks		3.4 oz				Rarely used, but added warmth in cold conditions. Seams need improvement if wearing next to skin.
Ski Gear (Worn)						
Voile Vector BC			48.2 oz		170 cm, per ski 118/94/107, patterned base	Perfect blend of weight and function. Patterned base is a must in rolling terrain. Wide enough for deep conditions.
Dynafit Low Tech Lite Bindings			5.8 oz		Per binding	Simple and light. Toe piece prone to freezing. Heel post prone to twisting. Minor annoyances for function.
Scarpa Aliens (Pepper)			29.7 oz		Mondo 28, per boot	Amazing comfort for a ski boot! Not durable enough for extended outings. Failure of BOA closure/Dyneema cord. Easy to get wet.
Dynafit PDG (Trauma)			28.8 oz		Mondo 29, per boot	Fitted at bootfitter to fit well; very uncomfortable before. No tongue, so added Mountain Laurel Designs gaiter to prevent wetting out.
Superfeet Carbon Insoles			1.7 oz		Trim to fit	Thin and supportive. Added needed volume in ski liner.
Ski Gear (Carried)						
CAMP Mohair Guide Skins (Pepper)			16.2 oz			Good balance of grip/glide. Quick to dry. Poor adhesion in extremely cold conditions. Attachment quick and easy.
Voile Skins with Tail Clip (Trauma)			25 oz			Good glue and good durability. Tail clip can be a pain when it comes off and skin gets iced up.

Item	Backpack (WA)	Snowshoe	Ski	Backpack (SoCal)	Pre-Trip Notes	Post-Trip Notes
Pieps Freeride Avalanche Beacon			3.8 oz		Lightest available beacon	Good battery life. Prone to turning on in sleeping bag. Noticeable lag time in search function.
CAMP Carbon Fiber Probe			4.7 oz		Lightest available probe	
Arva Snow Plume Shovel			13.4 oz		Double as stove base while cooking in snow; tarp pole foundation	Good balance of weight and shovel surface area. Durability of blade was poor.
CAMP Race 290 Crampon			10.3 oz		Integrate into AT boots	Didn't end up using, but carried. Easy attachment after adjusted. Compact and light to carry.

Ski Repair Kit

Item	Backpack (WA)	Snowshoe	Ski	Backpack (SoCal)	Pre-Trip Notes	Post-Trip Notes
Torx Screwdriver (Pepper)			1.4 oz		Dynafit binding repair	
MaxiGlide Glide Wax (Trauma)			2.5 oz			Gloppy snow conditions are a nightmare. This did its best to combat the conditions; short to last.
Foam Padding (Pepper)			0.6 oz		Pad pressure points, $\frac{1}{8}$ inch thick, 3 x 5-inch sheet	Worth the weight! Negated pressure points after days in ski boots.
CAMP Skin Wax (Pepper)			1.9 oz		40 grams with case	Extremely helpful in variable conditions. Candle would work for cheaper alternative.
Voile Strap (2) (Split)			1.1 oz		9-inch, 15-inch; attach skis to pack, repairs, etc.	Extremely versatile. Used to combine trekking poles for tarp, attach frozen skins, etc.
JB Weld Quick Set (Pepper)			1.3 oz		Epoxy for binding repair	

Item	Backpack (WA)	Snowshoe	Ski	Backpack (SoCal)	Pre-Trip Notes	Post-Trip Notes
Granite Gear Air Zippsack (small) (Both)			0.5 oz			
Zip ties (Pepper)			0.3 oz		Skin and binding repairs	Test zip-ties before using. Poor quality; did not work in the cold.
Other						
Gossamer Gear EZC 2 Line (50 feet)	1.5 oz	1.5 oz	1.5 oz	1.5 oz	Repairs, knot per foot, cutting cornices	
Leki Carbon Titanium Trekking Pole	8.3 oz	8.3 oz		8.3 oz	Per pole; backpack section, use for mid setup; duct tape on pole	Carbon poor choice for cold and snowy conditions. Carbon becomes brittle, easy to break. Broke four sections; Trauma, one.
Leki Venom Vario S Trekking Pole			9.8 oz		Per pole; stronger and cross-country style grip; duct tape on pole	Great ski pole. Amazingly strong! Twist lock can be problematic in cold conditions.
Helinox Passport Tension Lock 125 (Pepper)				6.0 oz	Per pole	Amazingly strong for the weight. Wish I had purchased the adjustable version for tarp setup.
Vargo Titanium Pocket Cleat				1.9 oz		Great purchase in ice/firm snow for under 2 ounces. Worth the weight. Very packable. Likely will only work with some shoe types.

Item	Backpack (WA)	Snowshoe	Ski	Backpack (SoCal)	Pre-Trip Notes	Post-Trip Notes
Clothing (Worn)						
Montbell Stretch Light Pants	12.2 oz				Lightweight soft shell for mild water resistance	Light and simple. Great fit.
Montbell Alpine Ridge Pants		17.4 oz	17.4 oz			Great balance of weight, durability and function. Full side zips key. Lack of pockets was a challenge.
Montbell Breeze Spun Shorts				8.5 oz		Light and simple. Great fit.
Icebreaker Oasis Legging		6.6 oz	6.6 oz			
Icebreaker Bodyfit 200 L/S	7.3 oz			7.3 oz		Great warmth. Low odor.
Icebreaker Mondo Zip 200 L/S		8.9 oz	8.9 oz		One-quarter zip, greater neck coverage	Great warmth. Low odor.
Montbell Tachyon Anorak	1.9 oz	1.9 oz	1.9 oz	1.9 oz		Most versatile clothing layer. Wore nearly every day. Fit is poor.
Exofficio Boxer Brief (Pepper)	2.8 oz	2.8 oz	2.8 oz	2.8 oz		Extremely durable, comfortable, quick to dry.
Icebreaker Relaxed Boxer with fly (Trauma)	3.2 oz	3.2 oz	3.2 oz	3.2 oz		
Suunto Vector Watch	2.0 oz	2.0 oz	2.0 oz	2.0 oz	Watch, altimeter, compass	Easy layout, useful functions. Prone to fogging up after replacing battery. Hard to reseal unit.

Item	Backpack (WA)	Snowshoe	Ski	Backpack (SoCal)	Pre-Trip Notes	Post-Trip Notes
FITS Light Hiker Crew Sock	2.7 oz	2.7 oz			Extra warmth	Great fit and durability.
FITS Light Ski Sock			4.0 oz			Great fit and durability.
FITS Pro Trail Quarter Sock				2.1 oz		Great fit and durability.
Montbell 3-D Mesh Hat (Pepper)	2.4 oz	2.4 oz	2.4 oz	2.4 oz		
Montbell Wool Beanie (Pepper)	1.5 oz	1.5 oz	1.5 oz	1.5 oz		Super warm. Prone to shrinking in wash.
Icebreaker Chase Beanie (Trauma)	1.2 oz	1.2 oz	1.2 oz	1.2 oz		
Icebreaker Wool Baseball Hat with ear flaps (Trauma)	3.0 oz	3.0 oz	3.0 oz	3.0 oz		
CAMP G-Lite Wind Gloves	2.8 oz					Durable but lacked warmth.
Outdoor Research PL400 Gloves		2.8 oz	2.8 oz			Power Stretch much warmer than anything else. Easy to wring water out and dry. Good durability for fabric.
Suncloud Conductor Sunglasses (Pepper)	1.2 oz	1.2 oz	1.2 oz	1.2 oz	Affordable sunglasses	Cheap.

Item	Backpack (WA)	Snowshoe	Ski	Backpack (SoCal)	Pre-Trip Notes	Post-Trip Notes
Smith Director Sunglasses (Trauma)		1.2 oz	1.2 oz	1.2 oz		
Montbell Spats (Pepper)	2.1 oz			2.1 oz	Keep powder, desert debris out of shoes	Great for sealing out minor precipitation. Need full gaiter for deeper conditions. Good durability on bottom strap.
Oboz Traverse Low BDry (Pepper)	36.5 oz				Waterproof for warmth	Had issues with fit in heel. Hard for feet to break in with extremely wet conditions.
Oboz Sawtooth Low BDry (Pepper)				33.5 oz		Good balance of weight and durability. Still look great after 650-plus miles. BDry helpful for Southern California storms, lingering snowfields.
Vasque Pendulum 2 (Trauma)	20.4 oz			20.4 oz		Used GTX version in Washington, non-GTX version in Southern California.
Clothing (Carried)						
Montbell UL Down Parka	9.0 oz				Camp and sleeping	Poor choice. Got wet from condensation under tarp since we were having a lot of precipitation. Switched to full synthetic outer layers. Much better.
Montbell ThermaWrap Pro Parka			15.1 oz	15.1 oz	Camp and sleeping	Perfect for continuous wet/cold conditions. Easy to layer over ThermaWrap jacket.

Item	Backpack (WA)	Snowshoe	Ski	Backpack (SoCal)	Pre-Trip Notes	Post-Trip Notes
Montbell ThermaWrap Jacket	9.8 oz	9.8 oz	9.8 oz		Use Mountain Laurel Designs Spirit quilt as secondary layer in camp in ski section	Lighter than fleece and more wind resistant.
Montbell Torrent Flier Jacket	8.6 oz	8.6 oz	8.6 oz		Gore-Tex Paclite	Nothing is waterproof.
Mountain Laurel Designs Cuben Poncho Tarp	4.3 oz	4.3 oz	4.3 oz	4.3 oz	WA rain/snow, shelter during breaks, cooking in camp, groundsheet	Amazing versatility! Kept pack drier in continuous rain. Extended life of rainwear. Pepper used as groundsheet in the snow.
Icebreaker Balaclava	1.5 oz	1.5 oz	1.5 oz			
REI Tech Compatible Mitts	1.5 oz	1.5 oz	1.5 oz		Camp and sleeping	Great warmth for weight. REI brand Power Stretch is very poor quality. Fabric pilled after one day.
Fits Light Hiker Crew	2.7 oz	2.7 oz	2.7 oz	2.7 oz	Sleep socks, spare socks	Great fit and durability.
Mountain Laurel Designs eVent Rain Mitts	1.0 oz	1.0 oz	1.0 oz		Storm shell and camp	Added marginal waterproofness. Poor fit but could layer underneath. Nearly impossible to keep hands dry in extended precipitation.
Icebreaker Oasis Leggings	6.6 oz			6.6 oz		
Montbell Versalite Pant	3.6 oz			3.6 oz		Surprisingly waterproof for the weight. Easily shredded by snowshoes.
Montbell Dynamo Wind Pant		2.8 oz	2.8 oz	2.8 oz		Great versatility for the weight. Nice in camp for added warmth or on sunny days to get out of stuffy rainwear.

Item	Backpack (WA)	Snowshoe	Ski	Backpack (SoCal)	Pre-Trip Notes	Post-Trip Notes
Toiletries						
Toothbrush	0.4 oz	0.4 oz	0.4 oz	0.4 oz		
Toothpowder/ toothpaste	0.4 oz	0.4 oz	0.4 oz	0.4 oz	Tooth powder to prevent freezing	
Head Hunter Sunscreen	1.2 oz	1.2 oz	1.2 oz	1.2 oz	45 SPF	Lasts a long time. Great protection with added zinc.
Second Skin	0.5 oz	0.5 oz	0.5 oz	0.5 oz	Blister care	A must for constant foot ailments. Recommend Compeed brand if you can find it.
Neosporin	0.9 oz	0.9 oz	0.9 oz	0.9 oz	Wound care	
Band-aids, 2 x 3-inch (10)	0.8 oz	0.8 oz	0.8 oz	0.8 oz	Treating frostbite	Part of daily routine for keeping frostbite clean and dry.
Toilet Paper	2.0 oz	2.0 oz	2.0 oz	2.0 oz		
Ibuprofen (50 pills)	0.6 oz	0.6 oz	0.6 oz	0.6 oz	Inflammation	
Sewing Kit (Trauma)	0.1 oz	0.1 oz	0.1 oz	0.1 oz	Repairs	
Super Glue (Pepper)	0.1 oz	0.1 oz	0.1 oz	0.1 oz	Repairs	Micro bottles were perfect for single use.
Mountain Laurel Designs Cuben Zip Pouch (medium)	0.2 oz	0.2 oz	0.2 oz	0.2 oz	Toiletries	Super durable ditty bag. Kept contents dry.
Electronics						
Canon S95 Camera	6.8 oz	6.8 oz	6.8 oz		HD Video, w/ 16GB card	Amazing camera. Highly recommend the Powershot S Series. Pepper's broke after 2,200 miles from negligence.

Item	Backpack (WA)	Snowshoe	Ski	Backpack (SoCal)	Pre-Trip Notes	Post-Trip Notes
OtterBox Camera Case	5.0 oz	5.0 oz			Fully waterproof	Great case. Closure is troublesome; Pepper's broke after 1,500 miles.
Aloksak			0.8 oz			Emergency backup for camera. Not ideal for full protection. Likely reason camera broke.
Spare Camera Battery	0.7 oz	0.7 oz			Cold will drain batteries quicker	Camera battery life was surprisingly good. Did not need. Camera battery good for two to three weeks in the cold if slept with, although occasionally died during the day.
Princeton Tec Vizz	3.3 oz	3.3 oz	3.3 oz	3.3 oz	AAA batteries easy to find, light and bright	Super bright and light. Good battery life.
MP3 Player w/ headphones (Pepper)	2.4 oz	2.4 oz		2.4 oz	Sony 16G E Series	Amazing battery life and durability. This MP3 player has been through hell and back! Way better than an iPod.
Spare Batteries	1.3 oz	1.3 oz	1.3 oz	1.3 oz	(3) AAA	
Iridium 9555 SAT Phone (Pepper)			8.8 oz		Emergencies, weather reports, updates	Light and simple to use. Added extra margin of safety through High Sierra.
DeLorme InReach Explorer (Trauma)			6.6 oz		Emergency response, GPS, texting, redundancy in case of avalanche—both would have communicator	Multifunctional. Able to receive weather updates, track location, and send text for logistical needs. Helpful with Halfmile app.
Smartphone and charger (Trauma)					For use in towns and on trail	Helpful in town.

Item	Backpack (WA)	Snowshoe	Ski	Backpack (SoCal)	Pre-Trip Notes	Post-Trip Notes
Miscellaneous						
Maps (Trauma)	~2.0 oz	~2.0 oz	~2.0 oz	~2.0 oz	Halfmile maps	Huge advocate of carrying paper maps. Mandatory for whiteout and snow conditions.
Delorme Overview Maps (Trauma)	0.5 oz	0.5 oz	0.5 oz	0.5 oz		Extremely helpful for creating route alternatives and bail-out options.
Yogi's Town Guide (Trauma)	~2.0 oz	~2.0 oz	~2.0 oz	~2.0 oz		
Aloksak Map Case (Trauma)	1.1 oz	1.1 oz	1.1 oz	1.1 oz		Extremely helpful at keeping maps dry. Zipper prone to blowing out after about 2 months.
ID/Credit Card	0.4 oz	0.4 oz	0.4 oz	0.4 oz		
Aloksak Case	0.3 oz	0.3 oz	0.3 oz	0.3 oz	Waterproofing for ID, money, etc.	
Mechanical Pencil	0.2 oz	0.2 oz	0.2 oz	0.2 oz	More reliable than pen in cold; better for writing in the rain journal	
Gossamer Gear Journal	0.6 oz	0.6 oz	0.6 oz	0.6 oz	Track weather, avalanche conditions, journal	Waterproof. Just enough pages for logging town to-dos, mileage, notes, etc.

INDEX

DISCARD

ABOUT THE AUTHORS

Justin Lichter, also known as Trauma, has hiked more than 40,000 miles and recently, along with Shawn, completed the first winter thru-hike of the Pacific Crest Trail. He has hiked many of the major long trails in the United States and worldwide. He has written articles for *Backpacker* magazine, *Trail Runner* magazine, SectionHiker.com, and the *Adventure Journal* and has helped design products that have won *Backpacker* magazine Editor's Choice Awards and *Outside* magazine Gear of the Year Awards. He is the author of Falcon's *Trail Tested* and *Ultralight Survival Kit*. Justin lives in the heart of the Sierra Nevada in Truckee, California, and works as a ski patroller during winter.

Shawn Forry, also known as Pepper, completed the Triple Crown of hiking (Appalachian Trail, Pacific Crest Trail, and Continental Divide Trail) by age 25. He has continued to refine the limitations of ultralight travel, having logged more than 25,000 miles of wilderness experience. Having guided dogsledding tours in the North Woods of Minnesota in temps below -45°F, he also holds the unsupported speed record of the Colorado Trail, covering the 465 miles in just over ten days. In collaboration with Justin Lichter, Shawn has pioneered routes across the world, including the spine of the Himalayas and the Southern Alps of New Zealand. Together in 2014–15 they became the first individuals to traverse the 2,650-mile Pacific Crest Trail during winter—a trip the *New York Times* dubbed "the most daring expedition since Lewis and Clark" and leading to induction into the California Outdoors Hall of Fame. Shawn is the program director for Outward Bound California, having spent more than a decade inspiring youth in the pursuit of leadership and character development. Based in the Tahoe region, he enjoys Nordic and alpine skiing, alpine climbing, cycling, and the occasional crossword.